A FEARFUL INNOCENCE

A FEARFUL
INNOCENCE

FRANCES DAVIS

THE KENT STATE UNIVERSITY PRESS

Letters by Walter Lippmann to Hazel Hammond Albertson in the possession of
Frances Davis are reproduced by permission of the Yale University Library.

Copyright © 1981 by The Kent State University Press, Kent, Ohio 44242
All rights reserved.
Library of Congress Catalog Card Number 81-11793
ISBN 0-87338-260-9
Manufactured in the United States of America

Library of Congress Cataloging in Publication Data

Davis, Frances.
  A fearful innocence.

  Bibliography: p.
  1. Davis, Frances. 2. Journalists—United States—Biography. I. Title.
PN4874.D37A298   070'.92'4 [B]   81-11793
ISBN 0-87338-260-9   AACR2

TO I.B.C. & F.B.C.

Contents

Foreword

Our century has been a time of violence and disillusion. This fact hardly distinguishes it from any other century; but the contrast between the sweetness of hope at the twentieth century's start and the accumulating shames of its dying fall has perhaps a special pathos, at least for the survivors. *A Fearful Innocence* is a twentieth-century story and therefore the story of the fate of humane ideals in a merciless world. It is also the record of a gallant life. And it is, it seems to me, a peculiarly American story—in its openness of mind and heart; in its initial optimism and in its later insight into that "power of blackness" which Melville found in Hawthorne; in its fusion, so characteristic in our literature, of dream and nightmare.

Frances Davis came of Russian Jewish stock. Her father lived in the slums of Chicago, entered the labor movement, was an early protégé of Jane Addams and went to Harvard in order to equip himself to be a better labor organizer. The *fin-de-siècle* idealism of the new settlement movement and of socialist trade unionism blended with an older American idealism when Philip Davis encountered a former Congregational minister named Ralph Albertson. Albertson's evangelical zeal had already led him to try and build a Christian community in the swamps of Georgia, and in the first decade of the new century he was attempting a second experiment in brotherhood on a farm along the banks of the Merrimack River in West Newbury, Massachusetts.

Frances Davis grew up in this twentieth-century reenactment of Fruitlands or Brook Farm. Emerson would have immediately recognized Ralph Albertson, the devotees of his Farm and their "gradual withdrawal of tender consciences from the social organizations. . . . What a fertility of projects for the salvation of the world!"

Hawthorne knew the type too; for he had gone to Brook Farm himself and later unveiled its illusions in his exquisite *Blithedale Romance.*
"There are always two parties," Emerson had said, "the party of
the Past and the party of the Future; the Establishment and the
Movement." The Farm was the home of the Movement, Massachusetts section, early twentieth century. At first glance the Farm was,
like Blithedale, an idyll, and Frances Davis lovingly reconstructs the
sights, sounds, smells of fragrant meadows, newly mown hay,
freshly baked bread, merry young men and lovely girls in New England spring and New England autumn. The students flocked out
from Harvard; Walter Lippmann came, and Samuel Eliot, Robert
Edmond Jones, Carl Binger, Lawrence Langner, Kenneth MacGowan, Lee Simonson. They admired Hazel, Ralph Albertson's young
second wife, and they adored Albertson's pretty straw-haired
daughters by an earlier marriage.

They had great fun, but they also had high purpose. They were
aware of the bitterness of poverty, as in the tenements of Boston
where Frances Davis's parents were pioneers of social work. They
perceived American society as out of joint and believed that men
and women could find more harmonious ways to live together than
in the brutal scramble of a competitive economy. They were the
party of the Future, dreaming a dream of decency, a dream at once
guileless and noble.

Pure idylls are brief moments in human experience. Ralph Albertson was a man of enthusiasms and frailties, feckless and restless, always ready for new formulas by which to save humanity.
Life outside the Farm defied the ideal of brotherhood. Young Lippmann, in whom the Albertsons invested so much hope (and who
later married one of the straw-haired daughters), discovered the
intractability of circumstance lucidly and readily, almost too readily.
He had been assistant to the new Socialist mayor of Schenectady for
hardly a week before he wrote a dismayed Hazel Albertson, "What
appalls me is the smallness of our power and our knowledge and our
ability in the face of the problems we are supposed to solve. . . .
We are, dear Hazel, a ridiculous spectacle. . . . I have all the sensations of a man trying to tie a string around a sunbeam." This was an
early blow; a greater followed when the outbreak of the First World
War mocked the faith in progress with which the century had
begun.

Frances Davis remained a child of the millennium. Reared in a
utopian community, she did not lose her passion to serve people.
She became a journalist, watched the rise of fascism, worked in

Spain during the Civil War, was grievously wounded and, in sequences recalled with affectionate irony, returned to the Farm and the children of light for a long and agonizing recovery. Her own will and fortitude, and the sustaining love of the man who became her husband, I. Bernard Cohen, the distinguished historian of science ("Adam" in this narrative), brought her back from the brink of personal disaster into active and fruitful life. Bernard Cohen encouraged her to collect the documents and testimony that, nearly forty years later, serve as sources for this book (among them, of particular interest to historians, the hitherto unknown letters of Walter Lippmann to Hazel Albertson). In after years Frances and Bernard Cohen have offered new generations of Harvard students something of the encouragement and concern the Albertsons provided half a century before in a simpler world.

Innocence is an attribute of people, not of nations. Writers sometimes go on about "the end of American innocence," a denouement variously dated according to dramaturgic need; but the phrase is empty. Governments are never innocent; nor can people reared in the dark wisdom of Calvinism, a people who began by killing red men and enslaving black men, claim a saving ignorance of the irremediable evil in the human soul. Individuals, however, are perennially innocent, which is why Brook Farm is reenacted generation after generation.

Nor is innocence necessarily a menace to society. The dreams of innocence are often generous dreams, and they may help to offset the meanness, greed, cynicism, destructiveness that pervade so much of human life. Some must dream guilelessly to balance those who never dream at all. Hawthorne knew better than most the perils lurking in the human heart, yet could write of Blithedale, speaking through his *semblable* Miles Coverdale, "Often, however, in these years that are darkening around me, I remember our beautiful scheme of a noble and unselfish life; and how fair, in that first summer, appeared the prospect that it might endure for generations, and be perfected, as the ages rolled away into the system of a people and a world!"

Yet innocence is never enough, and optimism crystallized into ideology can turn into evil. The lesson Hawthorne took from Blithedale was the danger of fanaticism: "The higher and purer the original object, and the more unselfishly it may have been taken up, the slighter is the probability that they can be led to recognize the process by which godlike benevolence has been debased into all-devouring egotism." So Miles Coverdale returned with relief to the common life, "the thick, foggy, stifled element of cities, the entangled life of many men together." Frances Davis has seen the century sadly decline from the radiant optimism of the Farm to the degradations of Hitler and Stalin; carries the wounds of the century on her person; yet retains her grip on life. *A Fearful Innocence* attests to the hope that the tragic vision need not destroy faith in our common humanity.

Arthur Schlesinger, Jr.

Preface

This book is the biography of a girl, a time, and a place. The girl is myself, who began life when America still believed that living could be an idyll (if rightly arranged). The time is the fifty years that spanned that impossible illusion until the countries believing in the sanctity of the individual confronted Mussolini, Franco, and Hitler. The place is the Farm, sixty acres of freedom to be yourself. All of it is true. Though it reads sometimes like a novel, there is nothing made-up. The events and conversations, except in certain obvious cases, derive from published and unpublished histories and autobiographies, correspondence, interviews that I conducted, and the recollections of some of the chief characters. Only the later *immediate* Farm family of my own generation are dispossessed of their real names, out of a sense of intimacy and affection.

Ralph Albertson's unpublished autobiography and his unpublished account of the Christian Commonwealth in my possession, and *The Social Gospel*, the pamphlet of the community, are the sources for the philosophies, speeches, and the pulpit preachments attributed to him. Some of this has been converted into dialogue. I have also drawn on my personal discussions, many years later, with him in New York City and with members of his family and "survivors" who knew him. The two basic unpublished documents deserve to be edited and published, an assignment I hope some student of American history will undertake.

The statements attributed to Walter Lippmann and others of the early Farm group are based on letters, on conversations, or on treasured memories of early conversations recounted to me. In particular, the letters of Walter Lippmann to Hazel Albertson, not published until now in any part, are extremely important as witnesses to the change in his point of view after his idealism was put to the test of everyday practical politics in Schenectady. I hope to edit these letters for publication.

When I began to interview Hazel and her family, and others connected with the Farm from the early period, they all had endless stories to tell: recollected conversations and events, and free associations. I had only to get the conversation going for story to follow on story. Whatever the original episodes, some stories had become part of the myths accepted by all of us. This, too, is a kind of truth without which history would be isolated bits and pieces.

It would perhaps never have occurred to me to write this book but for the constant concerns (expressed in books, lectures, and deeds) of my father, Philip Davis, for the immigrants and their families who came to the settlement house from the streets strange to them. This was the constant talk at our table, and my mother, Belle S. Davis (known to all the world as Polly) was an active sharer in these concerns—both in words and action. It was Polly who urged him, poor as we were in the world's goods, to get a law degree so that he could be a more effective advocate. E. A. Filene, wealthy merchant and philanthropist, used to say to him, "Philip, you are planning your life backwards. First you should attend to making a good living and securing your family and then, later on, give your time and attention to those who need help." But Polly, like Philip, wanted to help others *now*, not later when they could better afford it. Polly was proud that her husband was the City of Boston's guardian of school-age bootblacks and paperboys. For many decades, well-established, plump men would throw their arms around him with delight, "Mr. Davis, Mr. Davis, you remember me?" His "boys" believed in the promise of the new land and began their upward movement toward careers under his sponsorship. Polly's unshakable belief in the millennium "right around the corner" was part of the constant atmosphere in which I grew up. The early part of the book draws heavily on these family remembrances, plus many later conversations with my mother and father, and on my father's published autobiography, plus his books and manuscripts.

It will always give me courage that near the end of his life of unremitting labor in this hard land, he called his autobiography *And Crown Thy Good*.

I am deeply indebted to Ann Louise McLaughlin, who helped me to reduce a large, unwieldy manuscript into book form. Without her editorial skill and judgment, this book would still be shapeless. I thank Carol Green for her critical reading of the typescript, and Julia Budenz for her gentleness. Llewellyn Howland III sustained me during many of the agonies that authors go through. How can I sufficiently thank him for his steadfast confidence in me and in my project? The framework of the book owes much to his suggestions. Donna Gold's amazing mastery of her Selectric produced readable, comprehensible pages from a mass of starred, arrowed, crossed-out, scribbled-over notes, additions and changes which she deciphered and turned into a typescript—and at such great speed, too! Thanks to Carl Krebs and Kristie Macrakis for their work in the Widener and Houghton Libraries to ensure the accuracy of the history I had not seen with my own eyes, and to Greer Gilman for a conscientious reading of the typescript.

I am well aware of my good fortune in having in Laura Nagy such a creative and understanding editor.

I am particularly grateful to Hazel H. Albertson and Ralph Albertson for the gift of valuable documents on which much of the book is based, and for supporting and approving the project of doing the book. The Yale University Library has given permission to quote extracts from the letters written by Walter Lippmann to Hazel Albertson, which are now in my possession.

Finally, I acknowledge the Farm family's patience with my writing out, over so many years, the life that was theirs as well as mine— an intense activity which they tolerated in order to help me get well. They know my deep and affectionate gratitude, especially "Laurie."

It will be very clear to the reader that throughout the book there is a constant "acknowledgment" of Adam's compassion and continuous encouragement whenever going on was beyond my attenuated capacities; his refusal to allow me to escape the proper disciplines of making a life into a book; his practical knowledge of the setting down of facts; and his comprehension—often beyond my own—of the significance of what I was trying to say. It is beyond me to try to say "thank you."

The final narrative version was completed at the Rockefeller

Foundation's Villa Serbelloni, at Bellagio on Lake Como. Dr. and Mrs. William Olson were kind and generous in providing work space for me, although my presence there was under the wing of my officially invited scholar-husband.

Cambridge, Massachusetts   F. D.
Spring, 1981

A FEARFUL INNOCENCE

Plain living and high thinking are no more:
The homely beauty of the good old cause
Is gone; our peace, our fearful innocence . . .

Wordsworth,
"O Friend! I Know Not Which
Way I Must Look"

prologue

The End Is the Beginning

Fall, 1940: When the war was over for us, we came home. Among the first women to be a reporter at wars, I was first among casualties. I came back forever maimed, the strength sapped from me. What I had been was finished, the bright promise of my life destroyed. The body that had been the instrument of youth, and joy, and hope, was now the prison of my being. Its walls were pain and weariness, and there was no escape.

This is a story of the return home with nothing left; and yet, how that was not the end, but the beginning.

The maple holds the River Room in its arms. When I lie in the big bed, I am in the bosom of the tree. Its limbs embrace the corner of the house, the window and me. The sun flickers through the leaves.

In the center of the great, square bed, I lie immobile. My body is so meager that it barely disturbs the taut, flat surface of the coverlet. My head barely impresses the pillow. My thin arms are neatly arranged beside my body, my flat black braids beside my face.

In my throat is imbedded what looks like a silver ornament. Only by the movement of this inanimate thing would it be evident to any observer that the girl is living. Moved by the tremor of her breathing, charged up by the work of her heart, it jiggles steadily, its mobile parts brazen and clicking, a thing with its own irate existence upon that too-still body.

The body is not passively still, but rigid, held quiet by a furious demand upon it. In violent act of will alone, is she alive. All the vitality remaining within that body is gathered up in one single intention: to be immobile. She has retreated into the furthermost burrow of her being where, transfixed, frozen with fear, she looks out through dreading eyes at the forces of terror and pain everywhere in wait for her. She will not move an atom of her person lest by a tiny, unguarded gesture she weight the balance, and horror, falling upon her, annihilate her.

Through the open windows come the sounds of laughter and living. I look up at the ceiling and watch the reflection on the waters of the river below the bank. Why, of all the children who have grown up here, am I the only one with my future finished? I am isolated, an island.

Later, I will learn there is still life left in this static body of mine, a demanding will, and that I am not alone. Here at the Farm I am part of a community. My present is only an early omen for the future of all the others.

This is utopia, the Farm, the utopia where we all grew up, wherever we came from, whoever we were. There was always a place at this table, a bed somewhere, even if it was a burrow in the hayloft. No one was ever asked how long he might stay or what he or she could bring.

At night when the house is still and I cannot sleep, I flick on the radio and bring into my room another world—the real world, the world that, episode by episode, disappears from the map of Free Europe. All of Spain is now in Franco's hands. The *Empress of Britain* is sunk carrying British children to safety in America and in Canada. The Germans walk the streets of Paris. Seven thousand civilians are killed in Britain in a month's air raid. That world, the world on the radio, is falling apart, in irreconcilable contradiction to the fact of this world, the Farm.

And when I fall asleep, the radio is still tallying its beads of loss. I dream. The dream begins with the repetition of a scene I cannot forget, and then slips into nightmare. Again and again, it is the scene of a press conference in Burgos during the Spanish Civil War. Reporters slump around a table: crumbs, cigarette ashes, wine glasses. . . . At the table's head the press chief of Franco's armies has tilted his chair at his favorite angle. He whacks the leg of his high-shined boot with his swagger stick to emphasize the lecture he is giving us. "Spain is immaculate. Spain is the lover of Christ. Spain is the guardian of the Holy Ghost, protector of Christianity. But now

2

she has become the victim of modern sanitation. Too many diseases cured, too much food available; Spain's blood is clogged. This is a war of sanitation. We must reduce the masses who are the carriers of filth." In my sleep, my heart skips a beat. He thuds his boot. "Masses! Carriers of filth. Spain's arteries must be cleansed. Her blood must be freed of contamination." And thud! "There are too many who are like animals. Pigs! Filth!" Thud, thud, thud, goes my heart. I am of the masses! I sit before the enemy—my judge. Thud, thud. Heart and whip are suddenly one. I wake and am bathed in the sweat of fear and fatigue. The thud, thud, thud, comes from the hooves of Roany, pounding down the lane. He has gotten out of the pasture once again and is off at a gallop. Thud, thud. I, too, have a passion for freedom.

My father ran the first settlement house in the North End of Boston, where the immigrants—the "masses"—arrived from Italy, Ireland, the Balkans, the closed villages of the Russian Pale, small families crowded together, the men carrying their bundles wrapped up in string and paper, wives hung about with various-sized children. All the lost souls. My father's responsibility was to resettle them into rooms that they could—at least to begin with—call home. To us, each human deserved, whether we liked him or not, the right of place, the opportunity to equal rights.

My second home was the Farm. No mere proper Farm, but a place that continued the beliefs in sharing and in the brotherhood of man which were the commandments of all utopian communities. We were never conscious that we lived under commandments, but all of us children who arrived at the Farm quickly came to live under the habits of shared life.

When I grew up I went out into the world armed with a sense of obligation to carry on the work of utopia. I joined the company of newsmen in the search for fact. I soon came to see that we could not escape from the fate that was to come to all of us, Apollyon standing on the road to Armageddon. And the vision and the events that made me see it so clearly brought me full circle, back to the Farm, bedridden, mute, defeated, and not even a prophet for those close to me. For no one listens to a prophet—especially you cannot foretell doom in a whispered voice. There was a gulf between us, the Farm family and me, for I had seen the coming conflict, the clash of armies, and they still lived in the arcadian dream that the achievement of utopia needs only the finding of a correct formula.

In the end we all knew. America and her beloved illusion of "Manifest Destiny" were to suffer from the terrible encounter with the

3

slow, agonizing process of reality as that belief in her mission of equality confronted the forces of Mussolini, Franco, and Hitler. This is the account of a small segment of America's Coming of Age, as concentrated in the journey of a five-foot, one hundred-pound innocent.

chapter one

"Where Utopia Standeth"

The Farm lay upon the bank of the river. On two sides, beyond the cornfields and the kitchen garden on the one, beyond the hill and pastureland on the other, the woods stood up like walls. The third side was bounded by the river on its way to the sea, and the fourth by a highway paralleling the river, the road from Haverhill running down to Newburyport. In from that traveled way for nearly a mile the lane ambled; over the brook, up and down the rock pile rise, by the pasture, past the duckpond until, like the river in the marshes, it merged its identity in the dust of the farmyard.

Only to the gulls, slip-sliding on the high air streams far above the hills and the river, had the Farm the appearance of its neighbors in that thrifty countryside, a proper farm in the New England sense—exercise in husbandry: sowing, harvesting, storing against a cold, lean day. Our Farm practiced a gay and enthusiastic sharing, tomorrow to provide for itself. To what the Farm had, everyone was welcome. Welcome to a bed, welcome to a place at the always expandable board, and welcome to work in our fields and barns to labor as if on your own farm!

It is curious then, that the people in the village, on the real farms round about (for it was farming country) and even the trolley car conductor who clanged by our gateposts twice a day, called it by that least applicable name, "The Farm." Not a tribute to haphazard farming, but evidence of the fascination with which everything that went on down there was regarded.

When the Farm on the riverbank used to be the old Jacques place, nobody thought twice about it. As a child, though, Bernard Berenson, the great art authenticator, connoisseur, and collector, traveled through this same valley countryside with his father, a peddler

The old Jacques place, mid-nineteenth century.

with a horse and wagon. At the old Jacques place, "B.B." would be allowed to get down from the wagon and play awhile with the Jacques boy, who was his age; and then "B.B." would run across the fields to catch up with his father's slow-moving horse. Since Ralph Albertson (or "Rory," as he was called) and his young wife came out from Boston and settled in, "You never saw such goings on! Them blonde Albertson girls riding into the village on the high seat of that spanking new blue-painted democrat wagon, and wearing bloomers! That Mrs. Albertson too, often as not, swinging them good-looking legs over the wagon wheels and jumping down—all that white stocking showin'!" The men on the porch of Henry Bailey's general store watched with bright, appreciative eyes. "Bloomer Farm" they called it.

Ella Dale, who lived in the neat little house across the road from the Farm lane, was sure it was one of those free-love places. That Mrs. Albertson! She'd got no more sense than them girls in bloomers. Scrambling up Brake Hill with the strangest looking young men on the Lord's Day! "Likely a pack of anarchists, all!" Catholic anarchists, because Ella Dale had seen Albertson himself driving one of the women to the Catholic Church that the French folk down from Canada had built in Haverhill. Catholics, to Ella's mind, were as dangerous as anarchists. Henry Bailey, however, decided that the new folk were Germans, being all fair-headed except Mrs. Albertson. Germans were known to be Jews. Therefore: German-Catholic-Jews.

Rory, whose Dutch Calvinist family had settled Jamesport on Long Island in the early 1600s, was never quite pleased to be peremptorily divested of his pioneering forefathers by this chorus of village wits.

In the decade after the turn of the century, the Farm was invaded each weekend by batches of assorted people fleeing Boston. The marauders took the early evening train to Haverhill, where they boarded the trolley, overwhelming its usual passengers and destroying the decorum appropriate to public transport. Unlike Ella Dale, the conductor was charmed.

"Settin' on their upturned cases, there they be at the terminal, waiting. Lugging all kinds of queer-looking bundles. Bags busting with books; sometimes funny-looking bread, once, holy smokes! live lobsters. Got loose and crawled all over my car. And always talking, never knew there be so much to talk about! Arms swirling like windmill sails, jabberin' away. Body'd think their lives depended on it. And girls . . . hats off, hair blowing, eyes sparklin', giving the young men as good as they got." The trolley car conductor, telling this to his cronies, smacked his lips. "Or everybody singin'. Right there in the streets of Haverhill.

> A capital ship for an ocean trip
> Is a wallopin' window blind . . .

They have that car of mine rockin' all the way down the line!" At the helm the conductor whistled, tapping his foot to keep the time. Opposite the gateposts the Farm-bound crew jostled off, and with a sigh the conductor stamped the starting bell. But sometimes a straggle of unattended girls clustered at the Haverhill trolley terminal after nightfall. Those were real occasions for the conductor. When he reached the Farm he would leave his car standing, deaf to the exasperation of the remaining passengers, and escort the young ladies halfway up the lane, within sight of the lights of the house.

He was expert at recognizing which passengers were for the Farm, and delighted to startle those, fancying themselves clothed in travelers' anonymity, who had come for the first time, by announcing, "Here you are, folks. Here's where you folks get down. Right here for The Farm." At dinner the new arrivals demanded, "However did he know?" and the Farm family chorused: "He puts all the queer ones down here!"

The Farm never did know, any more than the conductor did, how many were coming, or who, or when. At the sight of each new-comer plodding down the lane in city clothes, the family rushed from house, barn, garden, or meadow to be first with embraces and greetings. Girls in pink bloomer suits and blue bloomer suits erupt-ed from the cornrows. The rule was that you brought with you five yards of cotton broadcloth in any color but white. White was Haz-el's prerogative. She could run up your bloomers, elastic waist, mid-dy and all, in half an hour. Babies, children of various sizes, popped out of the one-time chicken house, now called their Castle, some-times clad as Indians or pirates, likely in nothing at all. Around the corner of the barn dogs ran, barking. Hazel alone waited, waving from the doorway of the house. At the Farm, "family" did not mean just the Albertsons. Rory Albertson and Hazel, his second wife; the girls Phyllis, Faye, and Christine, daughters of Rory's first marriage (the eldest only two years younger than her new mother); Laurie and Dutchie and the baby Jude, who were Hazel's and Rory's; these were the core. But "family" as the Farm used it meant everyone who came. A shrinkable, extensible, entirely flexible family made up of whoever happened to be living there, for weekends, for months, for years, or forever.

Rory, rarely at the Farm except on the weekends, usually led the first contingent of boys from Harvard and MIT, a professor or two, sometimes a muckraker, Rory's various secretaries and ed-itorial assistants, and the daughters of the Boston social and finan-cial establishment. They would barely gain the rock pile rise before they were inundated by the waves of welcome. The Farm absorbed the newcomers, and what a metamorphosis then took place. The young women's long skirts and high-necked blouses were discarded for bloomer suits, intricate pompadours were shaken loose, or plaited in braids. The young men flung off coats and neckties; each unearthed from some corner or closet a favorite pair of ancient pants, to be held up with rope, or precariously anchored with a huge safety pin.

If it was good haying weather (and if Rory was there to com-mand), everyone went off to the fields. The young women and the young men shouldered the long-tined forks, Rory led "General Big Feet" harnessed up to the old hayrake, the children scampered after. Rory laid the load. Hazel, beside him high up on the wagon, her braids bound round her head, was queen of this pastoral court. Ro-ry's blonde girls, tall as Hazel, were princesses. They set the pace of the pitching. The children bounced on the haystacks or, sitting abreast on the wide wagon seat, flapped the reins and pretended to drive with mimic "gees!" and "haws!" The scene was a golden idyll of enthusiastic labor and exultant brotherhood.

In the spring of 1909 Rory and Hazel had come down the lane in search of a farm. Hazel had seen the gulls at play, the winding river, the chestnut trees—a grove blooming upon the hillside—and had heard the murmuring of the little stream that ran along the lane. Here, these acres their kingdom, her children would run free, healthy as little animals. Here, not too far from Boston, her husband would live and farm, free of the entanglements of the city, the interests that forever seemed to take him from her. She would fill his life with poetry, read Whitman to him. As another child is brought up on the Bible, Hazel had been raised by her oil-prospecting father on the poetic inventories of *Leaves of Grass*.

Had she inspected the kitchen? Was there a bath? In the summer the children would bathe in the river; in the winter, splash in a tin tub set in front of the blazing fire.

Rory saw a dilapidated house: paint peeling, fences down, barn to be rebuilt, land to be renourished, orchard to be replanted; such disintegration made him itch to get at it. But it was not as a man measuring his solitary strength against ruin that Rory responded to the blight and neglect everywhere. In his mind's eye was the vision of many backs bent in the fields, of many hands happily slapping paint on the house, tightening the barn against the winter storms, bracing the fence posts, stringing the pasture wire, setting the stone walls—a brotherhood of workers, laboring side by side to make these acres flourish. Not one lonely man, slave to his own acre, bound only to his own concerns, but a community toiling, sharing together.

Bronson Alcott, Rory's predecessor in this philosophy by something over a half-century—his geographical neighbor, fifty miles as the crow flies—had practiced these principles at Fruitlands, declaring "I cannot consent to live solely for one family. I would stand in neighborly relations to several, and institute a union and communion of families instead of drawing aside within the precincts of one's own acres and kindred by blood. The Family is good. The neighborhood is better. The communitorium is best." Rory, less pompous, wrote in his diary, "I like the fellowship that grows out of many people living together, the yeast of many ideas and opinions, the fair division of what there is to share, work and benefit." From the first summer weekend, when he and Hazel moved their household from Jamaica Plain in Boston to the Farm, they were rarely to sit down at table as a "family" of less than thirty.

The difference between Bronson Alcott and Rory Albertson lay in the directions from which they had arrived at the same place, each convinced that he possessed the recipe for the establishment (under his own uniquely destined leadership) of the Good Society.

Alcott's progression from the transcendental controversies of Concord to the "consociate farming" of an inhospitable ledge outside the town of Harvard was a philosophical journey. He had packed his daughter Louisa and her sisters, his devoted wife, and their somewhat scanty family belongings into a wagon and had driven them across the countryside to a small farmhouse set on a windy ridge. The few scraggly apple trees, desperately clinging to the hillside against the winds that swept up the valley, inspired the venture's name: Fruitlands. His Concord friends had begged him not to subject Mrs. Alcott and the girls to the hard winter bare of comfort. But Alcott had grown impatient with lofty talk, with all the theorizing about how man might best live to better the lot of his brothers, with the schemes and visions of the elect clustered around Emerson and Margaret Fuller and the group publishing *The Dial*. He would prove his beliefs through practice, offer a shining example of transcendental living, which all like-minded men and women would be welcome to share with him.

Rory, farm-bred, could have told him there wouldn't be much to share out of that rocky soil.

In Alcott's practice of farming, when there was a spiritual question to be resolved, work waited. Philosophizing came first. The hay went unraked despite the threat of rain, the crops waited in the ground despite impending frost. Alcott had perfect faith that "some arrangement would be made." He meant on the Lord's part. Rory would never have left it to the Lord.

Right diet was one of Alcott's basic tenets. "A gross feeder will never be a central thinker." It boded ill for any diet that Alcott, novice farmer, forswore manure as "foul ordures" with which he would never allow the soil to be "debauched." Nor would any animal substance, whether flesh, butter, cheese, or milk, pollute the Alcott table. Luckily for the future readers of *Little Women* this was to be a brief digression from the unpretentious amenities of Concord. Louisa grew up to write of her father's Fruitlands experiment as *Transcendental Wild Oats*, and since the fruit trees on which they were to be nourished in the absence of meat or milk were those scraggly apple trees, she (like her mother, in secret) called his New Eden not Fruitlands, but Apple Slump.

This was the promise of America, the New Land; here on the vast continent, men and women who believed alike could form freely into groups. However unwelcome for unacceptable beliefs they might be in one settlement, there was room enough for them somewhere else. The earliest devout exiles were those seekers after that place to be their sanctuary, where they could worship according to conviction. H. G. Wells was to call these groups "Communities of Obedience"; their obedience was to God and to the dictates of an inspired voice in their midst. Dutch Mennonites, Shakers, Quakers, the "Women in the Wilderness Contented of the God-Loving Soul"; Ephratans who built their Temple without iron, for thus did Solomon; Jean de Labadie's French mystical Protestants; Moravians; Rappites fleeing the decrees of the Counts of Würtemberg; Separatists of Zoar, Seventh Day Adventists, Mormons . . .

Brothers and sisters of the early Communities of Obedience struggled together to tame the fierce and stubborn soil that it might bear their crops; cleared forest, removed rock, that the earth might be turned over and sown; built houses to shelter them against the fearsome cold, fearsome beasts, and fearsome savages; raised up their House of God, usually without ostentatious steeple. No paradise, but purgatory; here souls were disciplined for heaven. Most practiced a biblical communism, as had the monastic groups of the Middle Ages, whatever they possessed dedicated to the good of all, and that all to the service of God.

In the nineteenth century there sprang up other brotherhoods, inspired less by God than by Rousseau, Fourier, and Saint-Simon, determined to prove by example the perfectibility of Mankind. These, Wells identified as "Communities of Will." Brotherhoods, colonies, commonwealths, communities, concordiums, consociates, cooperative thises and thats; associations, societies, unions, fellowship farms and mutual homes; each removed itself from abjured society, proclaimed unique doctrines, and—isolated as a beacon—was determined to demonstrate the particular formula by which mankind would be saved.

Inspirationalists and Respirationists, Perfectionists and Devotionalists, The Brotherhood of the New Life, the Ingathered Israelites, the Spirit Fruit, Phalanxes scientifically organized according to Fourier, ideal-town planners, Robert Owen's vanguard of pseudo-social scientists, Koreshans—their leader himself the Messiah and the universe a celestial womb enclosing mankind within the yolk of the cosmogenic egg. Emerson, writing a gossipy letter to Carlyle in the fall of 1840, commented wryly that "not a reading man but has a draft of a New Community in his waistcoat pocket."

New Harmony, the grand project of the world-acclaimed humanitarian-industrialist Robert Owen, the "Father of Cooperation," for all the fanfare with which it was greeted, collapsed within two years.

Brook Farm, on the opposite side of Boston from Fruitlands, had a short if intensely intellectual existence. Hawthorne, with noble purpose, had gone to labor there. But a writer can always make a book out of disappointment. In his *Blithedale Romance*, the hero, Coverdale, cries out:

> If ever men might lawfully dream awake . . . and speak of earthly happiness, for themselves and mankind, as an object to be hopefully striven for, and probably attained—we . . . were those very men. We had left the rusty iron framework of society behind us . . . we had stepped down from the pulpit; we had flung aside the pen; we had shut up the ledger; . . . for the sake of showing mankind the example of a life governed by other than the false and cruel principles on which human society has all along been based.
>
> . . . we had divorced ourselves from Pride, and were striving to supply its place with familiar love . . . lessen the laboring man's great burden of toil, by performing our due share of it at the cost of our own thews and sinews: . . . we purposed to offer up the earnest toil of our bodies, as a prayer no less than an effort for the advancement of our race.
>
> . . . our beautiful scheme of a noble and unselfish life, and how fair, in that first summer, appeared the prospect that it might endure for generations, and be perfected . . . into the system of a people, and a world . . .

With the passing of the first ecstasy, Coverdale is to discover the disadvantage of sharing "the laboring man's great burden of toil." "We had pleased ourselves with delectable visions of the spiritualization of labor . . . [But] the clods of earth which we so constantly belabored and turned over were never etherealized into thought. Our thoughts, on the contrary, were fast becoming cloddish. . . . Intellectual activity is incompatible with any large amount of bodily exercise. . . ."

"I am afraid you did not make a song, today, while loading the hay-cart . . . as Burns did when he was reaping barley," Zenobia rebukes Coverdale.

"Burns never made a song in haying time. . . . He was no poet while a farmer and no farmer while a poet," Coverdale replies, rather snappishly.

All these Utopias are no more; some fell early, some late, before man's ineradicable humanness. They fell to self-seeking; to the temptations of the exercise of power; to secession for private gain. One by one the communities succumbed to envy, greed, jealousy, intrigue; to bad management and to bad theory: "to all who knock the door shall be opened unto them." "No Community that has thrown wide open its doors to all applicants has long survived," said William Alfred Hinds, who traveled from coast to coast, visiting communities of every kind. This proved to be a sage judgment. John Noyes, with shrewd sense, transformed his own "Perfectionists" into the craftsmen who made Community Silver.

Of the "Communities of Obedience" some still exist, if barely. The "Communities of Will" were all to disappear, save for this one or that one that converted itself into a joint stock company for the manufacture of refrigerators and radar ranges (Amana) or the crafting of silver (Oneida). Without dictatorship or devout belief, (Marx or Christ), neither secular nor Christian communism was long able to withstand the contrariness of human nature—man's stubborn and independent self.

What if any one of those exercises in better worlds had become a pattern for the hoped-for heaven, sharing and forbearing practiced forever? The Rorys of the earth would have fled such monotony of goodness.

In the procession of prophets who were to usher in the Millennium, Rory has his tardy place. I wish I could bequeath to him not the Christian Commonwealth he founded, but a utopia called (since Jesus was a carpenter) The Straight-Edgers. No better Golden Rule than that symbolized by the carpenter's straightedge would have fitted Rory's sound carpentry and social gospel.

The young Rory (breaking free of the doctrine that bound his Calvinist fathers) would accept no predestined fate, no allotted place in the hierarchy of heaven. While a boy in Jamesport, on Long Island, not far from New York, he read the sermons of Henry Ward Beecher, and later, when he went on his own into the city, the editorials of Johann Most in the anarchist weekly, *Freiheit* (or, in Yiddish, *Frayhayt*). He glimpsed wider horizons than the life chosen for him, the life of a coffin- and cabinet-maker. Planing the coffin boards to a satin smoothness, he stood in the midst of the curling shavings memorizing Beecher's grandiloquent sermons. Preachers had access to books; with rhetoric and text they led their people out of the wilderness. Rory saw himself as a prophet of a new day, pioneer and top sergeant. He would become a preacher.

Rory's Christian name was Ralph. But those who knew him never called him Ralph. To some he was known as "G. G.," apparently because of the familiar "Good God!" with which he punctuated his sentences. But most people called him "Rory." Some thought that "Rory" was a corruption of "R.A."; but others were certain that the name "Rory" came from the fact that—ever the preacher—he "roared" his opinions and convictions for all to hear.

Irene, his schooldays' sweetheart, thought she was marrying a first citizen of their town and followed him reluctantly through the years of mean existence as a penniless student, to be rewarded at last when the "call" came to a congregation in Springfield, Ohio. It was a workingman's congregation, but the rectory was heaven after the struggle to keep herself and her new little family quiet in the single room where Rory's soul and theology wrestled. Even that humble rectory was not to be hers for long. Like Bronson Alcott, Rory never hesitated to sacrifice those who belonged to him on the altar of the larger cause of humankind.

The church building was a roofed-over wooden box of one room, with hard benches for pews, the pulpit a lectern rescued from a demolished school. The congregation was equally unpretentious: hard-working people, sober, tired faces without an ounce of zeal left after each day's work. Churchgoing gave them little comfort, not in this church where nothing delighted the eye, and not even a hand-pumped organ tuned their hymns; nor, under past ministers, had triumphant praises to the Lord uplifted their souls. God as well as society ground them down. To Rory it was shameful to preach to this congregation that worldly success "could serve as a sign that a man had been 'elected' by . . . God."

Instead, Rory preached of their right to share a better world. They straightened up on their hard seats, attracted by his vitality. He was rather short in the legs, but stocky and strong across the shoulders. His fair hair sprang impatiently from his scalp; the set of his chin was that of a man who sees a task and intends to get on with it; his blue eyes were wide open, taking in everything. The congregation, fascinated by this new species of preacher, came into their dingy church with a livelier step. In the opinion of the Elders he was to prove all too lively.

Rory came into possession of his first parish in that last decade of the nineteenth century when "wild" Chicago was the geographical center of bloody industrial warfare. Labor had no weapons except its newly conceived solidarity. The employer, however, had police, federal militia, strikebreakers who were protected by Pinkerton battalions sworn in as deputy marshals, live ammunition, barbed-wire fences, lock-outs, and lock-ins: a whole arsenal against the threat of a union of workers. The anarchists, believers in the propa-ganda of the deed, in that one last indiscriminate explosion that would awaken the masses, seized upon the labor turmoil as the sig-nal to act: their opportunity to direct the rage of the workers for the anarchists' ideological ends. The workers wanted an eight-hour day, a minimum wage, child-labor laws. The anarchists wanted to demolish all government, all privilege, all property. They were, most of them, desperately poor men who had seen children starve in basements, wives freeze to death on street corners while fellow human beings passed by, mothers fling themselves out of windows, too discouraged to go on.

It was never proved who threw the bomb in Chicago's Hay-market Riot, but that explosion cost the lives of seven police blown to bits and four anarchists, who were hanged. This sum of lives was charged to the struggle for decent working laws. Then there were all those wounded and killed in the Homestead Strike and the Pull-man Strike. Reverberations of these desperate battles could not leave Rory deaf and unconcerned. He was no dry theologian but a hot-blooded young warrior, impatient to be in the struggle.

On an anniversary of the Haymarket Riot Rory went to Chicago to see conditions for himself. He walked past the guarded prison walls of the factories, the tenemented ravines of the ghetto streets. His heart was stricken for the desperate poor. But nothing in his properly ordered life had prepared him for the shock of such vio-lence, fury, and mob rule; for strikers burning cars during the Pull-man strike; for the flinging of scabs into the river; for the killing and the being killed. He came to the Wednesday evening discussions in Jane Addams's drawing room at Hull-House and heard each man shouting the righteousness of his own creed, reviling the preach-ment of the others as unrealistic, as "palliative!"—that most offen-sive charge. There the anarchists denounced the socialists, the so-cialists denounced the trades-unionists. Single-taxers urged the philosophy of Henry George; Ruskin disciples advocated the theor-

15

ies of the cooperative colony. There were Christian Socialists, Scientific Socialists, and even an anarchist converted to Buddhism. Sam Jones, later the "Golden Rule" mayor of Toledo, was often at Hull-House. So, too, was Professor George Herron preaching on Caesar and Jesus. Aylmer Maude, translator of Tolstoy and expounder of Tolstoy's social doctrines, stopping on his way back from escorting Dukhobors from Russia to Canada, told the Hull-House folk about Tolstoy and his literal practice of Christianity. Only Jane Addams kept her head amid all this babel. Each man knew, and he only, "where Utopia standeth."

Rory took back with him to his pulpit the reverberations of this boil and bubble. His sermons got farther and farther from spiritual problems. It was not salvation *hereafter* that people needed, but salvation now. He preached against the use of the Federal troops who had jailed Eugene V. Debs. He preached on Jane Addams's work among the poor on Halstead Street, on Henry George's single tax, on Tolstoy's philosophy of Bread Labor, and on Marx. He filled the church. Some of his parishioners were stirred, most were bewildered, and the Elders were anxious.

Then Rory was blessed by revelation—he would preach the *Social Gospel*, the divine practicality of sharing all property, all labor. "The Sermon on the Mount," he cried, "is not intended by Jesus to govern the spiritual world alone. It is His direction for the government of our material world, here and now. It is the most possible, sensible, practical, rational thing to work for and expect that ever dawned upon the history of human thought! It is coming!" Rory promised his flock that "Commerce and industry will be inspired by divine tenderness. The monopolies and the great trusts have shown the way. For as by corporate greed the multitude have been brought into poverty and sorrow, so by corporate love shall the multitude be brought into the fullness of life . . . The cattle upon a thousand hills, the market place and the mine shaft are His. Farm, store, and factory are to be managed by His spirit. A Christian society will recognize that the meaning of the Cross to the industrial and commercial world is the crucifixion of selfishness . . . [and the] renunciation of private property . . . The love of God will place necessities in all homes before it places luxuries in any!"

It was evident to the Elders that such gospel should not issue from an orthodox pulpit. Fortunately, Rory had come to hate the word "preacher." He didn't want to be a talker; he wanted to engage in fellowship, life, progress, social enterprise—brotherhood! He wanted desperately to feel himself physically engaged in the struggle for social justice. But it was against his nature to destroy, to burn, to break windows, to smash good machinery. Nor could he surrender his faith that the right word or the right example would reveal unto the employer that he was brother to those he employed. Surely they were all men of good will! Together, man and master would produce the goods of the world. Rory's faith was rooted in the power of Love. He himself would put the Social Gospel into practice. He, and whoever would follow him, would build a Christian Commonwealth.

Rory left the church, taking with him his bitterly unhappy wife and their three young daughters, Faye, Phyllis, and Christine. In 1896 he led a small band of disciples into the swamps of Georgia. Whatever meager property each of his followers possessed was sold to help buy the thousand acres of swamp and lowland where the Commonwealth of Jesus—its civic laws the Sermon on the Mount— was to be built by their own hands. Here they were to carpenter up the Heavenly City, uncontaminated by the selfish world, an island of love and prosperity.

They struggled, those desperate pilgrims, their lives depending upon it, through the first terrible winters. The paupers of the neighboring poorhouse, hearing of the Commonwealth's welcome to all, moved over en masse and just as quickly moved back again. At the Commonwealth there was only corn meal and cowpeas for supper, as Jane Addams reported after her visit. She said that "the corn meal and cow peas" of "the colony fare . . . had proved so unattractive that the paupers had gone back, for even the poorest of the southern poorhouses occasionally supplied bacon with the pone if only to prevent scurvy from which the colonists themselves had suffered."

Backbreaking work and sweat eventually made that kingdom habitable. Day after day, month after month, the men of the community plunged into the woods with axes, into the ditches with spades, plowed the first furrows to turn that bitter, unyielding soil. In those days of unremitting toil, weariness, and poverty, there was brotherhood. Yet that winter Rory's principles cost Irene their first-born son. The seven-months-old infant died of cold and starvation.

In the end, three years after the colony had been established, it was not to be wretchedness that killed the ideal, but greed. "Whosoever will, may come"—this was the primary law of Rory's city of God—tramps dropping from a passing freight train to get a glass of water; scalawags, loafers, petty thieves—and worse; cranks, fanatics, dogmatists. All were welcome; all, according to the laws of Christ's Commonwealth, were heirs, equally with those who had built the mills, the press, the community hall, the neat houses, who had tilled that inhospitable soil, sown and harvested the crops.

As their labor blossomed, as the colony flourished, the tramps, nostalgic for the vices of the world they had left behind, and the cranks, anxious to have things their own way, joined forces and applied to the court at Columbus, Georgia, for a bankruptcy order to force the sale of the property of the Kingdom of Heaven, that the proceeds might be distributed and carried off in their pockets. Rory could no longer follow in the ways of Jesus. He could not stretch the divine tenderness over these despoilers of his vision. He would fight! He would fight them in the courts and on his, Rory's, land. In that possessive pronoun he gave himself away.

The mortgage for the Christian Commonwealth was held by a group of sympathetic bankers who called themselves for this purpose the Right Relationship League. They had wanted to have the colony "deeded to Jesus Christ," as Rory recorded, "but I objected on the ground that Jesus Christ would not pay the taxes." Though the lawsuit was won by the colonists, the men of finance were horrified: Rory had betrayed Christ's charter, the hope of the world. He had resorted to the laws of courts instead of the laws of Christ; he had not turned the other cheek; he had driven from the colony's land sinners for whom He died. Rory had denied to these greedy men their immediate share in the Kingdom of Heaven right here and now, as set forth in the charter. To the men of the Right Relationship League this was anathema. Christianity, by Rory's proof, was not commercially viable. The men of finance, disillusioned, foreclosed. The property was put up for sale and when the debts were paid, each of the remaining members realized $8.50 with which to return to the selfish world.

Rory himself fell ill of typhus. A few friends stayed by him, but Irene returned to her own people. Rory, when he could stand up again, sent the last of the faithful to his family's care on Long Island. The temperature dropped below zero; snow fell on the cracked ground; and Rory turned the key in the Community Hall. Behind him, deserted, was his Commonwealth of Jesus, cottages empty, sawmill locked, print shop locked, communal dining hall with the Christmas greens still above the doorway, schoolhouse and cotton mill, all boarded up and locked. The trees of the orchards so tenderly cared for had been killed by frost; the fields, once a pattern of crops, were rubble again, the paths obliterated.

18

Shaking with weakness, Rory made his way to Corry, Pennsylvania, where he had been offered refuge by Ernest Hammond, a sympathizer who would have become a colonist had not Nennie, his wife, less spiritual than her spouse, refused. Ernest was fascinated by the Christian Commonwealth and had closely followed its fortunes. Nennie had no faith at all in the scheme—a wild, idealistic, hare-brained idea, especially that part about taking in all who came.

"Just the same," Ernest insisted, "that young Albertson is a man with the courage of his convictions, a man trying to do what he thought was right, going in the right direction even if by the wrong route." Ernest respected Rory's effort and had sent him a thousand dollars' worth of sawmill machinery, now rusted, wasted, lost.

"Some men," pronounced Nennie, "never cease to climb Fool's Hill." She probably meant both her husband and Rory. But she, too, would never have closed her door to a man in need. Hazel, their daughter, a lovely green-eyed, chestnut-haired blooming young woman, romantic as her father and devoid of her mother's realism, nursed Rory back to health. During the long days of convalescence he told her of many things besides Christly living. She learned about Irene and the blonde daughters not much younger than she was. Rory took pains, as soon as he could maneuver, to see that Irene was comfortably divorced—and happily remarried to a "steady pleasant man"—Rory's words.

Neither Ernest nor Nennie was pleased when Irene's divorce became final. Nennie warned Hazel that Rory was a restless man who would make a poor husband; there had even been whispers that it was not just living like a Christian that had tried Irene's soul. Hazel cried, "I know! I know!" secretly pleased by the rumors of virility and sure of her own physical charms. "But all that is behind him! He isn't young any more," she reassured Nennie. "Why, he's thirty-five!" As for the daughters, "Oh, if they will not accept me as their new mother, then we will all be sisters together!" Rory was her prophet and she, Hazel, would follow where he led.

Rory's belief in himself returned; it had never been long absent. He gathered up Faye, Phyllis, and Christine, his daughters, married Hazel, and, having reconstituted a family, moved to New England. Hazel and he would engage in a new battle, turning from salvation by the Sermon on the Mount to salvation by direct legislation.

Some time after the demise of the Christian Commonwealth, Rory had met Bradford Peck, the owner of a large department store in Lewiston, Maine, a business he had built up from scratch entirely

Hazel soon after graduating from high
school, just before she met Rory.

on his own. Peck enticed Rory to come to Maine to help in the
Cooperative Association of America, which he had just organized
and endowed. Peck's utopian ideas had been expounded in a book
entitled *The World a Department Store*, described by Rory as a "feeble
rehash" of Edward Bellamy's *Looking Backward*. One of Rory's as-
signments was to become editor of the weekly *American Cooperator*, a
"peppy, radical sheet," but "never dogmatic or doctrinaire." Two
years later Rory and Hazel, with Rory's three daughters, moved
to Jamaica Plain in Boston. Rory was now Secretary of the Cooperative Association of America, and in addition held down a variety of
jobs, including a spell as employment and welfare manager of Filene's department store. Through E. A. Filene, Rory became more
and more involved with plans for making Boston a better and more
progressive city, largely through the Chamber of Commerce and
the "Boston 1915" organization. He published a weekly paper called
The Boston Common, "devoted to civic integrity and social service and

Rory at the time he settled in Boston with
Hazel.

free from the control of party or advertising cliques." Later there
were other journals. He was much in demand as a speaker for civic
groups, progressive organizations, and independent radical clubs,
especially in colleges. It was from the midst of these preoccupations,
a few years later, that Hazel and Rory left the city on that spring
afternoon for their first glimpse of the Farm.

By Labor Day of 1909 they would spend their first weekend at the Farm; besides the family, a dozen others came to help
settle. In the wagon with the furniture from Jamaica Plain sat, huge-
ly enjoying the bumpy ride, four-year-old Laurie, Dutchie, two,
getting tired and restless, and five-month-old Jude, asleep in her
mother's lap. They got some of the beds set up, and the bed-less
burrowed into the hay in the barn loft. Hazel found a room—not
really a room, a sliver of a room, a slice, corresponding in width to a
downstairs hallway—where she and Jude, her new baby, snuggled

Hazel in her white bloomer suit, "airing"
her hair, as she called it.

together on a canvas army cot. There she lay and watched the swirling pattern of the skies of the summer night.

Early in the morning, the sun in her eyes, Hazel woke and leaned
out of the window to look upon the fresh new world. The cows,
bought along with the buildings and land, ambled down the lanes of
young corn, their tails swishing, thrusting their heads among the
new ears. Hazel laughed to see their patient faces munching. In delight she sang an old scrap of song, "Hannah! Hannah! The cows are
in the corn!" Mr. Ward, the farmer staying on the place until "they
got shook down," had planted the corn in the spring to be ready for
the family. He came running, shouting at the cows, Rory behind
him. They put the cows back into the barnyard and Mr. Ward

stopped to secure the gate. "Hazel!" Rory cried, looking up at her in the window, her long hair framing her face. "I don't see what you find to sing about. Why didn't you come down and chase them! That corn's valuable. There's nothing to sing about when cows get in the corn."

Years later, we the children of the Farm put our heads out of the window and saw the cows in the corn. Nothing ever stayed behind fences at the Farm. Rory, you, too, might as well have sung.

chapter two

Days of the Idyll: 1909-1914

In the last decade before the 1914 war, the war that put
an end to early utopias, intellectuals of every stripe, students, professors, society ladies—all the ardent of heart—threw themselves
into the battle to legislate the better world into existence.

Rory was at the center of the attack. From behind a huge rolltop
desk he edited or published a succession of protest magazines, *The
Boston Common*, the *Twentieth Century Magazine*, the *Cooperator*. He produced editorials against monopolies, imperialism, and corruption;
preached on the virtues of direct legislation, public ownership,
cooperation, socialism, the single tax. He ran a street boys' club and
a working girls' club, chaired endless meetings, plotted political
strategies, spoke whenever he was given the chance. From the
ranks of Boston's Fabian Socialists, Trades-Unionists, Suffragettes;
from anti-war, anti-monopoly, anti-imperialism, anti–child-labor
meetings; from committees for the eight-hour day and the minimum wage—from these workers for every organization for social
salvation: volunteers, secretaries, chairmen, patrons and patron-
esses, Rory lured converts to the Family of the Farm.

High thought and "lowly" labor; the inspired mind and the strong
back; Tolstoy, rethinking Christianity, stitched shoes (Jane Addams
took his gospel of "bread-labor" literally, baking bread early in the
morning before the demands of a Hull-House day overwhelmed
her): for the young men of the Harvard class of 1910, this wedlock
of opposites was the allegory of the "good state." They took as their
ideal William Ellery Channing's eulogy of "the union of *labor* and
culture." Bronson Alcott, said Boston's great Unitarian preacher, "is,
perhaps, the most interesting object in our Commonwealth . . .
Orpheus at the plough is after my own heart. There he teaches a
grand lesson; more than most of us teach by the pen."

Walter Lippmann, the scion of a wealthy and stifling New York family, to whom "play" was the well-supervised driving of his own goat-cart in Central Park and vacations were visits abroad to museums under a rigid Germanic tutor, tried testing his own persona as the president of the Harvard Socialist Club. Like the young royalty of Russia who—on returning home from school in Switzerland where they had been studying Rousseau—vowed to bomb the Czar's train as atonement for having lived on "the backs of the peasants," Walter and his fellow Socialists became profoundly involved in plans to make a better world—though less explosively. He was greatly influenced by courses in British government and especially "The Psychological Conditions of Local Modern Government," given by Graham Wallas, a visiting lecturer from the London School of Economics, a Fabian and progressive thinker whose "work was directed to improve the mental processes of those who occupy their minds with public affairs." At the suggestion of Lincoln Steffens, Walter became a reporter on *The Boston Common* (R. Albertson, pub.) and a volunteer teacher of English to immigrants in the Salem Street settlement house in Boston's North End. There he encountered Rory, then the house in Jamaica Plain, and then the Farm. He, in turn, enticed others to come to the Farm. The young Harvard men were enchanted to discover that the arguments for Fabian socialism were not restricted to Graham Wallas's "Gov. 10," "18," and "31," but were actually in practice thirty miles from Boston. There they could participate in the harmony of poetry and plow.

Stragglers caught the milk train. Sam Eliot, grandson of Harvard's president, hair and clothes in disarrary after a violent protest meeting, rounded up his comrades. "C-come on, let's go out to the Farm and tell them about it!" He always stuttered unless he recited poetry. "S-sure there's room; if there are no more beds, you sleep in the hay in the barn or on the riverbank. Doesn't matter if it's past midnight, you won't wake anyone up! C-c-climb in a window if the door's latched, it never is! You don't n-n-need to know them— everyone's welcome! And the most beautiful g-g-girls . . ."

When the trolley stopped running for the night, these comrades from the "social wars" hiked from Haverhill, between the deserted trolley tracks. As day began they reached the gateposts, took off their shoes, and walked among the grasses of the lane's edge to cool their feet. Sam Eliot led: he knew the Farm best. The Kuttner boys gingerly followed after. Julius Kuttner had already been experimenting with Freudian analysis via A. A. Brill, for whom he would translate *The Interpretation of Dreams*, page by page, in payment for his therapy. With Sam carrying a lantern he'd found in the barn, they

25

The Farm house and barn about 1914.

tiptoed Indian file down the row of cots on the porch to see which were occupied. Sam Eliot was too impatient to wait for morning to discover who was there. He took a census of the figures wrapped in quilts on the porch, in the hayloft, on the riverbank. Charles Boni, who had come out with them—for many years to come a New York publishing house would carry his name—followed shyly, fascinated by the variety of oblivious faces. The sleepers stirred in the flickering light, and some, nesting precariously on the bank, rolled a little in the dew-wet grasses. The mists rose up from the river.

Others, arriving late without benefit of lantern, never knew beside whose still form they stretched out to sleep. Lucien Price, already writing editorials for the *Boston Transcript*, got up early Sunday morning to watch the sleepers wake. He said it was like the Day of Judgment to see who rose up. Herbert Seligmann, heir of the banking house Seligmanns, though he was to spend his life writing and painting, abhorring finance, couldn't be persuaded, the first time he came, to take a pallet and lie down among those sleeping forms. He slept all night upright, leaning against the wall of the fireplace room and was found in the morning sound asleep standing up. He'd "never slept in public before." The latecomers left their shoes in front of the fireplace. Whoever got up first knew how many had arrived during the night by the evidence of shoes and bookbags in the fireplace room. The breakfast makers were experts at judging how much oatmeal to cook.

Down the lane came the young men who were to found the Theatre Guild, which was to bring to America's small towns great plays instead of an unmixed diet of vaudeville. Kenneth MacGowan was not then involved with the stage, but was passionately concerned with what he believed were the miserable salaries paid by the Harvard Corporation to the "goodies" who cleaned the boys' rooms. He was convinced it was floor-scrubbing that gave the "goodies" prolapsus of the womb, and as a result, *ipso facto*, had a direct relation to low wages and injustice. Perhaps it was just this tenderness for the ordinary human being that was to assure him a great career in the theatre. Bobby Jones, a devoted student in George Pierce Baker's drama course, made costumes for charades and sat cross-legged on the floor of the big front room sketching the stage sets for *The Man Who Married a Dumb Wife*, while Hazel read the play aloud. Later, he would become a disciple of Max Reinhardt's new stagecraft, and do the sets for many of Eugene O'Neill's plays. He had been raised in a Vermont farmhouse with no pictures but the illustrations of Foxe's *Book of Martyrs*. The Farm with all its lovely, free, Burne-Jonesian women, was Paradise. Lee Simonson, also a student in the George Pierce Baker course, was to be a stage designer, of whom John Mason Brown would say, "As a designer, Lee Simonson is a practical man, a craftsman not a dreamer, a doer not a theorist." The Theatre Guild, however, would never have come into being without Lawrence Langner, a chartered patent agent from Swansea, Wales. Rory brought him out to the Farm to hay, but he was bitten by the theatre bug.

Lincoln Steffens was a regular, taking time off from muckraking in Boston; Charles Zueblin, an erstwhile professor of social history at the University of Chicago, lectured to the ladies of the Back Bay on "entering into the life of humanity"—an unnecessary exhortation at the Farm. Professor Frank Parsons, in the classrooms of Boston University, Ruskin College (which he founded), and the Breadwinners' College of the Salem Street Settlement House, taught the principles of equal freedom, personal liberty, and government action. His high hat was often crammed full of the evidence against the Railroad trusts. Hazel and the three grown girls would sit around the table with their long hair obscuring the rolls of figures. There were two young Indian nationalists who came, training in New England shoe factories to unseat the British raj. Maxim Gorky appeared briefly, bitterly denouncing the "freedom" of an America where hotelkeepers refused a bed to the lady with whom he was traveling simply because she was not his wife.

They churned the butter and turned the bread, shelled the peas, tipped and tailed the beans. They made up games, acted out cha-

27

rades, told ghost stories, and listened whenever anyone read aloud. Hazel would prop up a book and read, while her fingers ran up the pods, shooting peas out of their shells into the pot—one hand disposing of the shells, the other reaching for a new fistful—never pausing except to turn a page.

On Sunday mornings all the girls made the Farm circuit, doing up the beds, working in teams, one to the foot and one to the head, bellying out the sheet until, emptied of air, it lay flat and smooth. Lawrence Langner, Shaw's latest play in hand, followed after, reading *The Doctor's Dilemma* out loud, stumbling over thresholds. In the attic the Harvard medical students were still asleep in the cots among the trunks under the eaves. The girls turned them out of bed, and they sat rumpled upon the trunk tops while Lawrence walked up and down in a cleared space, putting himself into each character as he read the lines.

They weeded cabbages and hayed, gestures in an experiment of great social significance, by each wagonload a step closer to the better world. At least, this is what they did while Rory was around. Wherever he looked he saw jobs that needed doing: fences to mend, plowing, hoeing, harrowing, weeding. He had those young men doctoring the pump, building bookcases, painting the flagpole, milking the cows, feeding pigs.

With Rory to goad them and Hazel to inspire them, there were few who did not leave something of themselves built into the Farm. Bruno Beckhard, also in rebellion against his Wall Street financial family, made his first call in striped trousers. He was put to repairing the broken-down furnace, a struggle from which he never fully emerged. But it was sheer heaven for Bruno to be let loose on machinery, though the pump froze at eight degrees below. He was to find all his delight for the rest of his life playing with marine diesel engines. Henry Willcox, whose major life interests were construction and social justice, cast the two duck andirons that stand in the fireplace today. Walter Binger, who with his brother Carl was one of the "goat-cart" contingent, would become consultant to public works from Iran to New York City, where as Commissioner he built the East River Drive; at the Farm, he was a student engineer who directed the MIT boys as they set the granite blocks that wall the barnyard. Carl would become a leading psychoanalyst and play God in MacLeish's theatrical success, *J.B.* Then only at medical school, he nursed the children through mumps and measles and whooping cough, diagnosed the "swearing throat" of the hired man (given to "Hellfires!"), and attended the farrowing of the sow, Miranda.

Top: Working in the fields. The hay newly stacked, Hazel with fork over shoulders, her mother Nennie with a pail, on her way to feed the chickens. *Bottom*: Hazel in a pensive mood.

A despondent poet, whom I cannot rescue from anonymity, allowing himself a last weekend at the Farm before he was to dispatch his soul on Monday morning to another world, was set to cleaning out the chicken house. He shoveled filth throughout one hot day in a fog of chicken dust and so nearly perished of asthma at the Herculean task that despondency was forgotten in heroic wrath at Rory.

Such is a sample of those ardent builders of a new society: the journalists, the engineers, the doctors, the theatre boys, who were all to enrich life, and whose inspiration was born between Graham Wallas and the Farm.

When night fell, everyone gathered in the fireplace room, the first to come stretching out full length on the couch, a lucky one slumped in the deep comfort of the big tattered chair, the rest lying upon the floor around the hearth. The hours were punctuated with fresh logs as they argued Marx and Hegel, the philosophies of Santayana and James, the Socialist program of Wallas and the Fabians. Sam Eliot took turns with Hazel incanting Whitman; and with equal zest recited the nonsense rhymes of Edward Lear. They talked endlessly of the schemes by which the "new day" would be brought to dawning. According to Lucien Price, who would become editorial writer for the *Boston Globe*, it would be a four-hour day. With the other twenty every man would accomplish wonderful things! Waiting only upon such a feast of time to grow gardens, write books, compose music, paint pictures, pursue philosophy. They tore apart H. G. Wells's recipes for new worlds, took with utter seriousness Havelock Ellis's *Studies in the Psychology of Sex* and were charmed by Edward Carpenter's *Love's Coming of Age*. The medical boys, professionally capable, preferred to wrangle over Freud, Jung, and Krafft-Ebing.

Joe August, newly immigrated, resolutely attacking English at the Settlement House, his impossible accent not impeding his passion, described his poetic vision of the state of human perfection under anarchy. With equal ardor he discussed with the MIT engineers the techniques of making "bumbs." He was experimenting in the Lynn marshes with the construction of a bomb that would not only blow evil from the face of the earth, but by carbonizing sugar (or was it coal?) under pressure, would also create the diamond that would pay for the revolution and feed the poor. His technical advisers were not sanguine, but Joe was as stubbornly millenarian in his physics as in his politics.

Lucien Price had been in correspondence with Romain Rolland in France and read aloud his idol's letters. Julius Kuttner discussed Freud's ideas and the problems of translating Freud from the German. He was as convinced that in psychoanalysis lay the key to the perfectibility of mankind as the anarchists were of the efficacy of violence or the socialists of industrial democracy. Sam Eliot read each act of his play as it was completed; in it the world was to be taken over by a race of Amazon goddesses "who would put all wickedness to the torch." From these certitudes Walter Lippmann slipped away, barricaded himself behind the big desk in the front room and finished his editorial for that week's *Boston Common*. Hazel carried about the copy of Bergson's *Creative Evolution* Walter had brought her; she would absorb it by propinquity.

High purpose had attracted them all to the Farm. Still, I suspect it was the enchantment and gaiety of Rory's beautiful straw-haired girls and all the others who were young and full of laughter and very serious, that brought them back again and again. The warmth of basking in Hazel's faith kept them there. In time, Rory became the antagonist. He was a decade older than most of the others, and on him alone Calvin had imposed responsibility for getting things done. A cross-grained Canute, he could not order a halt to the tide of life he had directed into these channels. The flood would inundate all his plans. He would wake in the morning with an excellent program laid out for just what he wanted the young men to accomplish that day, only to discover that they were already up and that the girls (this included Hazel) had walked them over and down Brake Hill until they had energy left for nothing more than flinging themselves on the sweet-smelling grass.

"Sam! Walter! Bruno! Good God, where is that lazy crew?" Rory's complaints were forever announcing his appearance, as he searched the Farm to discover his errant helpers on the riverbank, or in the meadow, chins cupped in palms and elbows planted in the clover, or propped up against the haystacks, reciting poetry. Scattered about the Farm were all those strong young men and women. Everywhere the eye could see the work to be done: lumber delivered months ago to build the new milk house; bags of concrete waiting for weeks in the barn tack room to be mixed for the new barn cellar; the new pump still in its burlap wrappings ready to be hitched up. "Good God! Bruno! Hazel! Do you want to waste all the day? How can you sit around cackling forever! There's *work* to be done!"

The measure of Rory's own brand of innocence was his perpetual surprise that the ingredients of his fine organization never stayed organized.

Everyone was welcome to what the Farm possessed. Nobody paid except Rory. The bills for this ideal experiment were made out against its responsible financial, as well as spiritual, protagonist: Rory Albertson, debtor. They accumulated on the desk, a ceiling-high piece of furniture he had rescued from the demolition of an ancient banking house. Sporadically the bills were tucked away in their proper pigeonholes from which, as the month (and months) progressed, they spilled out in unmanageable piles. Rory then was forced to consider them. The Farm would become suddenly still, everyone had disappeared.

"Good God!" Rory would storm into the silence, "Who in Good God ran up this bill for feed? What the Good God are we feeding here, prize Herefords? Hazel! A gilded cock for the weather vane! Good God, what's wrong with the weather vane we've got? HAZEL! I gave you money for this bill for the fencing last month! HAZEL! Where the Good God is everyone!" There was no reply. (For these attacks of apoplexy, Rory was known to the Farm as "G.G.") At the first storm signal, Hazel wandered off along the riverbank, attended by her sympathetic followers. At the explosion point, no victim present to receive his fury, Rory would thrust himself from his desk, grab his shotgun and rush from the house. The first shots could be heard from the woods as he blew to feathered pieces the ever-offending crows. Bang! Bang! Bang!

One weekend, coming out alone from Boston after a late Saturday afternoon conference, Rory walked wearily down the dusty lane, under one arm the briefcase bulging with papers to be studied, in one hand his straw boater to fan up a small breeze. No children, no girls, no Hazel ran to greet him. Only a figure solitary as himself plodded toward him, the hired man dressed in his town clothes and carrying his cardboard suitcase.

Abreast of the rise Rory sat down on a convenient rock and waited for Oscar to come up to him. "Where are you off to?" he began, sensing disaster building up like the thunderclouds in the lowering sky. Oscar set the suitcase down in the dust and pushed his hat to the back of his head. "Gittin' out of here, Mr. Albertson," he said. "T'ain't no sense stayin'. Mind you, got nothin' against you. Fair boss." The hired man shook his head, "Mind you, ain't sayin' it would be like this if you was about. But you ain't. All the ducks daid. Doctor boys cuttin' open their insides to see what's wrong with 'em. By crack, I know what's wrong with 'em! All them pretty girls of yours too bizzy—buzzin' with all them boys to remember to water 'em. You tolt me the ducks was their bizness. Open 'em here, open 'em there! Maybe they got this! Maybe they got that! This ain't no hospital! And hay! How's a man to have a crew to get the hay in with all that lazy bunch sittin' around gassin'? Now it's headin' up fer to rain. Wal, I'm gittin', Mr. Albertson."

He paused, mopped his brow, stuck the red handkerchief back in his rear pocket, and exploded again, "Nobody sets out no lunch for me. Mrs. Albertson now, she's a good woman. Give you everythin' she's got, she would. But she don't GIVE ME NO LUNCH! No *hot* food. Man can't live on buttermilk. I'm gittin' along now. Had enough of this place. No offense meant." Oscar pushed his hat back over his forehead again, firmly grasped his suitcase and, clamping his mouth shut, continued down the lane.

Rory was too hot and dispirited to call after him. The man was a stubborn Dutchman; his mind made up, there'd be no changing it. Rory got off his rock and continued up to the house. Oscar was right about the storm coming; they'd better get the hay in.

No one in the house, Rory went through the fireplace room, not a soul. Through the kitchen—on the stove, a huge pot. He lifted the lid. The ducks, dismembered, were gently simmering. Oscar should have waited for his hot meal. Rory looked out over the river. The clouds had massed thicker, blacker. He went out on the porch and walked around to the front of the house. There in the big front room, her back to him, Hazel, humming a little song, was searching the bookcases. She spun about when the screen door slammed, her braids swinging with the movement, her white bloomers billowing like a ballet skirt.

"Rory, darling!" she cried, her green eyes crinkling. "I didn't hear you come in. How wonderful! Take off those dreadful hot town clothes and come out and join us."

"Where is everybody?" Rory asked. He would not embark on the lecture, all clear and ready in his mind, until he got the facts ordered. The thunderstorm coming up, Oscar gone; this was the turning point. The whole family must be made to face the wickedness of their negligence. Either remedy your ways or the Farm is destined to ignominious failure, never to be self-sufficient, never a productive organization, he its general, Hazel his lieutenant, the family its army of workers . . .

"We're out in the hayfield," Hazel answered.

The speech Rory was planning fell apart. Were they then bringing the hay in before the storm broke?

Hazel ran on, "I just came in to get Dad's Whitman." She held up the tattered copy, back bent with constant reading, leaves loose. "Everyone wanted me to read aloud the pages Dad loved best. And the hay smells so sweet and fresh. Come up in the hay with us!"

The light in the front room darkened suddenly. A drawn-out

33

rumble rolled overhead. Down the river a wall of rain descended and moved forward. Hazel and Rory were left with mouths open and noiseless. Beyond the porch, across the meadow, he could see the laughing crowd wading deep in the cut hay, in a concerted rush for the shelter of the barn. He also saw, draped over the railing of the porch, already sagging under the onslaught of rain, the three new mattresses he had brought from town last week; across the porch and lawn the trail of pillows, books, clothing, possessions the family had dropped in its wake.

The rain reached the house. Rory sprang to close the nearest window. It shut with a crash as he came away with the tool that had propped it open. The thunder crashed too. Hazel could hear nothing of what he was roaring, but she winced at the violence of the gesture as he shook the tool at her.

"Oh, Rory," she protested, in a sudden lull. "I've told the girls not to touch your screwdriver."

Everything Rory wanted to say whirled round inside his head. Oscar; the hay; ducks; mattresses; propping up the windows with tools. Screwdriver! Of all the insults to his world, this was the final violation.

"Screwdriver! Screwdriver!" he howled. "It is NOT a screwdriver! How many times have I told you it is NOT a screwdriver. It's my brand new GODDELL AUTOMATIC HAND DRILL! That's the highest grade in the Sears Roebuck Catalogue! I've been waiting for it for six months! Screwdriver!?" Rage robbed his throat of sound. Speechless, he fled the room, snatched the gun cabinet key, flung open the door, seized the old rifle, crammed a handful of shells in his pants pocket, locked the power tool in the gun cabinet, and rushed out into the rain, bare-headed, town-suited, to disappear in the woods. Bang! Bang! Bang!

The storm was over as quickly as it had come up. The Farm folk came out of the barn armed with pitchforks. In the lovely sweet smell of the rain-wet hay, a rainbow curving above them, sunlit diamonds dripping from the leaves of the tree-lined lane, the family sang and worked, shaking the hay out and spreading it to dry.

Mr. McDonald, the itinerant horse-shoer, met Rory carrying his gun, sodden, crowless, and uncommunicative, at the head of the lane and rode him down the lane in the wagon. When he saw the bare-shouldered young men, the bloomered girls, laughing and calling to one another as they worked, he pointed with his whip. "It's all right for you Germans," he pronounced to Rory glumly sitting beside him. "Now if you was Americans and them city folk come call-

34

ing, they'd eat up all your food and not do a lick for it. Takes furriners to set to work like that."

A knowing eye would have recognized the true "furriners" in
that bloomered, shirtless crew: they stood about uncomfortably
when work was abandoned for poetry, unaccustomed to forsaking
labor for hymns to its glory.

For Philip, my father, who at age fifteen had arrived in
America from the Pripet Marshes (in Poland), with seventy-two
cents in his pocket and two lemons left over from the stock he had
carried against seasickness, work had never been a matter of poetry.
The idyll of the Farm was, for Rory and Hazel, a voluntary embrac-
ing of the simple life. That court of ardent disciples had turned their
backs on privilege, property, position. But to be spurned, privilege
must first be possessed.

Philip and Polly, my mother, had no such option. Work was the
fact of life of their world. The Boston slums where they had lived
since Philip made a place for them in this New World, was their
America. Here in a converted tenement was the settlement house
of which Philip, disciple of Jane Addams and Hull-House, was a director, arbiter of street tragedies, spokesman for the helpless and
bewildered, new immigrants to the golden shores. Here the fight
was for first things, necessities that made the difference between
hopelessness and possibility for the men, women, and children
jammed into the tenements of Boston's North End. For the black-
haired Sicilian who needed—not as though his soul depended upon
it but because the lives of his children did—a scrap of paper, to be
folded and refolded, treasured in a pocket: the license that entitled
him to push through the streets a barrow piled with the rejects
from the market—damaged oranges, bruised tomatoes, sprouting
potatoes, wilted cabbages—shouting his wares in his own tongue
above the babel. Even the grey-beard had to have the city's permission to stand in the gutter, his tray of oddments—shoestrings, safety pins, third-hand neckties—suspended on a strap across his
shoulders. His wares had to sell themselves; classic Hebrew was no
help.

At first, Philip taught the immediately necessary English to these
peddlers and hawkers; to the ditchdiggers, shoemakers, tailors,
milk wagon drivers, and coal shovelers; to Italians, Greeks, Serbi-

35

ans, Poles, Slovaks, and Jews; to fathers of families, bone-weary after the long day's work; to young, strong men forcing horny hands to grasp the pen. The teacher, himself but lately come by this difficult road, was interpreter for them and their New Land. He knew the fumbling questions—and usually the answers: How do you become a citizen? Where do you go if your child is sick? Is it true the school is free? Why won't they let me work? He knew, too, the questions they didn't ask: How to avoid the "runners" who besieged the docks and stripped the greenhorns of what little money they had, "depositing" it for them into fraudulent banks; jobs promised in the middle of nowhere; rooms where no housing existed.

They must acquire the rudiments of English; without it one might as well be deaf and dumb. However elegant this one's Hebrew, or that one's Russian, or Greek, or Italian, without English he was helpless. Street signs could not direct his way, nor warnings keep him from danger. He could not tell the doctor what ailed his child, nor understand his instructions. Nor look for work. Nor learn directions, if work were found. Nor count his money. Nor comprehend what he had done that was right or wrong in the eyes of the law.

Philip was his neighbors' champion. He sat upon the tenement inspection committees; fought to condemn the back-to-back tenements; sunlight was commercially computed. "Six dollars a year per ray," verified Jacob Riis, and "where the sun comes right in your face, seventeen dollars."

Philip turned the teaching of English into instruction on survival in the Promised Land; on the right to minimum decency and living space, the existence of child-labor laws and pure food laws. He helped his students get their citizenship papers: two witnesses were needed; Philip was witness and advocate in one. Philip fought for all these new Americans not because Whitman urged him: "One's self I sing . . . yet utter the word Democratic, the word En-Masse," but because these poor, newly transported to a strange land, who desperately needed help in living, earning, dreaming, or in sickness and in dying, were his brothers, brothers in poverty, his and Polly's.

Later Philip and Rory and the lawyer turned political scientist, Frank Parsons (to be my godfather, his top hat in the Farm attic my proof of that commission), invented the Breadwinners' College. They recruited instructors from among the Harvard students to share the philosophies of James and Royce and Santayana, the illuminations of Emerson and the poetry of Longfellow with the newly arrived Americans-to-be.

Sometimes Rory brought Hazel to his Breadwinners' classes. She would sit in a straight-backed chair under the picture of Abraham Lincoln, belief in the mission of democracy shining in her eyes. To the fruit peddlers and the basting pullers, struggling with Rory's evening serving of philosophy or economics or history, she seemed the symbol of their belief in America, her presence a vision of a Brighter Day. Some of these, too, came with Rory and Philip from the settlement house to the Farm: Tessacini, the poet who drove a milk wagon; the hunchbacked Jewish girl who served the Breadwinners' College as (unpaid) secretary; Joe August, of the "bumbs" and philosophic anarchy, whom Bruno Beckhard, investing his year's allowance, set up in a taxi business with a Royal Tourist Motor car. This formidable, brass-bound equipage arrived at the Farm on Sundays laden with nonpaying passengers, puffing down the lane in a dust cloud of glory.

chapter three

Polly's Millennium

In another life, two wars plus a decade after the days of the Farm idyll, when we two girls who are Polly's family were grown and married—my sister to an artist, I to a teacher—we gathered weekly around her lavish table. My sister, a dozen years younger than I, belonged to a later Farm generation—she and her husband, fellow students at Antioch, were married at the Farm in 1942. After one of Polly's famous meals, when nothing remained but the crumbs on the cloth and the empty coffee cups, when everyone had pushed back his chair for greater ease, Philip, who loved to stir up the laughter that was for him the final fillip to well-being, began a customary sport: teasing Polly about the geographical gymnastics of the village from which she had come to America. He'd complain that they'd been married for forty years and he still didn't know from what part of Russia Polly had fled, at sixteen, to find the Promised Land. He was never able to fix securely on the map that village of hers, lost in the vast Russias.

Polly ignores him. She twinkles her brown eyes at the son-in-law the artist and at the son-in-law the teacher of history. The twinkle confides, "Philip's such a silly man. You and I know he is trying to get me excited. We won't pay any attention to him." But my husband, historian and scientist, says, in a tone of judicial concern, "Just where was that village, Polly dear? Po——Po——Ponev . . . What was the name?"

Bridling, Polly tosses her head. "Look how innocent he is! He knows the name as well as I do!" Still, she can never resist. "Po-Nev-ya-sa," she enunciates carefully. "It was on the Nevyasa River. That's what 'Po' means: 'On.' 'On-the-Nevyasa,' you see?" All this she explains as seriously as if she had never explained it before.

Philip brushes Polly's explanation aside as inadmissible evidence. He is now no longer a settlement house director, but a lawyer. "It's not on the map," he objects. He lays great store by the map. *He* can point, almost without hunting for it, to the dot on the bleak Polish marshes which was his village. "Get the map," he directs my sister. "Get out the map of Russia."

"What do I care about your maps!" In scorn for the entire discussion, Polly has begun to collect the coffee cups. But she doesn't leave. She cannot bear not to be part of whatever is going on. "In a minute you'll be telling me you can't find the Nevyasa on your maps." The river of her childhood moved, so broad, so heroic, across Polly's memory that the existence of her town was proved to all the world because it bore the river's name.

The map is spread upon the tablecloth. Philip hitches forward his chair, clears his throat, and proceeds, a man of logic. His finger follows the courses of the larger Western rivers—from the German border, through Lithuania, through the Ukraine across the Russian steppes and emptying in the northern gulfs. He cross-examines Polly, "Was the village in the Ukraine?"

Polly's eyes sparkle in the excitement of vindication. "The Ukraine! Of course. See! What did I tell you? That's where it was! It is there, on the map?" Polly leans over the map, half hoping to see her village in miniature, the people moving in its tiny streets, as in a crystal globe.

But sometimes Po-Nevyasa settles as certainly in the heart of Lithuania, or hops up near Riga in Latvia, or moves over near Vilna in Poland, or, losing all sense even of geographical fidelity, betrays its namesake and establishes itself on the Volga as Polly claims each name that rings familiarly in her ears. According to its meanderings, she becomes successively Lithuanian, Latvian, Polish, Ukrainian.

Philip appeals to his sons-in-law. "You tell me, what is she?" Polly laughs until the tears flow. Sometimes they are all silly and sometimes they are more so. Of course, she's *Russian*! What else would she be? Hadn't she run away from the Czar's Russia to come to America?

This family game of find-her-village was played by us for the sake of the memories it stirred, a prelude to Polly's describing her village. She loved to tell us, savoring every detail, what it was like. Philip would sit and listen, a little wistful. It bothered him that his own recollections were a bitter contrast to the rich fabric Polly wove. He could not understand how it was that they had lived in the same country, nearly the same province, yet in such different worlds. For Polly's town was wondrous for more than its wanderings.

"I remember," she would say, settling her round body into the earnestness of conveying the pictures in her mind and talking with her hands and her eyes and her face, "the Greeks who used to sell ice cream in the summer."

"Greeks!" protests her family.

"Great big men," Polly goes on, "with fierce moustaches that stuck out in points. They came in the summertime with ice cream in the tin pails they carried on their heads." She taps the wavy brown hair of her head. "They sold us children a spoonful of ice cream for a penny. So much."

The son-in-law the artist sketches huge moustaches and a head surmounted by an ice cream pail. The son-in-law who is historian and scientist sighs, thinking of the map of Russia. Wherever Po-Nevyasa was, it certainly was not in southwestern Russia, was nowhere near Greece. "Are you sure they were Greeks, Polly?"

"Of course, Greeks, you think I don't know Greeks? All kinds of people came through our town. Greeks, Armenians, Turks. The Turks wore those red hats with the tassels and gave puppet shows." The artist sketches a Turk with a fez.

"Greeks, Turks," murmurs her bemused family.

"For us children the day was full of excitement. That's why I have no patience with all these people who wrote about how terrible it was in Russia. Pooh—Mary Antin! Three times a day we had a parade; the soldiers from the barracks marched through the town singing, three times a day. I think they were going to get their meals. All the children would run after them. The soldiers were so tall and so handsome and had such beautiful voices.

"And in the fall the little dark people from the north came down the river on rafts, taking the logs down the river. We would run along the bank and wave to them and they would wave back. They were strange people, not like us, brown like Chinese. Mongrels."

"Mongols," gently corrects one daughter.

"Mongols poling rafts in Lithuania!" repeats Philip, but he does not interrupt. Polly now is carried away by what she sees. "Yes, Mongols, that's right." She cocks her head and twinkles, momentarily shy at having used the wrong word. "We would stand on the bank and watch them and wonder where they were coming from and where the river was taking them; and then when they had disappeared, all the children would go and run and play in the wheat. The wheat stood taller than a man's head. We played hide-and-seek in the wheat and the sweethearts hid in the wheat, and the revolutionaries, they held their meetings and read Tolstoy in the wheat. They read about Humanity, about the Millennium"—Polly pronounces it "Millainiyum." In Polly's millennium even the Czar would take off his crown and come into the fields—like Tolstoy—and the peasants would walk arm-in-arm with Tolstoy and the Czar and they would all be brothers.

Once Polly's teaching son-in-law brought a colleague to her table, a Russian philosopher-historian. He sat listening tranquilly to Polly and following her account with brisk nods and "ya, ya" in understanding.

The Nevyasa. Ya. Ya. But of course. A tributary of the Niemen. "Well, not a large river," this in answer to Philip, who was slightly disappointed to have the existence of the river thus authenticated, "but not a small river." Such authority on her side intoxicated Polly. In a single burst of confidence she told the Russian professor all about her village of Po-Nevyasa. After a little he attempted a half-gesture of interruption, was inundated and subsided. At times he moved his body forward and opened his mouth again as if to protest, only to be again immobilized by Polly's words. Finally he shrugged his shoulders and raised his eyebrows in the gesture of man's fundamental helplessness before the forces of nature.

Afterwards, on our way back to Cambridge, my husband, choosing his words with the deliberation of a seeker after fact, framed the crucial question. "Does such a village exist—in Russia?" His colleague stopped short. He put out both hands and seized the lapels of my husband's coat. "My friend," he began. It was necessary for him to take a deep breath in order to accommodate everything that had to be said.

"My friend, . . ." he chose his words with care, "one can see that your mother-in-law is a remarkable woman. She makes me to remember my mother. May she rest in peace. A good woman. A noble woman. A delicious—no, that is for food, it is not?"

"Delightful," suggested my husband.

"Delightful. A delightful woman. One can see these things." He took a new grip upon the lapels. "But this village? The Volga? My God, how the *Volga*? The Nevyasa is a tributary of the *Niemen*. Greeks, Turks! Ice cream? No! THIS I have never seen."

Too many particulars crowded his mind at once; he became entangled and had to begin again from a fresh direction. "My friend,"

41

he said with new resolution, "you understand, this was *my* country. This country of which she speaks, I was born there. We came from the same *gubernia*, how do you say it?—state. Mongols? You know where Mongolia . . . Forgive me—of course. But *my* father, you know what business he had? *That* business. The logs. The shipping of logs on the river. *Mongols?* They were Russians! Russian peasants from my father's land who left their crops to take the logs down the river. They were brown? Of course, they were brown; they had been all summer in the sun. They were little? Of course they were little—it's a wide river—and she was a child. But Mongols!"

The outburst relieved him. "I tell you," he said, releasing the lapels, "the country of your mother-in-law exists. But of course, *here* it exists." He tapped his heart. "In childhood it exists, but in Russia, never!"

The Russian professor having subsided, now prepared to resume normal living. He had put his world together again. Then he paused; amongst the welter of so much myth a fact stood out. "It is, however," he said, "true, strictly true, that the revolutionaries met in secret, in the wheat. That they were, as she remembers them, poetic people. Ideal people."

"Idealistic," corrected his colleague.

"Idealistic people. Strictly true." Looking backward from the perspective of fifty years, he hunched up his shoulders as if the next thought gave him pain. "Romantic people," he said bitterly. "A revolution begun by princes, princesses, sixteen-years-old girls. They were in love with The People. They read the poetry of Nekrasov, Pushkin; they read secret copies of Herzen's magazines printed in exile, *The Pole Star* and *The Bell*; they read Rousseau, Saint-Simon, Fourier. They came home from the universities of Moscow and Switzerland to atone. For centuries of luxury supported on the backs of the peasants, they were now ready to give their lives to atone. To give up everything. Titles. Kropotkin had a title as good as the Czar's. Gold plates. Carriages. To go and live among the people. To live in garrets. To be hunted by the police. To be put in prison. To be sent to Siberia. To be shot against a wall. Already this is forgotten—but by her, by her it is remembered."

"Not facts," the Russian professor subsided. "Not facts, but the *soul!*"

Polly's private millennium had always seemed to me to be suffused by a golden light. Now I know it was so. The sun glinting on the stalks of the endless fields of Russian wheat gilded her memory: the child Polly, flat on her stomach, roofed over by the nodding heads of grain, screened by the waving grasses from the revolutionaries—boys from her village—lying stretched out upon the cornflowers that carpeted the wheatfields, reading aloud.

What were these inflammatory tracts the young men had to hide in the wheatfields to read? Tolstoy's *What Then Must We Do?*: "What must I do?" demands Tolstoy, "Learn not to live on the backs of others . . . take every opportunity to serve others with my hands, feet, brain, heart, and all the powers you possess and on which people make demands." "Tolstoy!" dreamed Polly, the buzzing of bees making her drowsy—"Tolstoy!" She had once seen a picture of Tolstoy with a long beard that came to his belt buckle. Polly's father had a long white beard and so, believed Polly, had God. "Tolstoy, Tolstoy." The bees buzzed in the cornflowers. The warm sun closed her eyelids.

To Polly-in-Russia it seemed that the millennium must be going on in America. When the young men ran away from Russia they went to America. There even the streets were paved with gold—though nobody picked it up because people were watching from the windows. Hadn't her brothers run away from the Czar's armies to go to America? If no risk was too great to be undertaken in order to escape the army—and the army to Polly was so splendid, soldiers in their shining leather boots, lightly sitting their spirited mounts—if all the young men ran away to America to flee such a life, this must be because America was even more wonderful, the millennium the prophet Tolstoy had promised.

Her brother Boris had run away from the army to America and settled in Philadelphia. The year Polly was fifteen, in 1900, he had scraped together enough for a ticket to send for Toby, Polly's older sister; it was the obligation of those who arrived first to send for the next member of the family, who in turn sent for the next, until all were safe on the precious shore. That was the year of the typhoid in their village. Toby died. Polly survived. Surely it must have been Polly who was meant to go to America.

Now I must surrender my favorite myth: that Polly fled from the tyranny of the Czar, crossing the border in a rain of bullets. It was of no concern to the Czar whether Polly went or stayed. She was no young man of army age. She might have left Russia properly by train. But her mother refused to countenance so perilous a means of travel as a train trip alone; Polly could go to America only with the protection of the boys whom her mother had known since they were children. Polly's mother never considered that there was another way of getting out of Russia except by the devious ways of the underground, fleeing with young men who were avoiding service in the Czar's army at the risk of their lives. This was for her the usual method of going to America.

It was true that in the last spurt for freedom, leaping from stone to stone across the narrow stream separating Russia and Germany, the little company was fired on by border guards. But that was Polly's fault. She lost her footing, and sat down in the shallow water anchored by her long, black, and now sopping wet traveling skirt. The boys, safe on the opposite shore, were forced to return and rescue her. The Russian guards, alerted as the young deserters regained the German side, fired warning shots into the air. So much for the rain of bullets.

Philadelphia, however, the Promised Land, was a bitter disappointment. Not gold in the streets, but dirt, filth, debris swirling in the gutters. Walls of tenements blocked out the sun and the sky was to be glimpsed only if Polly threw back her head and stared straight up. Where was the golden vision? People shouting, pushing, teamsters cursing, peddlers crying their wares, children playing under the wheels of the huge carts . . .

In her second month in the millennium Polly went to work in a factory that made buttons and badges for elections and special occasions. She made buttons for the McKinley election and, not much later, his assassination. With McKinley buried, she found a job as a "finisher" in a firetrap of a loft where a hundred other girls worked jammed together, with no place to lie down if they felt sick except on the bales of goods to be finished. Steam came up in clouds from the pressing irons, heavy stagnant heat radiated from the stoves. A hundred girls, and one filthy toilet. Polly was so furious about this lack of common decency that she went straight up to the boss and told him what she thought of him. Sleeves rolled up and brown eyes flashing, she organized the girls to clean the place up with buckets of lye—although the only way that closet could really be cleaned would be to burn it down. In Polly's millennium there would be clean toilets for all.

The union organizer got wind of the unquenchable indignation of this new firebrand. It did not matter that she knew nothing of parliamentary rules and less of English; he appointed her to preside over the new finishers' local. In no time she had so many girls organized that they could afford to hire a fine little hall for her local to meet in. But when her local voted to strike, there were no strike funds. Polly had spent their money on a red carpet for the hall. She stormed a formal meeting of the Brotherhood of Carpenters and Joiners, no immigrant, greenhorn union, but one of third- and fourth-generation Americans, an outcrop of the respectable Noble and Holy Order of the Knights of Labor. In Yiddish she addressed the carpenters as "Brothers and Sisters"—and it didn't matter that there were no sisters. She told them what she was convinced Tolstoy had said: that all workers were brothers. She told them that her finishers' local needed money to strike for decent working conditions, decent hours, decent wages. Their children must grow up in the country and drink fresh milk! A non sequitur, but passionately spoken. She told them that because they were a strong, rich union they should help her union, which was weak. That was brotherhood. Everything she said was obvious to Polly. The carpenters, without understanding a word, comprehended perfectly. They emptied their pockets for the finishers' strike. Polly jubilantly reported to her girls in their newly-carpeted hall, "Already the strike is a great success!"

This is the moment when Philip enters. To Polly this young organizer for the Ladies' Garment Workers was the great man, the educated man. In the ten short years Philip had been in America he had climbed out of the sweatshop. His first instrument of survival in America had been a twenty-eight-pound pressing iron, wielded fourteen hours a day. By this means he ate and paid his rent. What gave life its meaning was his intention to get himself educated in this new land. He had arrived with fragments of a Talmudic training as preparation.

When Philip discovered Hull-House his upward progress began. "What do you want to do?" asked Jane Addams. "Miss Addams," he solemnly replied, "I would like to educate myself so that I may return to the garment industry and ameliorate (he was consuming the dictionary these days) immediate evils!"

"Philip," said Jane Addams, "I'm for it. Our country needs educated young men and women to help the others!" And so began the collaboration that was to lead through the gates of Harvard. To prepare him for an American college, Jane Addams arranged for Philip to be privately tutored, during vacation time, at a girls' finishing school just outside of Chicago. Then he enrolled as an undergraduate at the University of Chicago. After two years Philip was dissatisfied with the economics teaching and transferred to Harvard. He wanted to get the best education possible so as to become a good emissary from America to her newer arrivals.

President Eliot, greeting the freshman class of '03, had heard of the presence of the immigrant boy whose patron was Jane Addams, and who had made his way to Harvard by pressing clothes. When Philip, in the receiving line, came abreast of the great man, Eliot paused at his name, "So this is the gentleman who comes to us from the labor movement? And what, young man, do you intend to do with the education Harvard will give you?" Philip and the president were equally, though antithetically, innocent. In surprise that his purpose was not obvious, Philip stammered, "Why, why, Sir, return to the labor movement from which I came."

"What a waste of a Harvard education!" exclaimed Mr. Strawbridge of Strawbridge & Clothier to the Harvard man he had so cordially welcomed for Alma Mater's sake, but who turned out to be a labor organizer!

Philip had come to Philadelphia to help the finishers—Polly's union included—with their strike against Mr. Strawbridge. Philip first saw Polly weeping in a jail cell where she had spent the night, charged with hurling a brick through the plate glass window of Strawbridge & Clothier on behalf of the striking finishers. His first job was to get her out of jail. It was not *she*, she insists today, who had thrown the brick, but she couldn't let the police take away the old lady who did throw it . . . now, could she? Philip thought he had never seen anyone with so courageous a fighting spirit, and such bright brown eyes.

In spite of Polly, the strike was lost. After desperate weeks, the girls dribbled back to whatever jobs they could find. Philip left for Kalamazoo for a new battle. Polly, blacklisted, couldn't get a job. One day, in the depths of her despair, a letter came with a ticket enclosed. In it Philip begged her to come to Boston, to help in his work in the Settlement House, and in his union activities. On this new battleground they would struggle together for the poor and for the labor movement. He would organize the men; she would organize the women.

And so she came to Boston. In her heart echoed her sister-in-law's admonition: "Organize? And marriage? Anywhere does your Mr. Human Rights say marriage?"

Polly's woebegone figure, waiting in the train shed to be rescued, so moved Philip that he wanted to put his arm about her, wipe the streak of soot from her nose with his clean handkerchief, and say, "It's all right now, Polly. It will always be all right." What he said was, "Let me take that bag."

"No," said Polly. "I can carry it. Why should you carry it?" It was important to show Philip from the first that though she was alone in this strange Boston she was an independent woman.

At the Settlement House Philip sat Polly in the chair at his desk, still clutching the disputed bag, and told her to wait there for him. How was Polly, trembling, to know that the great man Philip trembled more than she? Ever since he had sent off that letter, Philip had been tussling with his great problem: How do you get married in America? Organizing he knew. The strikers, strike funds, picketing, blacklisting, lockouts, scabs, the police, the courts—but of marrying in America he knew nothing.

"Rory Albertson! That's what I'll do! I'll ask him," Philip exclaimed to himself. Rory was the *real* American. Didn't everybody concerned with making America the best place for people to live come out to the Farm! Rory would know how to get them married.

Rory had just dismissed the Breadwinners' class when Philip confronted him, "You know about the Philadelphia finishers' strike, Rory?"

"I thought it was lost."

"Oh, it was, it was. We lost it." Philip was impatient. "But one of the strike leaders is here now, in Boston."

Rory clapped Philip on the back with enthusiasm. "Fine," he said, "that's fine. Will he do an editorial for *The Twentieth Century*? A stirring story on how the strikers have lost the battle but not the campaign! The Harvard Socialist boys will want him to talk to them. Tell you what: bring him out to the Farm with you this weekend. Hazel will want to meet him. Lippmann will be there, and Price and Eliot. Bring him out. We're getting the hay in and can use every hand."

"I wrote to her to come to Boston," Philip murmured. "I said she would organize the women and I would organize the men and we would go on, together, working for the movement."

The uncertain tone struck Rory and opened his ears to the pronoun. "She? It's a *woman*? *She'll* organize! Philip, what did you bring to Boston? A labor leader, or a wife?"

"That's it," said Philip, immensely relieved. "How do you get married in America?"

"Good God!" Rory burst into guffaws. "Bully for you!" He clapped Philip on the back. "We'll get you married. We'll take her to Portsmouth and get you married at the Town Clerk's. Then we'll bring her out to the Farm and Hazel will fix the Castle for your honeymoon." Philip, in his mind's eye, saw the "Castle," the uninhabited of the two chicken houses, sitting off by itself under the orchard trees. After the chickens had been evicted, he had helped to scrub it down, reroof it, whitewash it, and it had become the children's Castle. Now the children would be evicted and it would be his

Castle, his and Polly's. For the first time this getting married seemed possible.

Rory was still chortling, "So she came to Boston to marry you and to organize the women. Two great causes!"

"I . . . I didn't say . . . anything . . . about getting married," Philip confessed slowly. "I didn't know how to put it in a letter. It seemed such a cold way of saying it. I only asked her about the organizing—if she wanted to come to Boston to organize." The picture of Polly forlorn, sitting, waiting on the edge of his office chair, nagged at him.

"You haven't *asked* her, man? Haven't you *told* her?"

Philip looked at Rory. "Don't you think she understands?" he begged.

Rory stared, then pushed Philip through the door. "Good God, man!" he shouted. "She probably does. They usually do. But go TELL her!"

Late in the afternoon of the day Rory was to bring Philip and his bride-to-be out from Boston and carry them off to the Farm, Hazel, braids bound around her head like a crown, strode down the side of Brake Hill carrying fresh pine boughs. The resin stained her hands and released the lovely smell about her. Behind her, one of the Harvard boys dragged the greater boughs like a sweep. In the orchard below they could see the Castle. The dispossessed furniture stood under the apple trees; the mirror of the old bureau shone like a still pool, the white rocker creaked as the rooster attacking it challenged its presence in his domain. Daisy Mae the cow, snorting, investigated the freshly sheeted cots.

Hazel tacked the pine boughs above the door lintel and wove them among the rafters, then stepped back to inspect their work. With a sudden inspiration Hazel dashed up the lane and returned, lugging that huge picture which had always hung above an offering of bright flowers or autumn leaves, as the ceremonial center of the Farm: the Camden portrait of the bearded Whitman. "Come, I will make the continent indissoluble," she declaimed to Sam, her voice resonant with love for all the world and especially for the little Russian bride Philip was bringing. Hazel saw herself offering America to her Russian sister:

> With the love of comrades,
> With the life-long love of comrades.

It was dark when Rory and the bride and groom got off the trolley. The fieldstone gateposts stood massive and square. Between them Polly could just see the dusty ribbon of a lane and a lamp burning in a distant window. She listened to Rory booming at Philip, he sounded full of friendliness and cheer. They walked down the lane, Rory on one side and Philip on the other.

This was Polly's first venture out of the little room Philip had claimed for her at the Settlement House. Where was she now? She knew from the soft cushion under her feet that her shoes were scuffing up little clouds of dust. It made her homesick for her childhood. The leafy trees lining the lane were thick shadowy shapes. A hill began and lost its rolling contour in the dark. There was a stretch of meadow under the lighter sky and the black sharp outline of the woods beyond it. She heard a flush of wings, as a late barn swallow swooped by. The crickets chirped in the dew-wet grass. A vague miserableness closed about her.

Had it really been a wedding? Was this all there was to a wedding: the bare smelly room; the indifferent clerk who put his hand out for the money before he had finished mumbling the words; the signing that was so quickly done? Philip had wanted to guide her hand with the pen, but Polly said she could sign her *own* name.

Was this the significant act that bound Philip and herself for life? In Russia the bride wore starched lace petticoats and red boots and the couple were driven away in a troika jingling with bells. The dancing lasted all night. In *her* millennium weddings would be like Russian weddings! She tried to thrust her sister-in-law's warnings out of her mind. Perhaps he had only pretended to marry her! She didn't feel any different.

Rory was saying, "Well, here we are. You two won't want to go up to the house tonight. Plenty of time to meet people tomorrow. You'll want to be by yourselves." He gestured into the darkness. "It's all yours, Philip. Goodnight to you both. There'll be coffee on the stove in the morning. Mind you carry your bride over the threshold!"

Philip and Rory shook hands. Polly drew back when Rory leaned to kiss the bride, but she staunchly offered her hand. Then they were alone.

"Now what do we do?" Polly asked unhappily.

"There's a little house over the fence, in there," Philip said. What would she think if he said it had once been a chicken house? He walked a little way.

"Philip," Polly said loudly, for fear he, too, would disappear in the night.

"I'm right here. Come this way. The fence is here." She moved in the direction of his voice. With one hand Philip held up the bar of the stile, with the other reached out to guide her. A cow lowed softly and a broad, ungainly shape seesawed from side to side out of the gloom. Philip and Polly came out from under the trees, it seemed lighter, and suddenly she saw the dim shape of a little house.

Philip wanted to take her hand. How do you say to a woman that you love her? How do you put your arm around her and comfort her? It had all gone wrong. This was not what a marriage should be. Perhaps they should have been married in Philadelphia, properly, with the rabbi standing under the canopy, and the glass of wine to be sipped from and smashed, and all the people in the rented suits and dresses. He had not done this wedding business right.

The little house stood before them. The warped wood frame of the screen door squeaked as he pulled it open. "Come, Polly," Philip said, trying to cover up his wretchedness, "let's call it a day."

He made no attempt to carry her. Polly would have said, "Don't do that. Don't be silly. I can walk." She lifted her skirt to step over the threshold, then leaped back and clutched his arm. "Philip," she whispered, "Philip, there's something in there. I . . . I can hear it breathing . . ."

Philip listened. He, too, could hear a breathing, many breathings, as though the night itself respired. It was nonsense, he decided. It couldn't be inside the house. It must be outside. "It's the cows," said Philip. But neither of them moved.

"Philip!" cried Polly suddenly, no longer whispering but aloud. "There IS something in there! Ooh-ooh Philip!"

In the darkness a suppressed giggle burst into a bubble of sound. "Now see what you've done!" cried a female voice in laughter. There was a great whoosh of pent-up breath released and laughter and cries of "Welcome Philip! Welcome Polly!" Somebody started singing Mendelssohn's Wedding March: "Da, da, da-daa. Da, da, da-daa" and from all about voices joined in. "Da, da, da-daa-da-, da-da, da, da-daa."

A match flared, lighting up laughing faces. And then, one-by-one, brightly flaming, the candles of the wedding cake as beautiful as a palace, blazed. White and pink shone the frosting, and the silver on the white cloth gleamed. The shadows danced upon the white-washed walls, upon the green, fresh-cut pine boughs. Polly saw the people who had been standing pressed back against the walls. Such beautiful people! The women with their long unbound hair catching the flickering candlelight. The young men and the young women stepped away from the walls and swinging their hands, moved close to the table, singing, "Da, da, da-daa. Da, da, da-daa." One woman's strong ascending voice led all the rest.

"Carry her, Philip. Carry her over the threshold." Rory's voice spoke up behind him. Philip stooped, lifted Polly up into his arms and carried her over the threshold. The welcoming singing circle closed in about them. One of the women came towards her out of the circle carrying a candle. A gust of air caught its flame, lighting up the gilded frame of a picture hung with the green pine boughs. The face looked down at her, the white-flowing bearded, benign face. Polly's heart, like the late swallow in the twilight, swooped in her breast, "Tolstoy!" it sang, "Tolstoy!"

chapter four

Orphans of Utopia: 1913

We children were to be the privileged heirs of that pastoral utopia, the Farm. We were to be nurtured in freedom: our souls, minds, and bodies were to grow untrammeled by the swaddlings imposed by a society confusing prejudice and superstition with the will of God. We would be liberated to stand up strong and straight, "socialized" by the joyous disciplines of Nature, the new souls who were to inhabit the Better World. To this end we were raised and dedicated.

On a lovely summer day a newcomer to the Farm had only to catch a glimpse of us to be convinced that here was the Kingdom of Childhood. If you arrived down the lane for the first time and unprepared, you might (depending upon who brought you out and whether he was a favorite of ours) either be besieged by the pack, or experience a kind of nonexistence, as if you were invisible, the gaggle of young screaming past you on its own affairs. It was impossible to discriminate among individual children in that first rush. We were all sizes, all shapes, but all had the same bare sun-browned skins, knees like the hide of the iguana, and feet shod in dust and dirt.

Once you could identify individuals, you recognized as leaders Rory and Hazel's three. By 1913 Laurie was a grown-up eight; Dutchie, tow-headed, Hazel's first boy and the apple of her eye, was a stalwart six; Jude was only a baby of five, as dark as an Indian child. The rest of us were a motley gang, added on to the family by all the winds of adult chance that buffet children, by whatever fate overtakes parents. Chosen or inevitable, however it is that a child is an encumbrance: because a mother or a father had died; or fallen ill; or because a set of parents divorced; or were penniless; or were off

Orphans of Utopia: from left, Laurie, Dutchie, Jude, and little Ming, who was born at the Farm and died there as a young child.

traveling in search of enrichment of soul; or as converts to the service of Humanity, were giving speeches, holding meetings. In whatever circumstances a child's presence was a diversion of energy and attention or an embarrassment to creativity, there was always the solution: "Take him or her to the Farm!" Any living thing found temporarily restrictive was disposed of here; any surplus dog, cat, duck, or child was deposited at the Farm, for the winter, for the summer, or forever.

Brian and Timmy, twins, were permanent: both redheaded. Timmy slight and freckled, Brian called Boru by Hazel after Ireland's giant-King. Rory had found Kathy, only a week since her landing in Boston from Galway, weeping in the Back Bay railroad station with two small boys peeking out from the folds of her skirts. She had been transported from Donegal by a Boston Brahmin family, and had been frightened to death by their big, dark Beacon Hill house. In its cellar kitchen, a discarded lithograph of Mary, Queen of Scots with her head submissively laid upon the block had been somewhat unfeelingly rehung above the kitchen chopping board. Kathy dreamed that the poor Queen's blood dripped at night, hot red drops upon the inoffensive household board. After seven nightmare-nights, she took her twins and fled the house, to get as far as the railroad station. She had no idea where to go from there. But there Rory found and rescued them, and they were to grow up as children of the Farm.

My advent was by circumstances more hilarious than tragic. From the Settlement House streets, now relinquished by the Irish to the Jews, Italians, and Poles, Polly would carry me out to the Farm in a basket hemmed in with still-warm rye bread loaves. But when I was two or so, I, too, was brought out to the Farm to stay. Polly had decided that I should be at the Farm after my first adventure in the real world. I had set out from my highchair at a third-floor window in the Settlement House, to reach the excitement of a fire on the opposite side of the street: the splendid brass-bound, red pumper, belching steam, and its prancing horses with manes tossing—a temptation not to be denied by the fact that I could not fly. I climbed out of my highchair, pushed out the screen, scrambled onto the sill and stood, teetering; then nonchalantly stepped off into vacant air—to be delivered from permanent damage only by a large trash barrel filled by a neighboring family of Italians with old stuffings of their feather pillows.

"We fight against the slums for other people's children!" cried Polly, when it was certain not much was amiss with me. "I won't bring my child up in the slums." And so I was packed off to the Farm. Philip, always logical, could not understand what my lack of respect for heights had to do with slums.

There were children who were precipitated into the Farm family by more ordinary reasons: a Titian-topped, green-eyed boy whose family couldn't handle him—he was a lamb at the Farm; a pair from a broken marriage; Raymie, with a polio leg, from the village, he just came and refused to be returned to a family willing enough to be shut of him; a sickly child, otherwise left to the impersonal supervision of nurse and servants while his parents were at Nice, or Baden-Baden; a schoolteacher new to the village school, together with her very young brother—orphans, they both settled into the family of the Farm. And so on and so on. We children accepted each new member with neither welcome nor question, much as a stream ab-

Top: An afternoon at the Farm, 1912. Philip surrounded by the author at left with bow in hair, Ming beside her and Dutchie behind. Laurie, also with bow, and Jude are at right. A young Salem Street boy is behind Philip.
Bottom: The author with Polly, about 1913.

sorbs all rivulets and by this absorption the chemistry of the whole is changed. So with the addition or subtraction of a child, the family of children took on another nature, a change perceptible only to the initiated adult. The unwary, disentangling himself from a charge through one door of the house and out the other, was incapable of telling which child belonged to whom; which he had glimpsed before, who was lately come, and who was missing.

The keep of those who came with nothing was balanced by the checks sent for others: it all became one. What the Farm possessed was infinitely divisible without accounting: the food on the table, the warmth of the fire, the costumes in the attic trunks, the dog-eared books, the incomplete Montessori sets with which Hazel would attempt, in fits and starts, to teach us our letters, the cot beds in the One-Step-Down Room; all the treasures of existence we were to share equally, no one's rights more legal than another's.

We who grew up at the Farm would from then on, as a matter of habit, accept the claims upon bed or plate of anyone who asked, from anywhere arrived. I remember, from my adult days at the Farm, Kippy, the third generation, throwing wide the door to two itinerant Mormons: "Come IN! Come in! There are plenty of beds!"

A "banderlog" of a tribe, hopping and peering on the periphery of the grown-ups' concerns: the unannounced comings and goings, constant surprises, friends who played and sang and told stories, and went off for walks in the woods, a never-ending delight. We were up and about in the earliest morning to oversee the changes that had taken place during the night: bedrooms, attic, veranda; yard, barn, haylofts, riverbank. At first we went whispering, bare feet pattering—this was for the benefit of the sleepers-in-bedrooms—to inspect those still dreaming. Attempts at quiet were often appallingly noisy as we tumbled over obstacles. Stealthily opened doors gave excruciating squeaks; at each fresh noise we broke into a hullabaloo of hushings. In the attic, on the riverbank, and certainly in the hayloft, we were most likely to find our friends. And then what a whooping! We held a firm belief that to leap astride an unprotected belly, screaming, "I'm going to jump on your middle!" was an acceptable method of rousing a sleeper. Last exploded upon was Rory, all of us piling on his bed so that he could act out the story of the cat who rolled himself in a dish of grain . . . and . . . leapt-out-at-the-mice! This dénouement was accompanied by enormous tumbling on everybody's part, out of which Rory rose up, shedding children.

Breakfast in the summer was a peripatetic meal. Pitchers of new milk, loaves of Kathy's freshly baked bread, were set out on the trestle table on the porch, under the great maple. But no child in the summery days ate breakfast from a plate. We garnered whatever came to hand on our way elsewhere.

During the hot, bright days, the doors and windows of the Farm stood wide open, no distinction between "in" and "out." Through the open rooms, from woods and river, fields and barnyard, an army of children and livestock rushed. The animals were our camp-followers: two pink piglets, assorted dogs, kittens, a file of garrulous ducks, pet chickens. Favorite was a featherless chick named Salome because she went around with so little on. Laurie, who was just learning to knit, made a red sleeveless sweater to keep her decent. One tragic day, Hermann Blumgart, then studying in the Medical School of which he was to be a great teacher, stepped on Salome. She was buried with full funeral rites. The children engraved her tombstone: "Salome: killed July 10 by H.B."—the poor young man's initials affixed as a perpetual indictment.

In winter life took on another nature. Our giggling, wriggling crew jammed into the steamy hot bathroom around the oil stove that gave off a smell of heat—delicious after the icy cold of the One-Step-Down Room where most had cots—and threw flickering patterns on the ceiling. Hooks ran around the bathroom walls at child's height. On these, piece by piece, clothes were draped. Last off at night and first on in the morning were the suits of droopy-legged, droopy-armed, droopy-seated, long winter underwear, like a row of shed skins. Laurie, the eldest, presumed to be in charge, helped with buttonings.

On these clear, cold mornings, we sat at breakfast around the blue painted children's table, cheeks glowing with scrubbing in the icy water, impatiently spooning up oatmeal. Outside, the white world crackled and sparkled, a million gems set ablaze by the sun, the light shining off the ice on the river, the rays reflected as from a mirror. The sky was as bright a blue as our newly painted children's table.

When dusk fell, Hazel would seat herself at the never-tuned piano and play our favorite songs. The smallest squeezed up onto the piano seat beside her. Standing, each head topping the next, were Laurie and Dutchie and Jude, the sturdy ones. Laurie turned the pages. We sang with all the energy of full lungs. Kangaroo and Yellow Dog Dingo ran "thirty degrees, from Torres Straits to Leeuwin, and they ran back as they came." Or much more gently from the German Lieder books: "immer in Gelaufe, hopp, hopp, hopp, hopp."

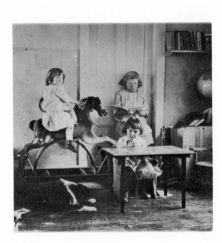

Top: The funeral of Salome. Jude, predictably, is the horse that pulls the hearse bearing the deceased, and Laurie is the chief mourner. *Bottom, left*: Ming rides Jude's rocking horse in the playroom, while Laurie, behind the author sitting at the table, reads. *Right*: The author and Polly in the living room at the Farm, about 1914.

The tall candles at either side of the piano flickered in the gusts of our breath; the lights and shadows chased over the pictures embellishing the music, rich in gold and color.

Best of all was the time before bed, after supper, toasting our toes at the fire while Hazel read. We wriggled in terror of the Red Queen; we were consumed with anxiety for Alice's lizard, Bill, scratching futilely on his slate with his toenail. We gingerly explored our own noses when the Elephant's Child's trunk got stretched for his " 'satiable curiosity." As Undine sank beneath the waves, Brian burst into sobs.

Yet today I think our sharing was not by conviction, but because we were expected to share. There was nothing one could claim securely as one's own, not one's bed, not even one's Mummy. No toy was long privately owned. That highly developed sense of "what's mine" which so helps to define one's self to one's small self, rarely worked in our lives.

Rory built shelves at varying heights along the playroom walls. "Every toy to be returned to its proper place." The blocks were to fit here, the books to have a shelf of their own. He had planned a space for Dutchie's monkey, Jude's rocking horse, Brian's cow. In practice no one put anything back where it came from. We all rode Jude's precious rocking horse, though we called it "Jude's." Dutchie's battered monkey, the chewable, huggable extension of his own aches and joys—was it "borrowed" by another equally needy of comfort? The premise that the Farm itself was shared, that life and love within its gates were shared, made it impossible to delimit "trespass."

And after loss, in whose lap was Dutchie to weep? There was always a plethora of mothers; Timmy called them " 'nother mothers." Yet some miseries do not yield to indiscriminate comforting. Our Heaven was the next circle above Purgatory.

Hazel planned that Dutchie, her man-child, would grow up to be the new Whitman, herald of the future. On a warm summer's day, the adored babe holds court upon a quilt in Hazel's garden. Hazel's garden was the only square of grass kept rolled and cut, made private from the porch by a lilac hedge and entered through the arch of overlacing branches, roses bordering Kathy's asparagus bed beyond. In that pleasant place all the family stops whatever they are doing to assemble when Dutchie has his levée, leaning over one another in all the postures of delight and adoration associated with the manger crèche. Animals are represented by a curious heifer, straining at her rope in the field beyond. This babe has no crib. He lies, the symbol of Nature's generosity, naked in the June sun, his skin tanned golden, his head covered with fine bleached fuzz, his eyes as blue as the weather-breeder sky above him—reaching, kicking, gurgling, grinning. "Hoopla," cries Rory, tossing his young son into the air; "I make such beautiful babies!" Dutchie screams with delight. The females in attendance are entranced. Catherine, from a household encumbered by nursemaid and upstairs maid, by butler and chauffeur, has never before joined in such public joy at a naked babe. She sees Rory alone as author of this marvel. And so, too, does the hunch-backed secretary of the Breadwinners' College. Rory, knight-crusader, soldier against injustice, defender of the weak, is the omnipotent male. His grown-up daughters are beginning to consider his baby-making capacity more nuisance than testament. There were already too many of Rory's babies here, there, and elsewhere. "He needn't feel it's an obligation!" protests Faye to Phyllis.

The court is divided. To the young men, this is a pre-Raphaelite romance of Motherhood. To them, Rory's part in the affair is minimal. The miracle is of Hazel's creation. Not simply the miracle of the bringing forth of a child, at least not for the young Harvard medical students, far too accustomed to the birth process to emote over mechanics. It is this ambience of the simple joys—the naked babe, the soft air, the smell of the grass—and Hazel, a new breed of mother, outstretched on her stomach in her white bloomer suit (by unwritten law no one else on the Farm wore white), swinging her strong white-stockinged legs, her hair unbound. It is she, basking in her affinity with Nature, whom the young men celebrate.

From Tuxedo and Asbury Park, the Hamptons and the Madison Avenue fifties, come these sons of heavily respectable families; from quiet, semidark houses, where half-drawn blinds protect the Chinese carpets, a stray beam of sun strikes color from Tiffany lampshades, and massive furniture sits somnolently in decreed positions. Their mothers are remembered as well-corseted: consulting diamond watches suspended by diamond bows from their tightly encased bosoms.

Because there are more young men than young women in this scene, the balance of attention is diverted from Rory's male prowess. He feels the shift, loses interest, and untangles the heifer wrapped about in her rope; then remembering the break in the pasture fence, he orders up the engineering boys. "Can't moon around women stuff all day, we've a fence to fix!" The young men follow reluctantly, but Rory's female entourage leaps up and goes off gladly, one to get the hammer, one the wire-cutter.

A roar is heard, a cloud tops the rock pile rise and travels the lane, to disclose, when the dust settles, the brass-bound Royal Tourist, chariot worthy of Apollo. All now dash off to greet this new excitement. The girls want a ride. Hazel is not so much older that she can resist.

The baby, lately king, is abandoned. The screen of faces protecting him from the limitless sky has disappeared. His world has abruptly emptied. Suddenly he is alone in the universe. A cloud passes over the sun, a cool breeze shivers his skin. He is, above all, surprised. He sucks in his chest and lets out a great howl of protest. Nobody rushes to comfort him.

The unspoken theory is that there on Nature's bosom no harm can come to him. Besides, *somebody* will see him, hear him if he cries. And it does him *good* to cry! It will exercise his lungs, rouse his blood, tone his muscles. Rousseau—defender of the child, free in Nature— has also warned parents against the "tyrannical infant," quick to snatch advantage. The babe must be taught that his caprice is not command. His caretakers are to be moved by their appraisal of his needs: hunger, pain. Poor frightened Dutchie, alone in the vast world! Rousseau did not perceive you as equipped to suffer loneliness!

The freedom of the child is only a portion of that greater freedom from which all men, and all women too, are to benefit. Hazel is to be free from the bondage of motherhood which would exclude her from the worldly preoccupations of men. Was she to be servant to Dutchie's demands, while Rory did battle for the miserable of the earth? When others played charades, was she to be exiled, comforting a young dictator who has nothing wrong with him? Surely a mother's right to escapades, charades, philosophy, or philanthropy was part of the just rights of all men and all women to be equal!

Because the struggle for equality, for justice and the equal sharing in the rights, riches, responsibilities of the world was the unchallengeable keystone of belief, and because we children, when small, were poor at dialectics, we exhibited our opinions, our side of the argument, in such fashion as we could. Jude, growing out of infancy, took to banging her head, sucking her thumb. Despite pepper, she sucked. Despite bandages, sucked. When her thumb was bandaged tight to her fingers, she sucked the whole thing. Why, amidst these ecstasies over freedom, was that poor thumb so determinedly imprisoned? Hazel never made conscious distinction between the ethos of freedom and the bits and pieces of her Puritan inheritance. No sugar on oatmeal, except with the *second* helping. Food could not be left on plates, no matter how cold and congealed a mess.

Jude rarely howled, but her face grew dark and furious and plop went the thumb in the mouth. There was no budging this child when she rebelled. She was granite, not to be blandished, especially by any of the crowd of nonparents when what she wanted was her *mother!* She was three-ish; had taken sick: hot, cold, wretched, at the end of a long afternoon of play. Her cheeks flushed and the glitter in her eyes too bright, she had been cordoned off from the rest of us by orders of one of our medical authorities and fretted herself to sleep in the crib she had so recently vacated. In the late night, she woke in the clutch of a terrifying nightmare. "Something dreadful! Something dreadful!" she screamed, and the door opened. "Oh Mummy, dear Mummy!"

But the hand laid upon her wet forehead was a man's hand—not even Rory's. Jude hated the medical boys for reasons of her own: when she wanted to climb into her mother's lap, why was someone else's head there? The incipient doctor held the candle closer, looked into that open, infuriated mouth, saw the spots, and with professional satisfaction diagnosed measles. Jude, clamping her mouth tight, set teeth marks in the tongue depressor.

Hazel was at a Votes for Women rally in Boston. Such a glorious success! So many wonderful people!

Not long after, Jude began to display odd preferences. She no longer clung to the soft, battered bear with whom she had nightly bedded, but had to have hard uncomfortable toys before she would go to sleep. Her choice was a small iron fire engine horse, a miniature Clydesdale, which she clutched in the hand that went under her cheek. The other hand bore her thumb directly to her mouth. Sometimes she cried in her sleep.

It was poor comfort to Jude to be one of the indiscriminate flock, welcome with all the rest of us under the wing of Hazel's love. How, without being claimed by Hazel and by Rory as their especial child, *their* Jude, they *her* parents, Laurie and Dutchie hers, how was she to shore up her sense of her own particular self: the unique Jude? Had one no unchallengeable claim upon a parent's lap or bosom? She

The author and her lop-eared dog in the playroom at the
Farm, 1914.

must compete not only with any other child who demanded a place
but clamber over grown-ups, prone upon the riverbank, or squeeze
in amongst the stand of legs, to tug at some attainable part of
Hazel—a bloomer edge, a white middy's bottom, a finger—or pound
on a leg. Then Hazel would laugh and rescue the importunate one,
and hug her close and lay her cheek upon that dark head. But not for
any satisfying period of time. Jude could never be certain she had
won her mother's undivided attention. There were too many of us,
nudging and pushing for the caress another momentarily achieved.
And too many grown-up people, always talking!

Timmy and Brian also struggled for their special mother, though
Kathy was always present. She could be sought out by her boys in
her private corner of the attic; or in what became known as "Kathy's
garden," where no one trespassed without invitation; or at the
marble dough slab in the kitchen, but she would *not* come forth to
champion her sons, nor fondle them where all the Farm were gathered. She could not publicly be appealed to against injustice. She
had, in some unspoken way, surrendered the twins' upbringing,
deeded them to Hazel and Rory in exchange for the roof that cov-

ered them, their place at table, and her seclusion behind the gates of the Farm, from the terrors of the real world.

We took it as a commonplace that the first devotion of all grown-ups was to the "underdog." We were not the underdog, that was someone else, someone called "Humanity." Humanity was what kept Rory and Philip in Boston all week so that they were fathers only on weekends. Humanity was what the books, especially the huge unwieldy ones on the bottom shelves, were full of words about. Humanity was what Walter Lippmann, trying to shut out of his mind the noise all around him, wrote about at Rory's desk at the end of the front room, scribbling away on his yellow lined copy paper. It was understood that Walt Whitman's picture, one-third face and two-thirds beard—having returned to its proper place after presiding over Polly's and Philip's wedding—under which picture Hazel always set a fresh basket of green leaves, or the first spring flowers, was a dedication to Humanity.

All the lives the children knew anything about were spent, it was taken for granted, in serving Humanity. Marriage, husbands, homes, children were incidental to that Great Work of Life. We, too, would one day go out and save Humanity—if it wasn't by that time all saved.

chapter five

Dissolution in Eden: 1912-1917

"Love" was another great word at the Farm. As Laurie
and Dutch grew older, more knowing at ten and nine (Jude at eight
was not yet to be counted), their ears sharpened to the variety of
meanings, the intimations of the word. There was Christian Love.
Love of the poor. Love of the working man. Love of the peasants, if
you read Tolstoy. And Walt Whitman's Love for all the world. Hazel
was fond of quoting from Tolstoy: "Christian Love, love of one's
neighbor, love of one's enemy, is worthier, sweeter, than the feelings which the beautiful eyes of a young man can inspire in a romantic and loving young girl." There was even talk about the more
abstruse aspects of Love: Havelock Ellis's vision, Freud's analysis,
the vagaries of Krafft-Ebing.

And Love had political aspects: the equality of the sexes and the
coming emancipation of woman; there were eloquent speeches on
women's rights, including "the first right of all—to have a baby."
Liberal groups passed resolutions vindicating Maxim Gorky's ex-
tramarital relationships. Professor Charles Zueblin preached "The
unfortunate sisters are not worse than the legalized prostitutes
who live with their husbands and don't love them. . . ." Emma
Goldman, revolutionary anarchist, championed by Sam Eliot
against the Harvard Establishment, wrote "if the world is ever to
give birth to true companionship and oneness, not marriage, but
love will be the parent."

In this apprehension of "Love" there was a growing presentiment by the two elder children that there was something personal
to themselves in this love business, not just adults' words floating
about. It began to be evident to Laurie and Dutch that there were,
existing outside the gates of the Farm, half-brothers, half-sisters of

whom they had no direct parental information, unaccounted for by the arithmetic of Rory's marriages; ladies with other relations to Rory than Hazel's claim as wife.

"My women are Free!" Dutchie, half asleep in the long grasses of the woodsy knoll where Rory was building Hazel a house in the trees, heard his father proclaim, "Free to do what they wish!"

And then Hazel, weeping, "Is my attitude wrong, then? Oh, Rory, am I just a selfish creature to want a selfish love?"

"Hazel, you are a lovely and beautiful woman, but you are romantic to the point of vagueness. You seem to think you were getting married forever."

"Oh! Rory, that's just what I did think!" Hazel cried, evidently to Rory's receding back. Dutchie, peering, could see his father striding off through the meadow to the barn. He could hear his mother's sobs. He imagined her long hair undone, she was the Lady of Shalott, deserted, alone in her half-built house.

Jude reported that she had overheard Rory tell one of Hazel's young champions, "Love is not like an unsliced pie: though some women claim the whole." But to Rory, the host, a good appetite deserved the hospitality of a slice. "Everyone is entitled to a piece of the pie." This hardly romantic phraseology sent the children into a state of giggles, and "piece of pie" became secret code.

Having read his journal of those days, I now can do some of the geometry deriving from that axiom of love by which Rory defended himself against the difficulties presented him by Hazel's "inability to be an Enlightened Woman." In the terms of his transcendental logic it was eminently reasonable that the love he offered Hazel was not diminished by his loving others. He believed in fulfillment for women; that living for the creation of life was a glorious purpose. He believed in the enrichment of experience for himself and the women he loved. Could he have arranged the world, he would have welcomed full responsibility. He would have put all his women under one roof, taken care of their children, and worked from dawn to dusk to see that they were well housed, well fed and clean; given them plenty of chores and plenty of books. If the world was unkind to children who could not point out their fathers with certainty, this was because the world was wrong. Was he not doing his best to set it right? He should have been born either a Mormon or a Sultan, not a Dutch Calvinist!

With so massive an arrogance as to be, at this distance, almost engaging, Rory set down in the account he later wrote:

wherever I have lived there were women [usually he ascribes the magic figure of eight to their number] more or less in love with me. All of them highly respectable and educated, of good taste and good manners. There were no open jealousies, no heartbreaks, no scenes. They are all today, I think, as well as those who preceded them and those who came later, happier than if they had never known me. At least none of them are old maids. . . .

My greatest weakness was in the fact that I could not refuse any woman who said she wanted a baby. There were more of these than anyone will guess. And some of them not only said it, but howled like the devil when they thought fate was cheating them. And I always hated a noise. . . .

Because of such digressions some considered Rory lost as a leader of the Socialist cause. Vida Scudder, Wellesley lady-professor and High Priestess to the Socialist movement, had hoped for so much from him: "And now you follow in the footsteps [. . . of those . . .] preferring the pleasures of the flesh to the joys of the spirit, rejecting the sacrifice, which the Cause demands of you!"

"You must think I am a romantic notion of a medieval Saint!" Rory objected, shocked that "so intelligent, socialist, suffragist, broadly cultured, widely traveled, so *American* an educator," could take such a narrow and archaic view. "You do not understand my true, red-blooded self!"

In turn, Hazel divulged her betrayal to her diary, her "secret confessional." She would be solaced, she wrote therein, by "my gray priest, my river!"

Nothing in nature being static, neither rock nor soul existing that is not thrall to time and process, the days of idylls are numbered; all worldly Edens, all earthly paradises are doomed to change and decay. From this distance the stages of disintegration are manifest: the early enchanted years were forever gone.

Rory had entangled himself with his "Madame X" whose enchantments he considered of a permanent nature. She abhorred the Farm and communal living, whereupon he set up a second household in Boston. She, possessing a fortune—and a baby by Rory—bought a house on Beacon Hill. He argued that it would be more efficient to have proper Boston quarters from which to direct his civic activities. Bedding down during the week in the Settlement

House was a nuisance. There was no privacy to write or to see people important to his various causes. He would spend weekends at the Farm supervising. Besides, his accommodating conscience continued, Faye and Phyllis and Christine would get better schooling in town. Phyllis could go into nurse's training, Faye to Boston University, Christine to a good high school. So he and the girls of his first family settled in with his third, though this time not legitimized.

Rory's girls were glad to be in town, where the boys were. They had begun to find Hazel's attraction for the young men irksome. She had no right to entice the best men, to sit on the block of tree trunk that was her throne at the fireplace, hands locked around her legs, cheeks flushed with the warmth of the blaze, hair like a mantle over her shoulders—and young men strewn about her on the floor. As a wife she should retire from competition. Phyllis and Faye pretended to spurn the intellectuals and took up with a local crowd. One owned a Model T Ford and another possessed a motorcycle.

The Farm saw Rory less and less frequently. The girls came out every weekend. Madame X and child, never. Of Madame X, Hazel never spoke, nor wrote of her in her diary. Not alone out of delicacy, but because she would always believe that if you don't *talk* about it, any fact of life can be made to disappear. "Sometimes," Hazel murmured, standing in the doorway to wave off those bound for Boston and a new week's work, "Rory seems hardly able to wait for Monday morning!" Bruno Beckhard would be up when the stars were still bright to make pancakes for the crowd going back to town. They had to catch the six o'clock trolley to connect with the seven o'clock train to get to work in Boston, or classes in Cambridge, at nine. Rory never had any difficulty in getting up. He'd be up and shaved and dressed and go around and shake everyone. His female admirers were roused and dressed promptly. Rory would shake the Harvard men only once. He had no patience with those who couldn't get themselves going when called.

At the last minute the academic boys arose as one flock, crowded into the bathroom, or used the kitchen sink to wash, threw toothbrushes and socks, if they could find them, into green bags, searched for books scattered over the Farm. With ties not tied and coats not on, they scalded their throats with hot coffee, besieged Bruno flipping pancakes as fast as he could and, each with a cake in one hand and a bookbag bouncing on his shoulders, sprinted down the lane. The trolley car conductor, more sympathetic toward laggards than was Rory, clanged, coming round the grade, to encourage a last spurt of effort. "We got another minute we can give 'em. Early by a minute this morning," and held the car as long as he dared.

In Boston, Rory's affairs became more complex. He was well into the theory of cooperation: editor of the *American Cooperator*, Secretary of the American Cooperative Society. What socialism could not yet accomplish, this new program for men working together in groups common to their interests, within the capitalist society, would surely achieve. With two families to feed, Rory slid into commerce by degrees. Madame X's money remained her own.

"Cooperation," pontificated Rory, accommodating a public philosophy to his own domestic needs—he was paid for these editorships—would "bridge common justice and free-enterprise economics."

An eminent Boston merchant commissioned Rory to make plans for the conversion of his large department store to democratic cooperation. The employees would be trained to take part and make decisions in the administration of the business that paid their salaries. Most were well paid, and content to leave things as they were, but Rory flung himself into their re-education.

"Yet even when we were talking about democratic control," he confessed in his journal, "something within me was saying, 'I want to get into the realities of business . . . to face the necessities of the market and the trade, to keep costs down . . . to show profits.' " He acknowledged his heresy: "The old communist in me shall be completely buried."

Rory set about becoming, still under the banner of Cooperation, a proper Boston merchant executive, member of the City Club, and of the Chamber of Commerce. He grew more and more preoccupied with new concepts, programs, proposals; sheets of figures on his desk; attention of secretaries; lunches in the company of Boston merchants; conferences with important men. He came more and more impatiently to the Farm, thrown into irritation by its perpetual inefficiency, irresponsibility, and disarray.

He stormed at Hazel. "A dozen cows and you sell no milk! You give it away! You don't even make butter! The horses don't earn a cent. Everything has to be fed—including the hired man! What you raise could be bought in the open market for half the cost. And those crowds you feed! You don't even charge 'em for a meal!"

"The Farm," he laid down in dogmatic terms, "should be an efficiently producing organization. I am its executive head. And responsible for the bills! You are my captain and the family your assistants. You must properly distribute among them the chores of the house and the work in the field!"

"Oh Rory," Hazel wept, "I'm not careless. The boys took the mattresses down from the attic. They must have forgotten to put them back before the rain. Six more than we expected came and I've been so worried about mumps. All the children have them and Carl said I didn't need to keep them in bed. But perhaps some of the boys haven't had them! It's so hard to remember everything!"

"Perhaps I'm not a good organizer," were her thoughts as she wrote to Walter Lippmann, who was about to go to Schenectady as assistant to the first Socialist mayor, the Reverend George Lunn. She asked him whether it wasn't harder to keep the Farm organized with the kiddies . . . and now the girls are in Boston . . . and the cows and the chickens and the pigs and the garden, and the hired man getting drunk . . . than to run an office with all his secretaries?

By return mail, Walter Lippmann, writing from the Harvard Club on June 17, 1911, comforted her. "I've talked so much about the farm that [my friends] . . . have begun to believe that it's a myth. We must prove that it's a reality."

Walter's cohorts, lately of the Socialist Club, saw his opportunity in Schenectady as the first test case of the practicability of the system they so eloquently, but heretofore only academically, espoused. Hazel was in ecstasy at a vision of lunchrooms, playgrounds, clean streets—all to be brought about by one of her boys. She, the inspiration; her influence, albeit a few hundred miles removed, to accomplish this metamorphosis.

The enthusiasm of the pioneer himself was more questioning. "Being in Schenectady isn't as inspiring as it sounds," Walter wrote from "City Hall, Schenectady, N.Y., January 8, 1912."

What appalls me is the smallness of our power and our knowledge and our ability in the face of the problems we are supposed to solve. It's really pathetic to see, as I do every day, twenty-five—fifty men, out of work, hungry, cold, come here with shining eyes to participate in this new heaven on earth which socialism promised them. Many of them lost their jobs because they worked for the victory. And we can't do anything essential for them. Inspect them a little closer for disease—give them a municipal skating rink and a concert! Tabulate a few more statistics of unemployment! Install what goes by the name of efficiency, talk in whispers about possible municipal ownership if the state legislature allows us, and hide our impotence in as sympathetic a face as we can put on.

We are, dear Hazel, a ridiculous spectacle. Between keeping the half hearted in line, and proving to the country that we're safe and sane, between the ignorance of real conditions which we share with everybody else, and the old blunderbusses which go by the name of political machinery, I have all the sensations of a man trying to tie a string around a sunbeam. I'm becoming more and more sure that political victories are comparatively insignificant; that we must know more before we can do more; that the obstacles are not the greed or bad will of capitalists one half so much as the unimaginative, dry, timid, mechanical boxes of wood which go by the name of brains. . .

You don't know how much love I'm sending with this to the farm.

In the shape of a restless wealthy Bostonian, the Devil proposed to Rory a scheme that would gross millions: a dozen corporations to be run by Rory—a network of cooperatives for the employees: food co-ops, clothing co-ops, co-op banks, co-ops to buy their homes. Rory would be the creative engineer, a latter-day Robert Owen, and here put all his theories to work; out of his visions he would make the stuff of actuality.

By now, most of the children went lagging up the lane, their course reluctantly set toward the village school. Dutchie had learned that what he could parrot of Rory's activities was poor coin in the exchange of vital statistics with the village boys: "humanity," "underdog," "the poor," "cooperation," all Rory's litany of service.

"What does *your* father do?"

"*My* father's a fireman, or a plumber, keeps a store, runs the post office."

If it was beyond Dutchie to describe what Rory did, it would have been beyond them to recognize. "*My* father's a farmer!" Was Dutchie's father a farmer? Though he owned the Farm, a *real* farmer was a twenty-four-hour-a-day husbandman of crops and cattle. Sweeping aside all Rory's talking, visiting, teaching, lecturing, the meetings he organized to construct the Better World—Dutchie hit upon the acceptable definition, "My father," he pronounced, "my father's the Boss!"

Dutch, unwittingly, had it exactly right. Rory stood no firmer against temptation than had Dr. Faustus. Lost to the pilgrimage towards social justice, Jesus' communism now far behind him, the Sermon on the Mount as an exercise in practical economics only a youthful folly: all was swept up in the revel of being "Boss."

The Farm, he did not altogether forsake. His conscience resided there and he came regularly on weekends. Hazel would not listen to his grandiloquent reasoning. "But we can do nothing about social reform without money!" Rory shouted at himself as much as at Hazel. He wanted her to believe that he was now engaged in building a million-dollar millennium: "We're going to spend every dollar on social reform. These social movements are so picayune," thus brushing aside the better half of his life. "We want to do things in a big way!" He even brought his affluent sponsor to the Farm. Hazel would not hear of these schemes which centered about money.

The lethal blow was dealt to Hazel's idyll by her favorite knight. Walter Lippmann was one of the few among that ardent company whose vision did not bemuse his sense. He had found machine politics as necessary to the socialists if they were to keep in power, as to Boss Tweed's ring. He was never able "to make what he saw mingle with what he hoped." These are his own words, used not as here in the negative, but in the positive and with charming affection to describe his classmate and fellow in that Harvard Socialist band, John Reed, in *The New Republic* in 1914. He added that Reed "has no detachment and is proud of it, I think." He could have been establishing, in reverse, his own ethos and identity. If his sympathies did not "march with the facts," he was not to be beguiled, neither by Hazel, by his friends, nor by his own heart, into a myopia towards the actual. For this independence of recognition, he had to pay.

As the months wore on in Schenectady, he grew as adept at recognizing how the skeleton of practical politics hung together as the medical school boys at identifying bones in their anatomy classes. He himself could never do the dirty work of politics. On March 4, 1912, he confessed to Hazel [a mistake!]: "From what I've written already you must have seen that the socialism in Schenectady was more of a name than a reality. . . ." "The general strike, sabotage and propaganda of the deed are dramatic and compelling, but they are dust and ashes in the long run. . . ." "I wish I could watch your face when you read this letter: I'm going to resign my position here in a few weeks."

This once, Hazel was neither all-understanding nor gentle. She rushed to attack such betrayal, backed up in her dismay by the friends who saw these as the excuses of a renegade. Hazel wrote Walter a lecture. He had been "too softly" raised, grown up too comfortably cosseted; she charged him with no longer seeing clearly because of his propertied background. Walter, hurt, cried out (on September 18, 1912):

> Surely you cannot mean that I have had comfort and no worry about necessaries. That [kind of] protection doesn't go very far! Protected against what? How can a person be protected against the banes of life if

Top: Rory surrounded by the Farm Family. Those who can be identified include, left, Nennie, Minnie Coles, then Rory. Standing behind are Herrman Blumgart and Hazel. Sitting in front of Hazel at center is Bruno Beckhard, his wife Isabel before him and Aja Katz, a dancer, at right. At far right is Laurie, with Jude in front. *Bottom*: Sam Eliot, his arms outstretched, declaims by the riverbank to an appreciative audience of Harvard boys and their female admirers, including, left, Stan Kelton, and top left, Horace Taylor and Dorothy Davis. Just behind Eliot is Rory's secretary, and behind her is Barbara Corwin, a cousin of Phyllis Albertson, who is at top right.

he sees them. Only an elephant's hide will do that, and I am only a partial elephant [he was tubby in those days] you know.

I have never cared for an upholstered life, and, please God, I never shall. . . .

There is a deep sadness in things. . . . "Ever not quite". . . . Perfection is a want that stays with us, philosophize about it as we will. . . . The great faiths are built on absolutism and when they are gone men have merely their own courage to beat off loneliness. An Odysee that never ends—it's not an unmixed joy.

One by one those zealous young of the early idyll drifted off into encounters in the world beyond the Farm gates. The nature of their adoration of Hazel the divinity, Hazel the dryad, changed too. One, on a wanderjahr abroad, writing across the distance of three thousand miles of ocean, having dabbled in love and in analysis since he had seen her, assessed and reassessed his love for her until he reduced it to tatters:

First you were a miraculously realised vision—then a priceless, because living and actual, ideal, then happiest of all, a flesh and blood woman that inspired me and filled me with joy. . . . I have seen many youths, ay, and maidens fall under your spell and out again, and rejoiced. . . . Now I know you pretend to object to this idolatry. But I think it pleases you. . . . I can only write to you now because you're so much older [she can't have liked that] than I and can take an impersonal view. Your mind is wonderful and I can trust anything to it and expect some answer . . . but part of you is a puzzle and a torment to me. . . .

But now [referring to his own psychoanalysis, not yet common in America], though I am still your Boy, is it possible that only two years ago I was writing wild love letters to you? I'm anxious to help you . . . I don't mean that I want you to be analyzed but drop the motherly attitude with which you look on most of us. . . . I long to save you, still. . . . Oh you could be so much happier, so much a better mother, a better farmer, a maturer, calmer, more confident inspiring person, if you could get cleared up. The world needs it, your children need it, you need it.

Will you permit me to enclose $15 [*sic*!] in part payment for the many times I've eaten at your big table without recompense? (I can easily make it $20 as $15!) I'm overflowing with salary; and I suspect financial difficulties are not the least of your worries.

The final moment of change, not just the ending of the idyll at the Farm, but the beginning of that time when idylls would never again be possible, came on a day in August, 1914.

Rory had decided that Hazel's bungalow on the knoll needed

shutters for protection against the storms that blew clear through it. Since there were no walls and Hazel would not have her view limited by shutters, they were to be hinged to fold upward. Rory supervised and sawed. Two of the MIT boys had gone for hinges heavy enough to take the weight of the big panels. Polly sat on a fallen tree and aired her long brown hair. Jude was a horse dragging logs to the lumber camp. Dutch hammered his nails in straight, a good apprentice.

The boys came back from town, waving not the hinges but the newspaper. Germany had invaded Belgium while they'd been planning Hazel's house. France and Britain were at war with the Germans. When Russia was attacked, only days before, the onslaught (at least to Hazel's mind) had come against an incomprehensible people. But now the French, and the *British*—these were people from whom she could not remove herself, no, no, not the English! She who quoted Shakespeare and Milton, who read aloud to us from Kipling, from Carroll; in spirit she had felt herself chained to the fences of Parliament with the brave suffragettes; or marching to the vision of the Webbs and the Fabian Socialists. Why! Hadn't Toynbee Hall and the People's Palace inspired Jane Addams? Even now, Walter was staying in England with Graham Wallas, who had written that wonderful book, *Human Nature and Politics*. Walter, before he left, had put it on her pillow.

She could not make herself believe in the war. "People are too civilized to shoot each other! This is a moral universe!" she wrote in her diary. But a letter from Walter a month later, from war-torn Europe, made pretending difficult.

On board R.M.S. "Adriatic." Sept. 25, 1914.
. . . Here I am back, and it seems as if a good pinch from you would wake me up so as to be able to say "That horror in Europe is unreal but . . . [you] and the kiddies and the Farm and the sanctity of human beings *are* real." It all came so incredibly fast. On Thursday in Ostende we were sunning ourselves on the beach; on Friday, I was wandering around fifteenth-century Bruges; on Saturday in Brussels people were weeping in the streets. We crept back to London through hundreds of war craft rushing into the North Sea, and then went through two days of unbelievable suspense while the English cabinet was deciding for war. The most peaceful people you met were praying for war, praying that England should not stand aside while Belgium was annexed and France crushed.

I lived with Graham Wallas almost the whole time till I sailed last week. We tried to live in the country and read history and think out a settlement. On August 26 we thought the British force had been annihilated and that the road to Paris was open. I tell you that was the blackest day I ever spent.

75

. . . The next week the refugees began to pour in—three little French children from Reims came to stay at the Wallas's. They had been running in front of the Germans for two weeks—their father was at the front, their mother a nurse. . . . The little girl woke up in the night screaming "les Taubes"—the name of the German armored aeroplane. On the streets of London the kiddies were forever looking up at the sky. . . .

I saw soldiers go . . . as the weeks passed there was a noticeable increase of people in mourning . . . the line of anxious women waiting at the war office . . . the searchlights playing over the sky at night, and this run across the ocean without lights, through fog and icefields.

We tried to find comfort in what we were pleased to call the "larger historic meaning" but I for one don't find any. If Germany wins the whole world will have to arm against her—the U.S. included—for Germany quite seriously intends to dominate the world: if Germany loses, Russia alone wins, and every country in Europe will arm for a struggle in which Asia is the stake.

The war burst the bubble of Rory's commercial extravaganza. His millionaire backer, credit mortgaged ten times over, sat himself down at his desk in his private office, and facing the irrefutable fact that he was no longer a millionaire, that he hadn't a cent but his life insurance (which might perhaps comfort his wife), shot himself.

"The son-of-a-bitch," Rory cried, "how could he do this to me!" When he could collect his wits, he vacated the Boston house—Madame X had long since quit that ménage, but left him in it as long as it served; he signed over the Farm to Hazel and thus resigned command. He was out of a job and penniless. His dream of power and achievement as the leader of vast business enterprises had collapsed, as had that earlier dream of the economic practicability of the Sermon on the Mount as practiced by the Commonwealth in the southern swampland.

With the two older girls, Faye and Phyllis, to care for him, he fled Boston for New York. For a year or two he made various desultory and dispirited efforts at earning an ordinary living.

Then came 1917, and the Revolution in Russia. If he was too old for the American Army—we were now well into the war—he would go off on this new adventure. Unfortunately for his curiosity and radical zest, it had to be, not on the side of the Bolsheviks, but as a kind of YMCA "Dad" to the White Russians, the English, the Canadians, the Yanks who, under a British General, flung themselves into that unrealistic, last-ditch attempt to hold Communism at the Vaga and Dvina rivers. Whatever the banner, Rory bloomed in the fellowship of danger, facing privation and misery with as stout a heart in Russia as he had withstood the physical miseries of those first winters in the Georgia swamps for the communism of Christ. Now he contended, glorying in martial rigor for its own sake, and for the sake of his comrades, whoever they were, or whyever there. "True grit." The nearly defunct government of White Russia gave him its St. George's Cross.

All the young people had gone from the Farm, exploded by the war out of Hazel's orbit: the medical boys sawing off limbs under improvised tents near the front lines, Phyllis nursing, Faye chauffeuring staff cars or ambulances at demand; all the other boys of whatever gifts, in those bloody, muddy trenches. Except Walter, who had been co-opted out of military intelligence into the entourage of Colonel House—to plan the peace.

"We are at war with Germany!" Hazel's diary reads. "Yet the birds in my woods still sing."

Philip went off to Florida, recruited to manage the Polish, Russian, and Ukrainian immigrant laborers in the shipyards; to enlist tin knockers, men who had learned their trade at samovars, pots, and kettles, to fill up the ranks of the solderers, blacksmiths, forgers, workers in iron and steel, desperately needed to build ships.

At the Farm the women were alone. Shutters came unhinged and banged in the wind all the long nights; these were well-established ghosts. Paint peeled and exposed grey shingle to the weather's bite; Hazel admired the patina. A stair-tread gave way and it became automatic to avoid it by always doing two steps at a time in that place. Crops were half-harvested. Fowls and animals of all kind forsook commitment behind wire or fencing. No wood was cut. No woodpile stacked. Hazel and Polly and Kathy established the practice of dragging underbrush home each time they went out walking.

These three women, encumbered by a dozen children, their own and others, some still only waist high, stood against the perpetual physical disintegration that takes the lifetime of one man to stem on any farm, the inexorable insistence with which all material things return to dust. Gallant they were, but disaster struck at the furnace, or the well, or the children. Hazel wrote Walter that her arm was in a cast, as a result of pitching oats for her country "with too great enthusiasm." Polly got lost in a drift as she tried to lug a galvanized iron mop-pail down the lane in a blizzard and, even when she got stuck in snow up to her middle, would not let go of her pail for fear she would never find it again until spring!

Sometimes at the moment of crisis there appeared one of the

77

scattered young men who had called from Boston just to say "hello," on his way to or from some wartime mission. He was at once commandeered. Bruno Beckhard spent a bitter night at 10-below, thawing the pump.

Hazel's faith was the miracle which held the Farm together. It was ample enough to stretch over barn and house, and even more miraculously, over the Farm pocketbook as well. A marvel that the women got through each week with food enough, so devious were the trickles that fed into that communal purse. The only steady monies were the drafts against Rory's YMCA salary and Philip's "keep" for Polly and me.

On one pane of the north window in the fireplace room, "H.H.A. '18" is scratched with a glass cutter. This inscription, idly incised on the glass, perhaps for no better reason than that the cutter had just been used to trim a new light and was lying upon the sill, temptingly close to the window, has always marked off for me the end of an era, as do the letters on a gravestone. In my mind's eye, I see Hazel carving those initials, standing for Hazel Hammond Albertson, with the north wind blowing, the pane upon which she cuts her name trembling under its buffets.

Occasionally, there were letters from Rory somewhere in Russia; or a note scribbled hastily by one of the girls from the hospital, or written in a moment of waiting at the wheel of the ambulance; or a note from Walter from New York on November 10, 1918: "I hear dreadful rumors that you are condemned to wear a corset. Not for your spirit, though—of that I'm certain"; or from a nameless soldier, even a poem, a poor one, composed in the mud of a trench on the Western Front, full of nostalgia. It is from such a poem that I have my own picture of Hazel-sit-by-the-fire:

> . . . the night time world is full of sounds,
> Such little sounds and low,
> The night wind makes careful rounds
> As soft as he can go!
> The old boards hold their breath for fear
> They crack and startle you
> Who listen by the hearth to hear
> The whole world listening too . . .

It is an instance of Hazel's artlessness that the poem and all the letters from her lost "boys," neatly tied up in a box, were furtively and regularly read by each new gang of children to discover the attic, all of us fascinated both by the conviction that we were reading deathless love letters and by our own wickedness. They were

Hazel sits on her log near the fireplace, about 1918. The duck andirons were cast by Henry Willcox.

known from generation to generation as Hazel's Love Letters. It is from that yellowed treasure that I have dug these forlorn bits. Only when, returning to the Farm from the wars, I reread them myself with full permission and at some cost to illusion, did I understand that it was not Hazel, the woman, to whom these ardent notes were written, but to a dream of youth.

One icy March day the latest hired man came home drunk. Polly emptied his oil lamp and refilled it with water for fear he would burn the house down. He tumbled into his bed and Dutchie, Tim, and Brian, under the instructions of Hazel and Polly, barricaded him into his room above the kitchen. Poor man! When he sobered up he pounded all night against his prison door, begging for a light.

The furnace went out. To get it going again proved beyond even

Dutchie's capacities, though he was now a man of eleven years. The plumbing froze and burst, flooding the kitchen floor and then, as the cold increased, icing over to make splendid skating.

Skating was not sufficient to warm us up. Jude, always first when it had to do with horses, and Dutchie hitched up the sleigh. With the two of them on the driver's seat, the three mothers, Laurie, and the rest of us, wrapped up like cocoons in assorted coats, scarves, and mittens, and covered with straw to our noses, set off down the lane. The harness bells jingled as gaily as though God was, and always would be, in His heaven. Off we went to town to invest the last pennies from the teapot in a dozen red roses. It was Hazel's birthday.

chapter six

Adolescent Anarchy: 1920-1928

By the early 1920s, when they lined up for a snapshot, Laurie and Dutch and Jude were as tall as their mother and bulkier. Laurie was a blooming sixteen; Dutchie at fourteen assumed postures very like Mr. America showing his muscles, exhibiting masculinity sufficient to dominate challenging females. Jude, then only thirteen, had in a year, in one spurt, gotten her full growth and stood equal, shoulder to shoulder. In the sere, curled-up pictures of those years, she planted her legs firmly, crossed her arms, and glowered at all comers. There had been Ming, born at the Farm, and in the family pictures always a sliver of a child. She died of what we children thought was a "right-handed" heart (it was probably an enlarged heart, untreatable in those days).

Those shapeless bloomer suits, so gay and free, so coquettishly revealing when worn by Hazel, hung upon the girls like sacks. Whatever implications of future loveliness might be hidden in that adolescent flesh, the bloomer suits concealed as modestly as any Mother Hubbard. Above the clumsy stuff rose Laurie's ash-blonde head, her hair as fine as when she was a baby, snatched back off her brow and held by a rubber band, only the sides fluffing up at her cheekbones. Her eyes had turned a green-blue that varied with light and mood.

It was accepted that Laurie's orbit was the house and its chores. Not because she was in any way domestic but because she was the prisoner of Hazel's loneliness. She knew her mother was a deserted woman, that without her, Laurie, to stand at her side, Hazel was utterly alone. Laurie was held captive by that same freedom which allowed Rory as husband and father, and afterwards, Hazel's court of devoted boys—devotion being even less a contract than marriage—to disappear down the lane.

Sizing the family, early 1920s. From left, Dutch, Laurie, Hazel, Ming, and Jude.

Laurie had become Hazel's household alter ego. Not Kathy, of course. Kathy was alter ego to no one. She selected what chores were to be hers: the baking of bread, the kitchen garden, and, for her soul's sake, her rose garden. She took no orders, however tactfully intimated. She never replied—just vanished. Laurie made beds. Laurie washed the dishes no matter who wiped, and spent the summer days in the canning shed. She swept; when vacuum cleaners became as common as brooms, you could find where she was by following the extra-length cord. She never saw the rooms she perpetually tidied; she never did any task in the house without looking out the window.

Hazel would come into a room and like a stage designer, enchant the set by pinnings and tackings. Here an old curtain tucked up to cover the tear where the stuffing stuck out of the sofa; there a bit of material thrown over a chairback to hide the fading, or the stains; then she would step back as an artist from her canvas, and at a distance see only the spell she had put upon the dingy furniture.

Laurie had no inner eye for any domestic scene. She did all her duties but her attention was not on them. She was perpetually torn between what had to be done, and what was going on elsewhere. She couldn't bear to miss a thing; whatever happened, from gate to house, was an event for Laurie. She forgot the wet-wash man's arrival because there was Brian bringing in his new prize heifer; deserted the pile of dust just swept up, to join Dutchie in the pump house. What ailed that pump this time? The canning jars boiled dry when Kathy called to come and see the eagle circling the lower meadow. In the summer she lugged the dishpans—one full of soapy, the other of scalding, water—out on the porch to the trestle table that she might be the better spectator.

Each slight occurrence, each subtle change in the shift of seasons—the blueberry bushes burning crimson on Brake Hill; the ice booming on the river in the January thaw—every incident in meadow, barn, lane, woods, hill, was gathered in by Laurie. She wove so close a net of all the day's happenings that it concealed chaos; she packed each day with what was visible, made a fine art of keeping her eyes fixed on the foreground.

Scattered from attic to barn were artifacts of the days of belief in the millennium: Lincoln Steffens's boots, now worn by Dutchie to shovel muck in the barn cellar; an old sweater of Sam Eliot's, hung up in the entry; a much-abused robe of Walter Lippmann's, warm and cozy on cold nights; and at the far end of the big front room were the exhortatory books that once had spurred the warriors on: Jane Addams's *A New Conscience and an Ancient Evil*; George Herron's *Between Caesar and Jesus*; Mary Antin's *They Who Knock at Our Gates*; Sam Jones on *Labor and Love*. Laurie knew the mission their yellowing pages preached and how engrossed the Farm once had been in the battles against injustice. But weren't they, the Family, also humanity? Abandoned on the riverbank, Hazel, Jude and Dutchie and herself left to grow up on their own?

The old ideals the Farm had once espoused, with which Hazel forlornly kept faith, never concerned Laurie. I alone of this new generation dedicated by our adults to win the victory for the wretched of the earth would take up that crusade. And not because I was, unlike any of the others, born an idealist, but out of my own necessity for a role in life, because I was to be a solitary, belonging nowhere.

In those years I demonstrated that I was the Farm's least valuable inhabitant. I was never to become a member of the technological age, Philip's child in this. His mind was the only sharp tool he ever managed. He could apply himself to whatever practical problem was set before him, but could never smack a ball with a bat. My hand and my mind were equally poorly acquainted.

I never got the swing of pitching a forkful of hay down from the loft for the cattle. In the barn cellar troughs the steaming muck slid off my shovel before it hit the wheelbarrow. My hands could not strip a teat. If I were to ride Junie, the Indian pony, someone else had to put a foot on his inflated belly to get him to subside to the tightening girth. Once saddled, he usually was quickly quit of me, somewhere up the lane, and returned on his own to the barn. Nobody trusted a hammer in my hands; the head flew one way, the nail the other. At one end of the crosscut saw, I lost the rhythm and the blade buckled. Dutchie tried using me to carry in wood but I could not manage door and wood at once.

Nor was I worth much more in the house. If I wiped the lamp chimneys Laurie had soaked clean in the hot suds and rinsed sparkling for the towel, I crammed the towel too tightly into one end and couldn't manage to get it out the other. Given the funnel and kerosene tin to fill the lamps, I slopped the kerosene. If I rolled the dough, slab, pin and dough adhered, too sticky to manage.

It was accepted that I was hopeless. Mine were the lowliest chores: dish-wiping and lugging swill to the pigs. I was willing, but a nonentity. My right to be one of them was never questioned, but it was skill that made you a member of the initiates, the inner crew, the circle of the accepted with its schemes and jokes and plans. I could only stand around on the outside and yearn.

I began drifting away from activities I was no good at, towards the companionship of the books in the front room. The presence of those books stirred up in my imagination a vague perception of those earlier days: poetic, heroic days. I'd settle on the floor, pull the books from their shelves, clap them free of the dust, read a line or two or sometimes get lost head over heels, stack up those, push others back to lean upon one another. I doubt that I read much in them, any more than Hazel read the tomes so hopefully brought by Walter to educate her in realities. Like Hazel I riffled pages and picked up bits of language, arguments, to decorate my supposed devotion to the Better World.

Philip removed Polly and me from the Farm not long after the war to end all wars was over. He had seen the last "bottom" down the ways and had returned to the Settlement House. He had become supervisor, for the city of Boston, of the newsboys and bootblacks still of school age. Now he had to build Polly her house. She refused to accept Hazel's continued jurisdiction any longer. She would have her own kingdom.

The house of Polly's dreams was to stand upon a hill—with a wood as its backyard. It was to be a house where the floors would be polished like mirrors; where books would be locked up from dust behind glass doors (she never had much sympathy for books), where the breezes would blow in through starched cheese-cloth curtains—an airy, bright and shining house.

Polly's ambition, since she couldn't make the slums vanish, was to remove its population for a weekly airing. For this, she wanted a house and land that would be her own, not too far from Boston: an extension of the activities of the Settlement House, able to embrace Sunday excursions of all the people she would bring away from the slums. She would stuff them with good "substantial" food; fill their lungs with good "substantial" air (the "substantials" are Polly's favorite identification of what was good for you), and thus fortify them against another week of evil in the slums. These were not to be the intellectuals who came to discuss the People, but the People themselves. If they had come to the Farm, as some few did—Joe August for one—Hazel would not have turned them away, but she would not have enjoyed their company. Although she did not always like them, she would still have included them under the great wing of Love. Polly and Hazel both made a distinction between the people who discussed the People and the People themselves. But where Hazel threw her arms around the students and the scholars and would never have kissed Joe August (whom she considered a "primitive"), Polly never really liked "professors" and considered herself to be one of the People.

Mine was a solitary existence on Polly's hill. I ate up the salamis of the Sunday inundations of the Settlement House folk; built myself a tree house to be above the adult world and gobbled Dumas there; fell asleep in the meadow watching the pattern of the daisy petals against the blue sky; decided I would be a writer. I had only to wait to grow up.

I did not recognize that I was lonely; never wondered why I did not walk home with an arm around a friend, or have a friend come to the Hill and play, or go and play at her house. I took my solitary state for granted. The difference between myself and those among whom I moved as though I did not exist, I ascribed to a mysteriously deduced state of "being special." I was growing up for the express purpose of accomplishing "something important" for the world. It was obvious that the decent, middle-class streets on my way to school had nothing to do with the world. The world existed beyond them. A world where Maurice Hindus, camped in a tent behind Polly's house, was writing his first book on revolution in Russia; where Alice Stone Blackwell expounded feminism, and refused to sit down to dine at the same table as my father's cousin, Chaim Weitzmann, because he had had something to do with TNT during the war.

Special or not, we were certainly, in that community, different. Respectable houses sat behind respectable fences on neat handkerchiefs of lawn. The whole street I walked on my desultory way to school might have been a stage set, for all I knew of what went on behind the half-drawn blinds, the carefully arranged lace curtains, the winter-deserted verandahs with only the skeleton of the glider left out to presage summer. I had never been invited across such thresholds into the dark halls where the stained-glass door panels lit the floors in varicolored patches, and the umbrella urns offered their bristling variety of handles. I could not have told you what kind of life was lived in those houses. I hadn't the seed of conception of the orderliness, of the virtues each family strove to present: the breakfast table with the paper lying unopened beside Papa's plate; the long-stockinged legs of the girls swinging disobediently; the time that had been spent with a hairbrush shaping the fat sausages of curls. No ladies I knew came to tea, nor did we, as children, curtsey before we were dismissed. No neighbors of ours came in to evening cards, no gentlemen smoked cigars. I was onlooker, outsider, when, brushed, scrubbed, in tidy best, such families issued in parade for Sunday church. Of the passions and ambitions, maneuvers and heartaches these respectable facades hid from sight, I had not a glimmering. Nor of what they talked about, nor of the games these children played, in mimicry of adult priorities of virtues: tea parties in miniature, the children's sophisticated grasp of social proprieties.

Our front porch was furnished, not with swings and gliders, but with beds for sleeping out; family and guests lay in a straight row against the rough stone of the house. In winter we padded forth in wool socks and stocking caps, lugging hot-water bottles. For daytime and against the weather—some mornings we dug ourselves out from under the weight of snow—the beds were covered by tarpaulins, which Polly managed to find in gay stripes. All this I'm sure was very good for the health, but what must the stranger to that front door have thought, passing this three-bears-row of beds? People who knew, came round to the back.

On holidays, weekends, whenever we could, Polly and I went out to the Farm, I, like an exile returning to the comforting solidarity of being one of the pack, even if a tag-end one. Here all the girls wore bloomers, all wore their hair Dutch-cut for comfort: no sausage curls, no petticoats, no matching coats and muffs; no gliders, no lace curtains—none of the paraphernalia of those incomprehensible streets. But each time I got back, I became aware that even here, at the heart of my place of safety, there were mysteries in which I was not an initiate.

Together we washed and wiped the interminable dishes. We curled up before the fire at night when Hazel began, "It was the best of times. It was the worst of times. . . ." In Indian summer we rolled ourselves in blankets and jumped into the low juniper bushes atop Brake Hill to spend the night under the stars singing to the heavens at the top of our lungs.

But Laurie and Jude, now giggling girls, tried lipsticks in the attic, puffed at cigarettes stolen from Hazel, and pranced before the mirrors, holding bloomers flat over their hips to mimic tight skirts. I watched, too naïve to comprehend new secretive games, and was uncomfortable. I didn't like the dandelion wine and choked on the cigarettes. I didn't like Dutchie's new blend of indifference—as though girls were doorposts—with sudden signals and whispers and touches. My pretense at understanding only incited Dutch to leers and barnyard bellows of laughter.

By the twenties, if Hazel had been willing to acknowledge it, there was plain evidence that the days of the idyll were never to be recreated. She had only to open her eyes to see, in its heirs, the beginnings of rebellion; we had grown long in the legs, thick through, were exploding with wild energy. Hazel, alone, never grew up.

Dutch and Brian and Jude made great show of being rude, hardworking farmers—no job too dirty. They loved to insult the latest variety of intellectual, newly come out to the Farm and sitting about on the lawn, by appearing from the barnyard in hip boots and smelling of dung. Hazel could play the lady and welcome them. No poetic sissies were allowed down in the barn cellar. Now, when a new figure came down the lane, we no longer rushed out in greeting. We disappeared, leaving all hospitality to Hazel.

We even grew suspicious of old favorites. The now-plump stomachs were not the firm seats on which we had bounced. Those sloping shoulders were not the bony saddles we'd ridden home from hikes when our legs gave out. We hardly recognized old friends and stood aloof from them, morose and disenchanted. Now and then some member of the first Farm Family made the mistake of depending upon old relationships, and tried to act *in loco parentis* over an issue of authority on which Hazel had been frustrated by size and strength. An emissary from Hazel attempting jurisdiction over Jude was bellowed at: "You're not my father!" Another sent to curb our lawlessness was pushed by Dutchie into the unused cistern.

The barn cellar was our territory. Here we could be as obscene in language and in gesture as we relished. It became established that Hazel's authority did not extend beyond the house and her own garden. That area with its books, its wind-up phonograph for music, and the visit of an occasional exile taking a moment out from the real world: that was the civilized ambience of the Farm. The barn cellar was refuge for rebels.

The barn's fieldstone walls, once whitewashed each spring, now were discolored with damp. The cows gave off their heavy smell of animals enclosed all winter, their breath making little clouds in the chill. Juniper, the Indian pony, and Jude's fine new jumper with the high-arched neck, Highboy, stomped in their stalls. The barn cats sat amongst the straw and litter in a patient row at milking time. The tack room smelled of well-used leather and soap. The dry smell of oats and hay mingled with the stink of the kitchen slops that Timmy fed to the pigs fenced off in the far corner.

Milking done, we all invaded the kitchen. Hazel kept her distance, shutting us off behind two in-between doors, and played to herself on the untuned piano in the big front room. She didn't like the barnyard smell we brought in with us, and the kitchen seemed intolerably crowded with uncontrollable forces. Sometimes Hazel would murmur plaintively through the dining room pass-through to Laurie, standing with one foot on the other, her arms in suds to the elbow at the kitchen sink, "Couldn't you all be a little more quiet?"

While Laurie washed, a batch of us wiped, grabbing the stinging hot dishes from the rinse water in nips and snatches, sopping at them with towels too wet to do more than spread the moisture.

There never were enough dry towels, and a battle regularly flared up over who had snitched another's towel because it was less soaking than his own. Timmy perched companionably on the marble dough-slab, hugging the pail of slops, loath to quit the kitchen for the hungry pigs. Brian sat upon one milk pail waiting his chance at the sink to scald it, with the others piled beside him. Jude was in the cool-room taking apart the cream separator. Dutchie supervised.

Hazel had attempted to win Jude back to the feminine side by assigning her the separator as a task halfway between barn and kitchen. Jude was furious with this infringement of the time she wanted to spend only on Highboy: to feed him, to water him, to curry him until his black coat reflected light, brush his tossing mane and flowing tail; to adorn him, braiding ribbons in the hair of tail and mane for the shows; to exercise him, holding him to a trot in the lane, jumping him over fences she and Dutch had contrived in the lower meadow, galloping free up the hill. Everything else was a damned nuisance and intrusion.

"When the goddamned hell are you going to get out of that sink?" she bellowed at Laurie from the cool-room. "C'mon, c'mon, I gotta get to the barn. Highboy and Junie haven't been fed."

The scalding water for separator and milk pails bubbled in the biggest kettle on the stove. But Brian, too, had barn responsibilities on his mind. He wanted to brush down the calf he was taking in the morning to the Fair. When Laurie, arms dripping soapsuds, emptied the dishpan and backed out of the sink corner, Brian snatched the kettle from the stove to get his pails scoured first.

"God damn!" Jude roared, outmaneuvered by the distance from the cool-room door. The separator handle went flying at Brian. He ducked, and it sailed through the window above the sink. For a moment there was dead silence but for the tinkling of the bits of broken glass. Shocked, our breath sucked in, we stood transfixed as statues. That separator handle could have cracked Brian's skull as easily as it had crashed the pane. Jude, sick and trembling at her own violence, lit out for the barn and Highboy's stall. No one said a word about that instant of disaster; we moved in concert, swiftly, to efface it. "C'mon," said Dutchie to Brian, "let's get a new light of glass in there before we catch it." Timmy helped Laurie pick out the jagged bits in the old putty. In the doorway, Hazel expostulated, "Children, what *are* you doing?"

The new college crop who straggled out from Cambridge after the war years, having heard a rumor of the existence of the

Farm, were as possessed with getting-rich-quick as their predecessors had been with getting poor. They rarely stayed long enough to change their city splendor for farm clothes. The talk was of the impotence of the League of Nations, of the Red Scare, the Munitions Makers and their intrigues; of the new Irish Free State and the heavy burden on Germany of reparation payments; of the ex-socialist Benito Mussolini who had marched on Rome. A few, at Walter Lippmann's urging, had read John Maynard Keynes's *The Economic Consequences of the Peace*, but most preferred to discuss T. S. Eliot's *The Waste Land* or Shaw's *Back to Methuselah* or O'Neill's plays. The doctors argued over the possible synthesis of Vitamin B.

The early idealists were now successful, involved, preoccupied: on hospital staffs, as partners in prestigious law firms; publishing, editing, running the Theatre Guild; engineers, business executives, men responsible for public affairs and families.

But Hazel had not changed. She was like the river, turning aside from resistance. She seemed a little sorrowful when her face was in repose. Amongst her giant children, Hazel of the free and romantic spirit, symbol of perfect motherhood, the ideal woman, became to the worldly eyes of those who had once been adoring disciples, a psychological phenomenon. They were confronted with the embodiment of their youthful ideals and found themselves a little taken aback. So removed were they from their old devotion to Cosmic Love that they could even talk of *dis*liking people! Hazel believed in loving people even if she disliked them.

"Congenital incapacity to look at the facts," Carl Binger, now a psychiatrist, diagnosed with professional irritation and a sigh for spent delights. In the old days he had met her wandering by the riverbank, picking sweet fern as a solace for some economic problem, and was filled with tenderness. Yet, however presently occupied, that first generation of believers could not sever their sense of responsibility for Hazel and the Farm. In some crevice of their hearts, at whatever waste of energy and effort she was destined to cost them, they wanted Hazel and the Farm, the Ideal, however foolish, to remain in the world.

They made up an informal club: a kind of "Save Hazel" club, an organization which had no ladies' auxiliary. The Farm's charm never withstood the occasional visits from the young wives brought out to this shabby Paradise that they might share its romantic impact upon their husbands' lives. Or when Hazel, shy, a little frightened and fussed by traffic, by the press of uncaring people, came to New York, there was, on the part of the wives, a unanimous "That's Hazel? Why she was supposed to be so wonderful!" How to convey the shapely white-stockinged legs, the skin glowing and golden from the sun, the chestnut braids—all now obscured by the dowdy hat and the heavy tweed suit. Even if they were Hazel's to begin with (which I doubt), such clothes always managed to look as though they had belonged to someone else.

Nevertheless she stirred a poignant chord in the men. Lawrence Langner, now lawyer for the people of the theatre, would telephone Walter Binger, New York City's sanitation engineer. It always went the same way between any two club members: "I say, Walter"— thus Lawrence, Welsh-born—"Hazel's in trouble again."

A pause while both men contemplate the improbability of Hazel's ever being got permanently out of trouble.

"What's it this time?" Thus Walter Binger, knocking the ashes from his dead pipe. And both men sigh, preparing to retackle the problem. No one pretended that they would not have it to do again tomorrow, whatever today's solution. They knew they were being asked to resume the illusions of their youth concerning the perfectibility of mankind.

"We'll have to try and fix up another mortgage," Walter Binger would finally bring out.

A grunt from Lawrence Langner, torn between laughter and harassment. "There are seven mortgages on the Farm right now," he says finally, having consulted with one hand, while he held the phone with the other, the file kept in his private drawer, amazement in his voice that he, a tough-minded realist, could be involved in anything so fantastic.

The mortgages were the result of almost yearly tax crises and a tragic Hazel bemoaning to Carl or Walter or Bruno or Lawrence the blind ways of bankers. She was always certain that *they* would understand. In fact, they did, but not exactly in the way Hazel meant. So little was needed to bring the newest scheme, believed Hazel, to fruition. Not that it was the paying off of the new mortgage that long held her attention, but the wonderful plan in itself: the beautiful colors and smells of the jams they would make; or the fine little pigs the Farm would raise.

The funds collected to build the pigpen somehow escaped their allocation—much as the piglets did. The Farm family spent their days catching the three red pigs with which the project was to start, named in honor of the times: Lenin, Trotsky and Gorky (Kerensky being in disgrace and too long a name anyhow). We called them the "racing pigs." Even after the pen was built, the piglets were never in it, but raced round and round the Farm so that they never grew fat.

So also with the moneys for more fencing and more feed: those sums, too, were difficult to keep penned up. Where the money went, nobody could account. Certainly it was never spent by Hazel upon herself, and Kathy could have lived on air. Besides, as far as Lenin, Trotsky, and Gorky were concerned, they would never have been allowed to be slaughtered. They, too, had become legitimate members of the Family. The economic value of the pigs for the Farm was as a kind of garbagemen. They spent happy, piggy lives until they died of old age and indigestion.

In this way, with variations, Hazel met her loyal legion of practical advisors and, by evading battle, defeated them. Perhaps it was they who were romantic and her position realistic, unless the Farm were to cease being what they dreamed it was—the embodiment of the ideas they wanted, despite good sense, to preserve—to deny facts was the only solution.

chapter seven

The Coming of the Hero

Kit didn't want to have anything to do with the Farm after he'd had his first hard look around in the early 1920s. To begin with, he had come unwillingly with Grandpa Ernest, Hazel's father. Ernest Hammond found Kit, an eighteen-year-old boy of Scotch-Irish and German parentage, in the oil fields of West Virginia. Kit had taken time off from his job in the Pittsburgh steel mills, puddling the red-hot metal, to give a hand to his brother by driving south for him a two-ton truck with a goose-necked trailer that hauled drilling machinery. He'd come back by way of the West Virginia fields to see how the oil men brought in the gushers.

Ernest was supervising a field of eighteen wells. He and his crew were cleaning them up, pulling up the casings with a donkey engine, testing foot-by-foot for weaknesses and cracks. A cable had to be put on the casing; somebody had to ride that block sixty, seventy feet in the air, and noose that length of pipe. No one came forward. Ernest cursed his men with everything he could lay his tongue to, and those old oil men didn't spare any words. Near him on the bank sat the skinny young man in city clothes, watching. Presently Kit laughed, and Ernest, explosive-mad, turned on him: "What the ———are you laughing about,———you!"

"None of them men good enough to put your cable on?" Kit taunted. "I'll ride your rope for you." "You!" and Ernest let go another string of oil language, having no use for anyone from the city. "Let's see your hands." Kit put out his hands—palms up.

Ernest looked at the callused palms. "Guess you've done some work at that," he admitted, and Kit went up the rope. He didn't ride the block. He rode the rope with one leg in the loops, one fist clamped around a monkey wrench. "You leave go of this rope," he yelled at the men below him, "and you'll get this monkey wrench!" They hauled him up—and when the cable was fixed, he slid down. "Boy," Ernest shouted, thumping him on the back, "I thought you were lyin' to me!"

Grandpa Ernest had just bought a new Packard. Now that the wells had come in, he was going to drive up to New England, to take a look at how Hazel and that danged Farm were getting on. Difficulty was, Ernest hadn't been driving long. He eyed the lean young man whose big hands were wide across, and so skillful and gentle.

"What say," offered Ernest to the young man wiping his hands on a piece of cotton waste, "you drive this new tourer of mine East? Ever get a look at all that ocean off there?"

Kit allowed he'd never seen that much water and had some curiosity to get himself a look, but it was really his dismay at the thought of that fine new Packard touring car ruined by the clumsy handling of the old man, that swayed him.

"All right," he said. "I'll take you there. Don't like to see a good piece of machinery ruin't. But I dast not stay long. That's a good job I have up in Pittsburgh. Not going to give it up even so you won't drive hell outta that auto of yours."

So it happened that Kit drove Ernest and Nennie down the lane toward the Farm. Kit was reluctant to come out from under the safety of the big steering wheel.

"How do," he acknowledged introductions, looking as though he'd like to let in the clutch and get gone. What a crazy lot this was—all those women in them danged bloomer suits. What did they want to do that for? Sure didn't help their looks much. But when Hazel came running out to throw her arms about her mother and father, Kit, recognizing that this was a lady in spite of the outlandish clothes, got out of the car, took off his cap, and shook hands. "You must be Christopher," Hazel said.

"Kit, ma'am," and forever after he was Kit to us and Christopher to her. We just stood and looked at him: tall with a shock of upstanding hair, his face sober and his whole body, its long arms and heavyset shoulders, in repose until whatever was to happen next, happened.

Jude, who'd been taking Highboy to the upper pasture when the big car rolled up, waited under the trees, holding the horse's head down hard by his bridle. Now she came to stare with the rest of us, and greet her grandparents, the "Grands." Highboy didn't like getting too near that strange machine. He snorted and tried to free his head, his rear hooves dancing in the dust. Without his seeming to have thought about it, the new young man's big hand went slowly to the horse's head, stayed motionless for a moment upon the velvet nostrils and then stroked. And Highboy, high-strung hater of anything new, thrust his head forward and nuzzled; his tail came down and he stood. Jude was chagrined. No one had been able to handle that horse but herself.

Kit didn't notice. He helped lug the cases into the house, Dutch and Timmy giving a hand. We would ordinarily have made ourselves scarce until after the first inspections of unpenned pigs, downed fences, barnyard deep in muck, corn to be thinned, hay to be mowed, leaks in the roof, shingles loose, shutters loose, paint needed everywhere: until all these evidences of neglect were scored up and enlarged upon by Grandpa Ernest. Nennie would already have inspected the chicken house, vacant again since her last visit. But since Ernest took Kit along to check out the wreckage, we went too, an untidy string of us. This was a new kind of young man. Even Jude and Dutch had the sense to temper their language. We all had a presentiment that we'd not like the shock of a sharp look from those steel-grey eyes.

At the supper table that night we were, every last one of us, cleaner than we'd sat down in a long time. Dutch had seen Kit's callused hands; his own weren't in it for toughness, but Kit's hands were hard-scrubbed, and Dutchie's had been boastingly filthy. Dutch put on a shirt and water-slicked his hair, and so did the other boys, all watching the hard-muscled young man who evidently had no intention of coming to table without his neck clean, his shirt fresh and his hair wet down.

We girls, too, brushed out the snarls and changed our middies. Laurie tied her topknot with a blue ribbon.

"Children!" Hazel exclaimed, delighted. "How nice of you all to clean up for the Grands!"

Nennie, wise to every human foible, said "Humpf" and applied herself to dishing out the vegetables.

"Now tell us, Christopher," Hazel began, being charming and drawing out her guest, "was the countryside beautiful driving here?"

"Good enough farmland, Ma'am," was all she could get out of Kit. "Highways ain't much yet. Better drivin' roads round Pittsburgh with that new macadam stuff."

Hazel, who had expected to hear about the beauties of the scenery, was put off. She tried another tack to set her guest at ease. "Do you go to school in Pittsburgh?" she asked, a little mistily because she couldn't remember what college there was in Pittsburgh. Probably one started by that tyrant Andrew Carnegie against whom the poor workers had had such dreadful battles.

"Steel mill's my school, ma'am; been working in 'em since I was a nipper. Quit school by time I was ten, ma'am."

"Should your family have allowed that?" Hazel was horrified. "We've fought so hard against child labor."

"My poor Ma didn't have much say, ma'am. Pa was long dead. Ma worked harder than the lot of us. Broke her heart like to have me quit school. But we all had to work if we wanted to eat."

"Goodness," was all Hazel could think to say. She should have left well enough alone. But there was something about the refusal of this young man to succumb to her enchantment that challenged her. "Poor Pittsburgh," she rushed on. "I suppose we *need* all that steel? Though I'm sure it was the steel manufacturers who helped to get us into that wicked war. But it must be hard for your dear mother to keep her curtains clean with that nasty smoke."

"She's long dead, ma'am. My sister's been a mother to all of us. She don't allow no dirt."

"Doesn't allow any dirt, dear," corrected Hazel under her breath.

Nennie came to the rescue. "What's become of all my chickens? I don't see any sense buying eggs if you live on a farm. Though I don't see how you can call this a farm, neither."

That weekend each of us took Kit off to exhibit a special treasure, or get his help. Jude wanted him to feel the sore on Highboy's hock where he'd struck a stone wall.

"Shouldn't take him over what he can't clear," rebuked Kit, and together they put clean bindings around the sore.

"How do you understand so much about animals if you come from the city?" Jude wanted to know.

"My brother and me, we worked on the big Jackson place next ours in Aleppo County since we were kids. We'd get up at four in the morning, help milk sixty cows. Clean the barn." He looked at the flies settling on the uncleared manure troughs, but said nothing. "We'd done half a day's work with them animals before we'd go back to hot biscuits and fried spuds and ham and eggs for breakfast. Then we'd go to school and I'd sleep most the morning. Didn't learn much, I expect."

He shifted the horse's hoof from his lap and set it gently on the stall floor. "Always did like horses."

Brian exhibited his prize calf; Dutch got Kit to spend the afternoon taking apart the old mowing machine Grandpa Ernest had given the Farm in the hope of getting something practical started.

For this job Kit shed his coat and shirt and put on a pair of old pants; by midafternoon, all the young people of the Farm were squatting around the dismantled carcass of the machine under the great maple tree. The group around the old mowing machine presaged the time when the big tree would shade the litter of cars, trucks, tractors, that were to be the focus of the attention of the new generation of the Farm.

Rory had built the Grands a neat annex, their own house, in the fallacious hope that he could seduce them from wandering to settle and run the Farm in his place. He, too, could never get the Farm, or Hazel, off his mind (I think he was in love with her until the day he died). Back from Russia, now established in New York with a third wife, he continued the habit of popping out "for a look" at the Farm, building something, and going off before he could see it begin to fall down. That the Grands would stay and take over the Farm, so that he, Rory, could have an easier mind: that, too, was delusion.

After a month or so of tidying up the fences, bringing the cows back into shape, tacking shingles on the roof, and so on and on, Grandpa Ernest would begin to be restless for the oil fields and the gamble of bringing in a new well. In their snug cottage, under the sighing Norway spruce, the night would come when Grandpa Ernest would say, "Come on, Nen, our ancestors had sense enough to leave this place a hundred years ago," and they would make preparations to be gone. As soon as they disappeared beyond the gateposts, things fell to pieces again: the chicken flock to dwindle to a few straggling hens, the beans to wither on the vine without Nennie's fingers to pick them and her tongue to drive us into helping her to get them in, canned, and stored in the cellar. We missed her. We would all gladly have exchanged our liberty for the stern security her presence gave us.

They never left without a sense of guilt and, as a kind of conscience money, sent Hazel a steady procession of hired men to accomplish what they themselves could not; nor could Rory; nor all the men of business, of law, of engineering, or medicine, in their advisory capacities. The hired men were unlikely souls: there was kinky-haired Jim who loved to shinny up the flagpole and announced frequently " 'ow he uster be a 'ostler in the Riyal Naivy!"; and Abbott who quoted Virgil, and whose room the family dubbed the "Abbott-toire." When Hazel tried to tell him at what hours he might have free use of the bathroom, he said, "Don't you mind, ma'am. Winters I wear long underwear—summers the river is good enough for me." He stayed all one winter. Thomas Porteous, whenever he got drunk on hard cider, presented himself to Hazel. "Mrs. Albertson, I want to shake your hand." "Yes, I know, Thomas." And the two would solemnly shake hands, a periodic acknowledgment that he was born a gentleman. John Barr had no use for women. He would *not* do, on principle, what Hazel asked him because he would take no orders from a woman. If Hazel settled that "today they would bring in the squash"—that day he dug fence holes.

Ivan Galli and Peter Simkavitch were called by us "the Russians." Peter had a long scar across his cheek from the 1905 Revolution. Nadya, the sister of one and the wife of the other, was supposed to help in the kitchen, but each mealtime they all began "Comes the Revolution!" and exploded into excited Russian, while Hazel, bewildered, wished she knew what they were saying and obscurely felt this wasn't the lovely revolution she believed in.

Finally, Albert Stromso arrived, he of the shining brown eyes, all willing sweetness. Hazel asked him if he were married and he said in infinite sadness, he "guessed they'd call it so." We learned what he meant when Mary Stromso came. She and her two babies were to live in the Grands' little house. Mary was slovenly and stupid, witless and spineless. She had no upper teeth and chewed her meat 'twixt thumb and gums. She would stand, her hip outthrust, knuckling an apple into mash soft enough to swallow and talking through the food, the knuckle, and the lower teeth.

Another Mary came out to the Farm to stay, Mary Birch. The only thing in common with Albert's Mary was the name. She was the daughter of an artist. Once exquisite, now in her early fifties she wore men's high boots, men's socks, a long black skirt, with hot-water bottles hung fore and aft to warm her. She decided that Hazel was Christ in bloomers.

Mary Birch attached herself to Albert "for his welfare." By her family's count, he was the twenty-seventh worthy young man in whose cause she had involved herself. She took him to her room and played Bach and Beethoven to him; fed him on pickled walnuts and fancy cheeses from S. S. Pierce's in Boston. She wouldn't let him work after five o'clock in the afternoon and called him in from the hayfield, leaving the rest of us to get the hay loaded by ourselves.

Mary Stromso was going to pull out all Mary Birch's hair! Hazel talked to Mary Birch, begging her not to interfere between Albert and his wife, or Albert and his work. Mary Birch called Hazel a wicked capitalist fattening off slave labor! She wouldn't stay another moment in Hazel's house. She would pitch a tent in the field to be near Albert.

From this effective immobilization of Albert's value to the Farm, Ernest and Nennie had been forced once again to the rescue. It was to abet this purpose that Grandpa Ernest kidnapped Kit. The coming of Kit was to change the fate of the Farm.

One Monday morning, Kit announced to Ernest that it was time he was getting back. Was he and his missus stayin' on a piece? Kit had made up his mind, before he'd stuck a leg out of that Packard, that he wasn't going to be caught by no run-down Farm.

"Didn't contract, Mr. Hammond, to do more'n drive you here."

"Yes, yes. I know that. You've the right to go now. But I've a mind to get them some good new machinery. You and Dutch come into Haverhill with me and let's see what can be done."

"Not much sense leaving good machinery to be wrecked by that gang," objected Kit. "That bunch doesn't know a damn thing about machinery."

"Well, well! Perhaps I can find them a good hired man." Ernest had already established himself in the Packard and was honking for Dutch.

"None of my business." Kit slid behind the steering wheel. Not only Dutch but all the kids piled into the Packard. Ernest made them stay in the car, out of the way of the men, while he and Kit and Dutch disappeared into the farm machinery showroom.

With Kit examining and Dutch standing close by in an advisory capacity, Ernest put his hand in his pocket and pulled out a thick roll of bills; he bought a tractor, a disc harrow, a single-bottom plow, a double-bottom plow, a one-and-a-half-ton truck, and a new mowing machine.

"Damn shame." Kit was horrified. "Mr. Hammond, that's real money you're putting out. They won't earn that money back in ten years. Waste of that good money. All that good machinery! It ain't right, sir!"

"Well," said Ernest, "suppose we stay a little while longer. Suppose you and I teach them how to farm, how to use all this stuff. Then we can both get off. Suppose we stay until after the harvest. Hey?"

They got Jersey cows and new pigs and fenced them in, found another workhorse, restocked the chicken yard, plowed up fields that had never known such deep furrows as that tractor made, and planted them to rye and buckwheat. That summer the swing of man-sized farming caught up the Farm. Kit, Dutchie and Raymie, Brian and Jude, the barn chores done, were in the fields at seven.

Dutchie, almost as tall as Kit, bare to the belt, his hair bleached and his skin golden, was inseparable from his new idol, the two of them always at the machinery, Kit riding the tractor as though he were part of it.

Raymie, the village boy with the shriveled leg, pitched hay with Brian Boru and Timmy all the long hot summer. Raymie's shoulders and arms grew stronger, his chest deep, to compensate for the withered leg. They all slept out in the new cocks, and when the fall came and cold set in, moved from the meadow up to the attic.

In Kit's army Dutch and Jude became top sergeants keeping the troops in line. Raymie was frequently of the mechanized corps; only Laurie, nominally in charge of cooking and canning, had to steal moments to join in the skirmishes. The presence of Kit anywhere in barn or fields was an irresistible magnet.

Romance changed its nature over night. There was no one now to listen to Hazel's enchantments. The days were spent squatting, staring, climbing up and over and under the machinery that Kit and Dutchie and Raymie were forever taking apart and putting together again. Jude, like her brother, would no longer work on the ground, but would work all day if the job could be done from the seat of any piece of machinery. Kit loved machinery. He loved the smooth working of one part against another. Grandfather Hammond never could have gotten him to stay to farm; it was the tractor and the machinery that beguiled him. The same wholehearted attention Dutch had once brought to hammering a nail straight he, too, now spent upon motors. As he became a man, he assumed aspects of Rory's personality. It was he who tried to establish what was to be done and who was to be drafted to do it. Kit's way was to announce that the lower fields should be mowed. "Let's get about it." He was always sure of hands. Dutch designated *who* was to get about the job: he himself was to ride the rake or the tractor. Nevertheless, being the Farm, it didn't come about that way. No one challenged Dutch's right to make announcements, but each went about his day just as he intended to.

Hazel was excluded from this hierarchy. She still thought of Dutch as her lieutenant, but it was Kit whom we followed without his having issued any decree that she had heard. Hazel made lists of the day's chores and read them out at breakfast in the dining room, but Kit took his breakfast in the kitchen and the serious farmers went with him. When he had finished his last cup of coffee and said, "Well, how about that back meadow?" all willing hands flocked after him, each in turn slamming the screen door. Hazel and Kathy were left behind the coffee pots in the dining room.

In this tug of war Laurie was in the middle. She gave all her attention so urgently to what went on outside, that in the house she looked as though she'd only come in to get something and was going right out again. Any excuse brought her into the fields or the open-air machine shop: to take a huge pitcher of lemonade to the sweaty workers in the sun of the open meadows; or simply to stand, on one foot, poised between the house and the car-parts shop beneath the maple. She was intensely attracted not only by what was going on, but to the place where Kit was. And he felt her presence. He understood the tribute to his way of life acknowledged by her adoption of the mechanical language native to him. "Is it the gearshift, Kit? Do you think the trouble's in the spark plug?" She didn't know beans about gearshifts or spark plugs but she delighted in the sense of companionship and advocacy of Kit's world that this use of privileged, professional language gave her.

Laurie and Jude, now in their late teens, became rivals, each desperate to be by Kit's side. Jude was victor during the day, in the fields, taking apart the tractor, standing up to Kit, job for job. But at night he sat beside Laurie on the porch step and she listened enraptured while he talked about the steel country: the whole sky on fire, the flames leaping up, fading, from the furnaces of the mills. The men stripped to the waist: "If you don't wipe off the sweat, you can't see what you're doing. When I first come to the mills, I'd blink every time them hammers come down, then I tried stuffing things in my ears and the old-timers they'd say, 'Son, you pull out those plugs, you take your mind off that hammer. You think of what you're doin' and you'll stop blinking.' " A world of men, whose muscles bunched in sweat-streaked arms. Kit under cover of summer dark held Laurie's hand. "You have to stay with your job until another man comes and relieves you. You don't take three steps. You're pinned right down to that spot, you kick the lever when that hot steel flows by, all day long, kick the lever, open the flue . . ."

I don't know how we first discovered that Kit not only talked intelligibly in his sleep, but without reserve would answer questions put to him. Perhaps it was when he slept in the attic where all the boys had chosen beds in a dormitory line that went from eave to eave. Now Kit had resettled into the room over the kitchen. He liked it because it could be reached by a ladder that went up behind the kitchen from the back entry, by way of a trap door in the bedroom floor. This way he didn't have to come in and out through the house. He was his own man.

We were all wild to have Kit say he loved Laurie. Except Jude: she didn't want him to say a thing. Except Hazel, who refused to believe there was anything poetic about a young man who walked off when she talked about books. The rest of us whispered about the looks we'd caught exchanged between the two. We were avid for any new speck of evidence to mull over, giggle about.

It was Timmy's idea. "We could sneak up when we know he's asleep and ask him." It was dangerous, he might wake up and get mad at us. Kit's personal privacy was not to be lightly invaded. "You're goddamned fools"; Jude, wretched, had slipped back into her old ways. She'd have nothing to do with this, and took a roll of blankets and went up to Chestnut Hill to fling herself into a spreading juniper and watch the stars until she fell asleep.

Laurie knew it was a dreadful thing to do. He might never forgive her if he woke, but she couldn't stand not going along. Dutchie, Timmy and Laurie: they were the ones to go. The rest of us waited below for word. We were all barefoot and wearing whatever we had gone to bed in. It was past midnight, with no light but the moon through the window above the narrow bed where Kit was asleep. All of us assembled at the foot of the kitchen stairs, shushing one another. Dutch went up the ladder first, holding the trapdoor for his sister and Timmy. Laurie, wretchedly ashamed, squatted at the foot end of the bed in the shadow, keeping the trapdoor up for quick escape. Timmy had begun to be afraid, too. They wished they weren't there. But Dutch squatted on his heels by Kit's pillow. The moonlight shone on Kit's defenseless face.

"Dutch! Don't!" Laurie hissed; suddenly she couldn't bear the trick he was about to play. If Kit loved her he'd tell her when he wanted to.

But Dutchie shook his head at her. She'd wake him up if she didn't quiet down.

"Kit," began Dutchie in a low voice, not quite sure how to go about questioning a sleeping man as to where his heart lay.

"Kit—you going to stay here at the Farm? Are you going to stay with us?" This was really what Dutch wanted answered. His sister's fate was secondary. "You're not going back to that old Pittsburgh, Kit?"

Kit stirred. His eyelids quivered, his eyes beneath them rolled.

"Kit," Dutchie insisted, putting his head closer to the sleeping man's pillow.

Kit, in a voice that was not his own, murmured, "Place . . .of his own . . . for a man and his wife . . . place of his own."

Laurie, in anguish, knew just what he was talking about. She couldn't take any more, and scuttled back down the ladder, Timmy after her. The trap shut softly. "What did he say . . . what'd he say?" the waiting audience hissed at her.

"He didn't say a thing," said Laurie, furious, and left. Timmy had nothing to report either.

But Dutch, persisting, had demanded, "Do you love Laurie, Kit? Are you going to marry her?"

"Sure," said Kit in his sleep. "Sure," as though this were the easy question and not at all the problem. But when Dutch, slipping out the door had closed it softly behind him, Kit's eyes opened and he grinned in the moonlight.

"Well, doggone, it's as good a way of telling her as any other. She doggone well has to decide. When a man marries, he wants a place of his own. No doggone public Farm." He rolled over, burying his head in the pillow. She knew now what the choice was. "She doggone well has to make up her mind." Then he went truly to sleep.

One night at the summer's end Kit drove the flivver he'd put together from spare parts down the lane under the row of maples, no lights on, engine barely purring. He picked up Laurie waiting with Jude at the rock pile rise, Laurie in her only go-to-town dress, all her things in a little bag. Jude in black melancholy walked back up to the house to tell Hazel, now that it was too late.

Over her diary that night, in the privacy of her little house on the knoll, Hazel wept, the tears blurring the ink on the page. It is, today, difficult to read. "You, two lone pines, not afraid to stand alone, to live your lives in solitary grandeur, let my soul grow tall like you. Comfort me, roll on, oh river."

Driving over the Alleghenies in the brass-bound flivver, Kit said, "When you first get married you want to do things for your wife and family your own way."

A winter was to come when there would be nobody at the Farm: no living creature, neither cow, horse, duck, hen, pig, dog, nor cat, only the birds who fluttered in the barnyard undisturbed by larger animals; the grasses grew, and dried back uncut; the aspara- gus ran to seed, the new blooms of Kathy's roses tumbled over, unplucked dead flower-heads. The sumacs grew back on the river- bank, screening the empty, closed-up house from the river. That was the only time, the first and the last, the Farm was ever to be utterly deserted. It doesn't bear thinking on!

Jude had gone off to college in Cambridge, riding round the se- date town in a Tin Lizzie that had neither doors nor top. Myth has it that she drove up the stairs of Radcliffe's Briggs Hall. My guess is that she confused Highboy of the arching neck with her four-wheeled steed Highburry Halpin—its name an overtone of the horse's, but otherwise etymologically undecipherable. Nevertheless, such is the character of a Cantabrigian woman of a certain vintage that Jude was the favorite chauffeur to Dean Cronkhite. The dean found the lack of doors rather like riding in a phaeton, but she did demand an umbrella in case of rain.

Dutchie was concentrating on higher mechanics at engineering school; Brian specializing in selective breeding of bulls at the agricultural station; and Kathy had gone to New York to keep house for Rory, temporarily without third wife, mistress, or live-in daughter. Timmy went with Kathy, and in those early days of radio spent the predawn hours as what is now known as a disc jockey. There needn't have been an audience awake and listening; he was content with such a wealth of recordings surrounding him to play all that music in lovely solitude, for himself.

Raymie? He refused to return to his family. The livestock having been boarded in the barn of a farm downriver with space to spare since the farmer had sold off his own, Raymie went with them, to comfort Junie and Highboy, and to keep to Daisy Mae the Second, who was content to ruminate her cud anywhere.

Hazel, the indomitable, was now defeated. For the first time since she'd gone off in such high heart with Rory, her inspirer, her leader, her Whitman, her lover and husband, she retreated to stay with Nennie and Ernest. One grey morning she turned the key in the Farm front door, never locked before—she'd had to have a lock and key newly made for this—and she went off, forlorn, down the lane in the town taxi that would take her and her one suitcase into Haverhill and the train. Stillness, emptiness, settled upon the Farm, and, as the winter came, desolation.

In Pittsburgh, Laurie and Kit and the twins Debby and Donny lived over a railroad station, the hours marked by the trains rushing by. The very idea of such a home made Hazel shudder for her "poor dear Laurie who had lost her way." But Laurie loved it. She knew which were the express trains, which the local, and which the famous-named trains arrogantly signaling their right to precedence on the track, running coast to coast, across mountains, rivers, wheatfields, prairies, deserts, stopping briefly at big cities, then roaring past the sleeping houses, hooting in the night. Laurie's excitement was infectious. The twins, who were two, would rush

Top: Laurie at the time she and Kit returned to the Farm. *Bottom*: Kit and his young son, one of the new Farm generation, 1944.

from the window crying, "Lim-ted, Lim-ted, Mummy," and Laurie would consult the clock and all three rejoice that the Limited, or the Merchants or the Twentieth Century, was on time.

Kit's older brother had set him up in the garage business. He and his crew worked on the city's cars, the big, black, official vehicles. They got their share of orphan cars to fix up and resell: stolen cars smashed in a police chase, hot cars used for getaways that failed, deserted cars of jailed bootleggers. The cops came in off their beats for a cup of coffee. They talked about graft, about the kind of crook who packed a gat with less thought than he settled the angle of his snap-brim hat. About politicians and policemen, about pool parlors and "speaks," about protection and stoolies. Kit built up a sophisticated body of the knowledge of violence; how far a man could be pushed, and who was yellow, who dangerous. He listened to it all but none of it touched him. When he watched a man work on one of his cars, he watched to see who kept at the job until it was finished, who set his teeth and without patience, forced a part. That's what he cared about. He'd step back and wipe his hands and listen to the motor turning over.

Kit had repossessed a twin-six Packard that had belonged to a bootlegger before he ran it into a telephone pole with the cops gaining on him: "You'd never have caught up to me in that baby if I'd had her wheel. Some punk driver who can't get away from you guys in that baby!" His friends, the cops, took the ribbing in good part.

But it wasn't to last for Kit, that fine life of motors and grease and the rushing to and fro of the Limited, of friends who understood the same things he did; keeping his own small family out of his own pocket. Hazel was stronger than Kit. When the letter came from Hazel in Ohio, describing the Farm shut up, locked, deserted, he knew something had to give. Laurie could not live with her mother's sadness.

"Tell you what," he said in bed that night. "We'll take the twin-six and go this summer. Bud can take over the shop. Give the twins a chance to get their bottoms browned. How about that, Laurel?" He was the only one of us who called Laurie by her given name. Laurie flung herself on him, her face hidden in his shoulder and soaked his pajama-top, weeping. "Danged women," grumbled Kit, getting up to find a dry top. "Weep when they're sad, weep when they're glad."

Kit, who was never touched by Hazel's enchantment, to whom Hazel was the Old Lady, and most of what she did and said pretty silly, women's stuff; Kit who would not even sit in a room when the talkers were there, who would not read a book; who was raised to believe that every cent counted, and waste was a sin—it was he who was to inherit his lifelong burden of the Farm.

chapter eight

To Know the World

Like Zeus disposing of the world upon the shoulders of
Atlas, Rory settled the Farm on Kit's back. Rory was attracted to
this young man who was enamored of everything mechanical for
he, too, believed in the gasoline age. Rory envisaged that in the new
era of cars the Farm could have a splendid advantage simply because
its land fronted on the highway. The trolley had given up the ghost
and the grass had grown over its unused tracks. "That's it!" Rory
announced to Kathy. "Build a garage. Right down there by the
lane's end. That's how we'll keep 'em on the Farm. You think that
husband of Laurie's can run it, eh?" That summer Rory came back
to supervise the building of the garage. When the concrete floor
was poured and the roof on, he went to dicker for the lease of a gas
pump.

The twins settled into the landscape as though they'd never lived
a day punctuated by the passage of trains. Kit knew when he was
licked, and sold his own garage to Bud.

In Hazel's eyes the pump disgraced the gateposts; nor did it
prove, after all, a profitable arrangement. If gas was sold, the family
raided the till. If the till was empty, the pump itself was raided to fill
up the empty tanks that stood between the vehicle-mad mob and
adventure. With a gas tank full, they were possessed of that most
wonderful gift to youth—mobility.

Like little foxes' our ears picked up the signals of the first surrep-
titious movement toward a car. There were not, I think, cabals and
conspiracies. It was part of the game to get away without the others; high glee was intensified by the discomfited, outwitted, left behind. What we went for, where we went, were secondary to getting
away: Ella Dale's for an ice cream cone; Plum Island after a storm to
see the surf; or just riding round, just riding.

What a sneaking off at night went on! Car lights off, smothered giggles as the car was eased down the lane. It was not Hazel's authority from which we were escaping; she had fled from the wild spirit which now infected us, and nobody heard her say goodnight. Usually we crept away because one half wanted to avoid the other half. To miss out on a ninety-mile drive for a hot dog was tragedy.

Kit had wangled a dealership for second-hand cars; cars were scattered about the near meadow as daffodils once had been. He and his crew fixed up the cars and sold them around the countryside. Everyone had something to ride in. Dutchie roared off to school in the twin-six Packard that had belonged to the bootlegger. It had no top; and a baker's dozen, plus, of us would pile in, one on top of the other, to go hooting, shouting off for a moonlight swim in Pen Pond. Anything with four wheels, an engine, and a chassis was fit vehicle for a joyride. If Kit drove the twin-six, Dutchie alternately commandeered the hearse converted into a tow car—a chassis with two seats and no body. Later Dutchie found his pride and joy, a beaten-up, broken-down hybrid Duesenberg, to which he was as devoted as Jude had been to Highboy. There was always a collection of flivvers: Brian had a safely enclosed coupe in which he herded the young bulls at the breeding farm where he had a summer job; Raymie's Penelope the Mudder had a gravity-feed tank. He eked out the gas by putting nuts and bolts in the tank to raise the fuel level. Jude would come home in Highburry Halpin, and was as inseparable from that banged-up buggy as she once had been from her stallion Highboy. She rode the tin Highburry wherever she went—whether from barnyard to chicken house to gather eggs or into Cambridge for Radcliffe classes.

The garage was not Kit's. The garage was actually Hazel's, with Kit as unpaid mechanic. There wasn't anything going on he missed, but if the "Missus wasn't goin' to yell at Dutch" neither was Kit. He got himself a job that put a little money in his own pocket: he rode the first motorcycle that the town police ever had, looking handsome in leggings and tight britches. "Only you kids keep out of that car of mine. Don't you be playing no stunts in *my* car. I'll wop ya." Dutch was sick with envy of the motorbike, and the dust spun under the wheels of the Duzie as he gunned the engine in frustration.

There were times when those two fought savage battles, not with their fists, but with their cars, their alter egos. This could take place only at night. The challenge was a game of tag within the Farm acres. Nobody ever planned it; it just happened—a battle for mastery, determining who in this new mobile, mechanical world of skill was top dog. It went on all summer. We, the lesser beings, were audience, judges, jury and participants. We clambered into one car or the other, having no role except to be in at the kill. The fight was private between the two antagonists.

You'd never know which one would start it, or when, or whether it just happened because they were sitting in their cars and it was dusk. But one would sneak off—across the pasture, over the dry fields, up the bank, down the lower meadow; the other, becoming aware of the absence of the first, gave chase: the search began. It was never done with lights on. It could only have been done by those who knew the terrain over which they urged their cars as well in the dark as in the day. The trick was to move like a big black soundless hulk, cutting the motor to coast down a hill out of gear, then gunning in the nick of time. When the adversary had been located, the other combatant would spin the wheel, slam into reverse, back up, and change course.

I don't know why we weren't all killed. The cars scraped against the trees, nipping between them with nothing to spare; we would have been thrown from the cars if they turned turtle down hilly banks. (Later I was to go rushing across battle lines, hurtling down foreign roads; and later still, these same boys were to fight on beachheads, through villages seeded with booby traps.)

I was then a prisoner of Polly's hill and of the school year, exiled from Farm excitements but for weekends and holidays. What does one do before the door to the world swings open? How to pass the interminable time waiting to grow up and be admitted to life? In Boston I had taken to haunting the Public Library. I liked the reading room where all the seats were filled by people bent on such a variety of searches. There (having become at sixteen undeniably female) I found companionship—by naughty pursuit. Usually the young men were a good bit older and safe enough, since I managed to get them out to Polly's hill where they were shocked out of any conventionally wicked intentions by finding themselves in an atmosphere of hilarious innocence.

Or I wandered among the bookstalls on Cornhill and picked up a certain expertise in recognizing first editions. There, too, I shang-

The author as a senior in high school, a "prisoner of Polly's hill."

haied bookish young men. Anyone who liked libraries or bookstores was obviously another frustrated citizen of the world.

The improprieties involved in this collecting of young men never crossed my consciousness. Polly, too, must have believed that young men who talked about books were, ipso facto, safe. I don't remember her ever having been dismayed by that parade of captives from bookstores and libraries. Certainly among such companions I found more ease than with the son of the town's haberdasher on my one excursion to a high school dance, wearing a red dress encircled with ruffles like a flamenco skirt. (Polly once had such a dress when she was young.) But even the alchemy of the dress could not disguise for me the difference between dancing to the wind-up victrola at the Farm, in bloomers, and the deportment proper to a country club.

A less incongruous setting than the clubhouse was the press room of the town's weekly newspaper. Big green flies buzzed on the factory-glass windows; the hot sun brought up the smell of the wet ink and the oil and dust. The bony spinster beside me at the long counter under the window didn't think this kid of sixteen, part-time, was much help. She had no patience with my forgetting the proper proofreader's symbols and having to look them up; forgetting how words were spelled and having to turn to the dictionary; laboring to write the corrections, scrubbing with my eraser, gripping hard at the pencil, my fingers pink with the tension applied to make the letters clear. My colleague pursed her lips and handled with distaste the smudged galleys passed on to her. I had small competence for reading proof, but I did it with zeal because it was concerned with newspapers.

Then, in addition to proofreading, I ran here and there in the town, digging up fillers, "space" stories, wherever I could. At the end of each week I brought back to the Hill the newly printed, ink-wet papers and sat on the floor of the upstairs hall with scissors and paste pot and measuring tape about me, clipping with care my "copy." I was paid by the inch. Sometimes there were long columns to be clipped and pasted, column after column to be added to the streamer of type. Other times I could not find what had become of my story. Surely, this couldn't be it? These few sentences out of all I'd written? When the scraps were pasted up, I took the streamer to the railing and hung it over the bannister into the stairwell. Then I let the measuring tape down, side by side with the strip of news columns. I knew by practice that if the ribbon of print touched Jane Addams's picture, I'd made more than three dollars; if it grazed the midway landing I would collect five dollars! It took a lot of copy to add up to five dollars.

A year or so later I picked up, in one of my bookstores, the first issue of a modest imitation of the witty young *New Yorker*. It was being printed in a loft on T-Wharf, where one paid as little rent as was possible without stepping off into the harbor. I rushed to offer myself as general printer's devil and editor's dogsbody, after school. I got into the way of doing pieces here too: gossip from the bookstores; a column on Boston food—a *pensione* table where the Italian politicians lunched in an alley off Hanover Street, or a St. Botolph Street house where local sculptors came in to have an omelet and a carafe of red wine. I learned to "make up" the little "book" and count off spaces for captions and heads and "put it to bed."

It is a wonder I ever turned up at the dreary high school at all. "Real life" consisted of taking the subway to Boston and loitering about T-Wharf. The fishing fleet tied up on one side of the pier; men worked in their high boots and rubber aprons to get the catch up from the belly of the boat. Sometimes propped against a bollard, I would watch a freighter or even a liner with people going abroad slip out of the harbor to the sea. And if nothing else moved in the harbor, there was always the penny ferry, shuttling from its dock to East Boston.

With the new competence and the air of consequence the work on the magazine gave me, I began to appear on the doorsteps of the city papers. Harold Wheeler of the *Boston Traveler* lifted harassed eyes from his desk, blue pencil still working on copy. "Yes, yes, what do you want? . . . Boy!"—this shouted at the copy-boy—"What is it *you* want?" "Who let you in here now? Don't you know it's press time? *Boy*!! A job? For God's sake! Go home and grow up. When you do come back, don't come at press time! *Boy*!!!" After a year or so we got to know one another. Then he'd say, "Hello, you again! So you think you're grown up now? What do you want to work on a newspaper for anyhow? That's no job for a girl. Have I got your telephone number? You'd better give it to me again."

One day my phone rang. "This is Harold Wheeler. *Traveler*. You still want that job? Think you can help on the movie column? Our regular girl is out sick. Well, come in Monday. We'll see." But when Wheeler saw me he smacked his forehead with his free hand. "Oh! for God's sake, I keep forgetting you're a kid." Then, more gently, "Not this time I'm afraid."

At last I was hired—not by the *Traveler*, but by the *Boston Transcript*, that literate virgin of a newspaper. I went up on the shaky *Transcript* lift and found the feature and book editor entombed behind his Chinese wall of unread books. He gave me a book to review, delighted to have one less. As old and dusty as his tiny, book-stacked office, he made no estimate of my years, or lack of them. Later he took a feature story I suggested, then suggested one himself, each a half page of lovely space and big lettered heads. Space the *Transcript* had in plenty. Advertisements had faded from its pages. Who read the *Transcript* those days? Not the suburban housewives watching for sales in Filene's basement. The Boston Brahmins went to no sales.

Times were getting difficult. My undernourished magazine withered away; the *Transcript* got thinner and thinner. I answered a "writers wanted" advertisement and found myself banging out laudatory biographies for a puff sheet, printed according to the number of copies sold. I booked talent acts for smokers. (What blind eye picked me for such an occupation?) I went to a yacht club as paymaster for a traveling act, but a sensible Norwegian locked me up in the "ladies" for security until he could get me away from there. I tried ushering, only to be given the "rush" down the aisles to the stage by a flying wedge of toughs, who then ushered themselves to their own seats. Employment was reduced to tugging one-size-too-small dresses onto perspiring ladies. High school years laboriously over, I enrolled in journalism school—only to leave after a month, scornful of such finger exercises. I was ready for wider horizons.

The year I was eighteen, in full possession of adulthood, I talked Philip into subsidizing the balance of the winter in New York. There my typewriter and I settled into an unfurnished Seventh Avenue cold-water room. From floor to ceiling, mirrors stood in their ornate frames; the empty fireplace was marble, but the sink was reached by standing in the bathtub. In the courtyard the skeleton of a tree rattled dry bones in the winter cold. The first night I slept on the floor, rolled into a gendarme's cape that one of the young men of the earlier generation, returned from the 1914 war, had left in a Farm closet.

I subsisted mainly upon day-old loaves of bread and milk; the bottles were returnable for the nickel deposit. These I neatly ranged against the wall to provide the subway fare for chasing jobs. I lived by means of publicity jobs, ghosting, occasional freelance features, anything that had to do with writing and would feed me. Rents were low enough, and for that place, minimal.

One day I discovered other housing, absurd in New York City: a white clapboarded house with a peaked entry roof, a wrought iron gate to the macadamed-over front yard that once had been a garden, fenced between two tall apartment buildings. The windows of small leaded panes swung open on a sliding arm, like those in Polly's house; there was even a wood-burning fireplace and a brick chimney. I should more properly say "a piece of a house." It must once have been the kitchen ell of a farm building, the big house long since shorn off to clear ground for the apartment houses, and this hapless end, a slice of another time, left still standing.

And how could I afford to pay the rent for such a treasure? Because it was not a treasure; nobody had succeeded in living in it.

The vulnerable little house, its bedroom on the street just inside the easily vaultable fencing, stood on Bedford Street. On one side was the territory of the Hudson Dusters; the other side was run by the Bleecker Street gang. When the wars between the two gangs subsided, they attacked in concert the small leftover bit of a house. Firecrackers tied to a brick were sailed through the street window, as a paper boy might sling his daily delivery, an almost offhand sport if you happened to be passing and it was evident that someone was reading, eating, or working within. Better fun on chilly evenings was climbing the roof to let a cannon-cracker down the chimney, and waiting for the fire to be lit. Invariably the tenants moved out. The real estate office would have been glad to give the house away to anyone who could manage to live in it.

The boys, when I moved in, waited for me to jump at the first satisfactory bang, eager for the fun of the chase when I called the cops. It didn't occur to me to call the cops. When the boys came back from their first spurt to see what had gone wrong, I was waiting with broom and dust pan. We struck a bargain: they'd help clean up and then I'd play them at craps for the price of a new window. I lost. Who was I to shoot craps with these kid-professionals? But the brother of one was a glazier and in his pile of trash he had some of those nutty little panes—who'd want 'em?

The boys were by now in the house. They'd never been inside before. My typewriter sat upon the newly painted, bright blue table—dining table, work table, everything table, with benches original to the ell built in on either side. "You make this thing go?" demanded one, poking a finger at a key. "Don't!" said I, a workman protecting her tools, an attitude they understood. "There's no paper in it and I need that typewriter; that's how I earn my living."

A boy got off the floor where he'd been searching for glass slivers the broom had missed. "Write me a letter, huh?"

I sat down on the bench, businesslike, and rolled in a sheet of fresh paper. "Who do you want me to write a letter to?"

"Write that old bum, the principal. Tell him I ain't never coming back no more."

"What do you want to do that for?" I was primed to embark upon a Philip-type of sermon on the advantages of education. The boy turned sulky and serious.

"My old man's sick," he said, face averted. "Somebody's got to bring in the dough."

I wrote the letter, politely as I could and with attention to the reason. After that I wrote letters for the entire neighborhood. Letters to families in Italy and in Boston. Letters to husbands, fathers, brothers in jail. Letters to the ward heeler. Letters seeking admission to trade schools (enclosing recommendations which I signed with an imposing hand). Letters to landlords and bill-collectors; letters arranging betrothals. Besides village scribe I was the neighborhood soft touch. "Can I use your phone, huh?" Or, "Hey, you gotta buck for medicine? My ma's sick." Or, "How about a couple of dimes for coffee all 'round?"

In return, I was their ward, the little house and I, their joint protection. If I had a story to do, both ends of the short street were closed against any loud crap game, or playing catch, or sometimes—over-doing it a bit—even to traffic. When Christmas came, delegations arrived laden with unwrapped presents, fruits of a two-gang raid on Hearn's, the 14th Street store. If I refused to be a depository for stolen goods, neither was it my affair to preach.

I sold a story, and then another, to the old *World*. Walter Lippmann was then its editor, but to announce myself to him as a Farm child, mourner with him at the burial of the chick Salome Hermann Blumgart stepped on, was beyond even my brash self. Philip, however, for whom the name of any of his Harvard classmates—magic words—was open sesame to wider worlds, sent me to thrust myself upon the attention of Richard Washburn Child, lately recalled from his ambassadorship to Italy, where his approval of Mussolini had been too vociferous. Child was then doing a series for the *Saturday Evening Post* on crime in New York City. He was delighted to pick up (and cheaply) an amanuensis innocent enough to amuse him and no threat to the call girls, pimps, politicians, sharpie lawyers, ambulance chasers, and bail bondsmen at the downtown Democratic club. These last, the bail bond boys, were his prey. He was doing a series on the toleration afforded them by the Democratic machine, for his own political reasons and those of the Republican and very conservative *Saturday Evening Post*. My ignorance not only diverted this motley bunch; they'd come and visit me, any hour of the night. I made friends with some of the call girls, who would visit me at my house. But my young, sophisticated neighborhood protectors did not like the presence of girls who left after quick phone calls, to come back with their money and pick up their pimps a few hours later. I kept the peace only by saying I was doing a story.

They would have liked less—for they were very moral where I was concerned—the offer of a share in a speakeasy. It must have been intended to use me as a "straw," but I signed nothing and after I had kept what I had mistaken to be a morning appointment with the big, bosomy, blousy girl whose show it really was, and discovered myself in her bedroom—bedclothes tumbled, maribou robe upon maribou mules on the floor, windows and blinds tightly closed, the dim room reeking of stale cigars, perfume and whiskey, and the lady snoring—whatever sense I had from Philip backed me out the door.

The gang of Bellevue interns I fell in with offered more comprehensible fun. One snowy midnight we went off to sleighride in Central Park and were met at the stable door by a line of caparisoned camels, daintily lifting their feet out of the cold, wet muck in the streets. It was the Christmas season and the camels were on their way to join their Wise Men.

When spring came we rode the nickel ferry to Staten Island for the delight of seeing the mystical city rise out of the waters, never really believing this city of spires was not illusion. We went to so many D'Oyly Carte performances that the leads recognized our enthusiasm by coming to a midnight supper for which we pooled all resources to offer champagne and hothouse grapes. (They probably would have preferred scrambled eggs.)

And when I was alone I rode on the top decks of Fifth Avenue buses; was rained or sunned on, enraptured by the city's streets. Or, solitary but for a galumphing sheep dog I'd acquired—who passionately liked to become a passenger in police cars or taxis if anyone unwary opened the door—I stood under the prows of the tall vessels snubbed so close to the sidewalk in their berths that I could reach out and run my hand over the lovely edge of the *Normandie,* its name written in calligrapher's gold. Of all that New York offered this was my favorite, private haunt, here where the known land stopped at the edge of the pier; here where the tugs would nudge the great ships backward, until they had room in the river to turn and set their course. One day, one day, I would see the shore retreating, from the ship's rail . . .

Another story for the *World*—and this one, alas, my final one. Alas not only for me; by now this was 1929, and the *New York World* collapsed. Better newsmen than I would ever be walked the streets.

Those were the first days of the Depression, of the soup lines and the apple sellers. Freelancing dried up at the source. And yet at the proverbial "last minute," when my fortunes were down to the last cache of milk bottles to exchange for subway fare, I was offered—undeservedly with so many others in desperate need—a fat job. An industrial designer who had seen the final story I'd done for the *World* needed a private copywriter. Through those miserable years of the Depression I would survive, well paid, well housed, well fed—and discontent.

In a black and gold tower on 40th Street I wrote booklets about the "Dowager" deluxe bathtub with spigots of gold, its handles carved like opening roses. Often I came in before the day had decently begun, drew a drafting table up to the window, climbed onto my stool and, with my legs wrapped round the stool's rungs, beat my brains for adjectives to devote to the bathtub's immortality.

Across the street in Bryant Park the homeless men who spent the nights on newspapers on the grass performed their morning ablutions. For some it was enough to run a hand over a stubbled jaw. Others, who had not yet accepted despair, still carried about with them a razor, a mirror fragment, and a scrap of soap. They gathered around the water fountain, and I could see them squinting, twisting up their chins to catch their reflections in the bits of glass.

My head was empty of the words they paid me for—"The Neo-Classic lines of this architectonic tub . . ." Was this the brotherhood of man?

Early summer of 1934; the country was already a year into Roosevelt's New Deal. Even to those who still had comforts to cling to, to whom Roosevelt was "That man!", no churchman now dared preach: "The Lord Maketh Poor and Maketh Rich. . . . For the Poor shall never cease out of the land." The helpless poor were now to be helped, not by the urging of the Lord to the virtue of Charity, but by fiat of government. We were, by law, become our brothers' keepers. Rory's old social gospel—"Commerce and Industry to be inspired by divine tenderness"—was now to be put into practice, with divinity or tenderness having little to do with it. Hazel's celebration of Whitman, "One's-Self I sing . . . Yet utter the word Democratic, the word En-Masse," was not to be realized by conversion of the spirit, but by inexorable sharing of the same fate—for all alike, the newly poor with the always poor, the equality of "no jobs."

Why didn't I—daughter of millenarian dreamers, child of the Farm and the Settlement House—rush off to Washington to serve in this new army of social democracy? Become a contemporary Jane Addams, or a young Lillian Wald; or, if I must write, report: become a junior Lincoln Steffens policing a new politics; another Ida Tarbell, half grown, a new watchdog of industry?

Filled with dismay at my preoccupation with poetic paeans to bathtubs, the job that fed me; guilty to be fed by such stuff, when those poor men down there across the street in the park were hungry and jobless: why didn't I take up a ladle in the soup kitchens, pin up notices on the job boards?

I never thought of it. My eyes were fixed on another horizon. Dorothy Thompson had been deported from Germany by Hitler—red roses from every foreign correspondent in Berlin. The story was glowingly described on the front page of the *New York Times*. There was a heroine! Vincent Sheean's *Personal History* I swallowed whole the next year. To such demigods belonged the world.

Did I tell myself, as Dorothy Thompson had, that I would report on the "little people" whose cause was my inheritance? Nonsense. I was born, not a worker in the vineyards of the poor, but a small Ulysses. At night I lay awake and listened to the deep farewells as the great ships left the harbor for the sea. Nothing "could conquer in me the ardour that I had to gain experience of the world, and of human vice and worth." Thus, to Dante, Ulysses spoke in Hell.

The thirties and the ascent of Hitler: reporters assigned to Berlin stood upon the curbs while the first brownshirt formations marched four abreast singing "When Jewish blood gushes from our knives . . . things will be better!" Year after year the press corps watched the boldness grow. They saw bodies dumped in alleys; were impotent to protect bearded old men scrubbing sidewalks, beaten by young bullies, guards armed with rubber truncheons; heard the frantic appeals of women whose fathers, brothers, husbands, sons had disappeared. They listened in horror to the shrieking voices in mass meetings, frenzying the crowds. With every human being dispossessed, beaten, interned, dead, it became clear that there was loosed upon the earth, a satanic contempt for humanity.

I was determined to join the ranks of these prophets of doom, Depression or no Depression. This was history. I would live it and record it and so make myself participant. Reproving "those who cry of any story 'but we know already!' " Thomas Mann was to chide, "that is a foolish thought. Anybody can know the story. To have been there is the thing."

How do you go about becoming a foreign correspondent? I got through the secretaries into the formidable presence of Edwin L. James of the *New York Times*. "On the *Times*?" he barked. "With the Old Man not dead a year? He'd turn over!" The Associated Press foreign man said, "I've no objection to hiring a girl. I don't care whether you're male or female. All I want's the news. If there's a mass hanging in Poland I want a cable full of detail. I don't want, 'Sorry, I fainted.' Anyhow, all our foreign men have to work in the domestic service first. AP rule. Anyhow, we're full. No openings."

I had heard enough about "Peace" at the Farm and on Polly's hill: Wilson's Peace, the Protocols of Peace, Permanent Peace, the Fourteen Points of Peace that Walter Lippmann had helped Wilson's Colonel House to formulate, the League as Instrument of Peace. I looked up in the phone book all the names that began with "Peace," or "League." And so found in a shabby building, J. W. Terry, an old newspaper man, now nearly blind. When the volunteer workers and the squabbling salaried heads had left for the day, when he could be alone at night, he wrote and made-up for the printer an eight-page sheet of foreign news for a League of Nations lobby.

He listened and then said, laying his pipe down on the sheets of yellow copy paper, "There's very little chance for a woman in the foreign field. If you can be discouraged, I want to discourage you."

"No." I couldn't be discouraged.

"All right, I'll be glad to have you work with me. I'll teach you what I can. Have you any languages? Have you got enough money to take French lessons? You want to plan to get over there by next summer." He tapped the newspapers with his cold pipe and bits of tobacco spilt upon the pages. "You want to get over there before all hell breaks out."

For the next two years, at the end of every day, sucked dry of words to describe bathtubs, I worked with JWT in the echoing building, rewriting the news, distilling, through the editor's despair, accounts of the crumbling hope. He, teaching me the facts of politics and war, taught also the facts of newswriting. "For God's sake, stop trying to write a great story—just write the STORY!!"

It was March of 1936 when JWT said, "There goes Germany back to the Rhineland—so much for the demilitarized zone! That's the end of the Versailles Treaty. There'll be war all right. 'Right forever on the scaffold, wrong forever on the throne.' All to do, again and again. You'd better plan to go pretty soon. Now, what are we going to do to get you over there? Why don't you work up a column? Mail stuff. Sell it to the country papers. You need a sample to show. Let's see, pretend you were in Geneva this week. Write up a column and we'll see what we can make of it. No interpretation. Experts doing that. Use your eyes. Make your reader feel he was there. Keep it simple."

I used the bathtub money to buy my passage to Europe, certain that I would go. JWT slashed at the verbosity of trial columns until he had one pared down to where he wanted it. We got it printed up and I took the train home to Boston.

Polly and I got into Polly's car, her first. Philip was far from convinced, he would have liked to talk it over. But I knew it would fall apart if talked over. Philip sighed, "Another Polly," and waved us off. In two weeks Polly and I drove through New England, through New York, through Pennsylvania, and as far west as Detroit. We stopped in every town that had a newspaper with a circulation over

50,000. Polly sat in the car while I was swallowed by yet another building. Sometimes I came right out, sometimes I was gone for hours.

There was an editor in Pittsfield whom I found at three in the morning at the end of a sportsmen's dinner. I had no trouble selling him, but would he remember what he'd been sold when he woke in the morning? Polly in her bed in the tourist camp worried and stayed awake until I came stumbling back in the dark. There was an editor in Buffalo, whose paper was housed in a marble-faced building, with elevators and wood-paneled corridors. "Sure," he said, "good stuff. We'll take it. When does the service start? Foreign stuff is going to be more and more important. We'll be giving it space. This'll be good color stuff."

Not all encouraged me. Some editors said they would take it if they liked it. Others said, "Well . . . you could send copy," but they did not see how it'd do me much good. "Folks aren't much interested in Europe."

chapter nine

Small Ulysses

I stood at the ship's rail wearing a patent leather hat with a visor, stylishly made for scrutinizing horizons; a slender adventurer something less than a hundred pounds, something more than twenty years; five feet tall, on the button; dark hair, dark eyes, pupils large with avidity; explosive as a firecracker packed with concentrate of curiosity. Ignorant and innocent I sailed off, carrying no baggage of judgment, no discipline of proper training; nor, despite JWT's efforts, a grain of comprehension of the nature of the tyranny, the terror, from which the American world and I were still separated by three thousand miles. New York, two-dimensional as a theater backdrop, slid by.

Paris, spring, 1936

Heil Hitler! Ninety-nine percent of the Germans vote Nazi. The Nazi program is now overwhelmingly approved. The dream of the thousand-year Reich is proclaimed. The crooked cross replaces the double eagle. Exultantly rearming, the Nazis cry "Sieg Heil!" Hitler shrieks, "Today Germany is ours! Tomorrow the world!"

In Germany those who have the mischance to be born Jews are excommunicated from the human race. Nobody, anywhere, is willing to pose to himself the syllogism that runs like this: the Jew participates in humanity; I, too, partake of humanity; ergo, what happens to the Jew can happen to me. It is a question of vulnerability: Jews first, since they have no protectors, save the conscience of Mankind. But gradations of vulnerability change with growing appetite. Gypsies are classed with Jews—expendable. The S.S. demolish the trade unions. It is a waste of the nation's strength to permit labor to combine for "rights." Words are *verboten*—there is only the word of the Führer. "Intellectuals are carriers of the plague of ideas"; books are burned, Mann, intellectual, chooses exile. Einstein, intellectual *and* Jew, doubly diseased, goes into permanent exile. Despite this evidence, everywhere men believe in their hearts that they, unique in God's grace, are safe.

Such is the Europe into which, with glee and impatience, I propel myself. Arriving breathless in Paris, carrying a letter from JWT to the dean of foreign correspondents, Edgar Mowrer of the *Chicago Daily News*, I am taken to lunch by that harassed but compassionate newsman. He is aghast at the idiocy of this young cub appearing upon his doorstep on the day before Armageddon.

"So you're doing a mail column?" Mowrer begins. "How many papers have you got? Got them signed up? Got contracts? Can you live on what they pay you? You kids who come over here thinking you're going to live on air! Have some more soufflé? Don't you know good food when you see it? You'd better eat while you can. You won't be eating this food often on what a mail column'll bring in. . . . Do they know about you at the Press Department? Want anything else? Dessert? Liqueur? Well, come on back to the office. We'll have to get you fixed up."

All the way back through the streets Mowrer walks a half step ahead of me and talks so fast and of so many things that, trying to keep up with him and to see all there is to be seen and not to miss what he is saying, I have nothing to say for myself. Mowrer pushes open the door of his office, calls out "Get me Fleury at the Quai d'Orsay!" and sits down at his desk, still in his hat and coat. "Fleury . . . there's a young American here doing a mail column. No, no, a girl . . . not bad-looking." Mowrer looks up at me over the phone and grins. "She's got a good string of papers. Country papers. France is not understood in the American countryside."

Mowrer puts the telephone down. "Three o'clock tomorrow afternoon. O.K. for you? Comte de Fleury. Napoleonic title. Probably buy you an orange juice. Well, don't underestimate him. Now, what do you know about the government set-up? Better talk to somebody. Ed Taylor of the *Chicago Trib* can give you some good stuff. Lousy paper, but good man. Knows what he's talking about. Get me Taylor! Ed? What are you up to this afternoon? Want to give a cocktail to an American kid? It's a she. O.K. I'll send her over. She's here to do a mail column. She's got a funny hat."

I am dismissed in a state of glory, excitement shining from me. I trot up the Champs Élysées with such delight in the spring of my step and the set of my head that passersby, amused, turn to look.

Then I have to run a little because otherwise I will laugh aloud. I am invincible.

Ed Taylor, stretching out his long legs under the table at the café, smiles and asks, "What'll you have?" When the drinks have been brought he falls into an abstraction looking at the people going by on the sidewalk, and finally begins, "Take Blum. The premier is neither so well-meaning, nor so much the wavering idealist as the U.S. thinks . . ."

The Comte de Fleury introduces me into a tiny *pension* on the Rue St. Benoit. My window opens out on the Impasse des Deux Anges. I set my typewriter on the table, there I sit and look across the alley into the room opposite where a sailor and a girl live. They have their table, too, before the window; on it a loaf of bread and a knife. The sailor and the girl keep a monkey, who wears no trousers or vest but has a little fez. He is chained to the window sill and sits there putting his hat on and off with quick flicks of his tiny wrist. The hat never misses his head. He always gets it on at precisely the same angle.

At a corner of the Rue St. Benoit and the Blvd. St. Germain is the Café Flore. It is because of its proximity to the Flore that the Comte de Fleury recommended the little *pension*. The Flore is the meeting place for the French intellectuals; for writers, film people, theatre people; and for the foreign newspapermen in Paris. The newsmen eat here, meet here, work here. When there is a think-piece to write out, the tables become their desks. The rent is a cup of coffee or a *fine à l'eau*, depending upon proclivity. Here they read the papers, exchange background bits and argue about the end of the world. The café phones ring. These, in practice, belong to the newsmen, as each bureau calls in its man with a new lead, a newsbreak, or a message that his wife wants him. The conversations are muffled into the mouthpiece but every other correspondent in the café lifts his head from his paper, his page, or his drink. Talk is suspended. "What's he got?" These men are best of friends; and deadly rivals.

Into this crew I am accepted; I have been introduced by Ed Taylor. At the Flore I learn to use the tentacles of all my senses, to be a receiving set for every scrap of information, every change in atmosphere. I have no office to call me when there is rumor of a story. If I go home to the *pension* and bed, who knows what great scoop I might miss? Reporting was still, then, a game of scoops.

By the vigilance of the newsmen around me I manage to be in the midst of the mass meetings of the Popular Front in the Val d'Hiv and get myself crushed in the mob with red berets and red scarves howling, "Vive le Front Populaire! À bas La Rocque!" I don't even understand. But I have a mail column and can plod through the next day's papers to add background to "I was there."

I go off with the contingent to Geneva to watch the little Emperor, Haile Selassie, the Lion of Judah in a derby hat—his Ethiopian empire now lost to him—descend the marble steps of the newly completed Palace of Nations. No nation sitting has any intention of fighting to regain his throne for him.

I rush off to Brussels. The Rexists, aping the Nazis (as do the Mosleyites in England, the Croix de Feu in France, the Sudeten Germans in Czechoslovakia; all the fascists let loose by the victories of their Nazi prototypes, all dreaming delusions of power) have staged a great demonstration in the square of the Cathedral. Gendarmes mounted on huge horses chase the demonstrators—and me—down the Boulevard, whacking heads indiscriminately with the flats of their sabres. The mob gives way but does not scatter. I find myself knee deep in the fountain of the Manneken Pis; a safe, however wet, place to take my stand as observer.

None of this expensive rushing about is essential to the writing of a mail column, but it is the breath of being alive to me.

In the solidarity of these reporters; in the gossip they exchange: the news, leaks, rumors, names of people, names of places; in the language of their trade: dateline, deadline, rewrite, think-piece, scoop, informed sources; in all the jargon of getting the story and of putting the paper to bed; in the immediate response to the frenzied urgencies of coverage; in the instant putting aside of private purpose; in the pride taken, the priorities demanded of professionalism—I have found my first comradeship.

The glamorous career of the foreign correspondent began with the great peace conference, preliminary to the Treaty of Versailles, in 1918. The word "career" is apt—definition number one: "a profession"; definition number two: "to gallop"; therefore, the profession of rushing off at a gallop. The fraternity was created whose lives were regulated by the ring of a telephone: the summons that broke in upon meals, meditation, love, and sleep, and that sent its thralls off to any spot on the globe by the first possible conveyance, traveling light—a few shirts and pairs of socks, toothbrush, typewriter, passport; no door remaining closed to them, no confidence too private to remain unspoken. They will gain access to ruler and to rebel, interrogate the poor and the powerful, exercising the divine right of newsmen. Their persistence in being present at what Ed Taylor called the "collective dramas of humanity" will catapult them into confrontations of governments, explosions of rebellion, wars, and disasters of man's making and of nature's. Whenever two or more foreign correspondents find themselves together again, at some new spot upon the earth, drinks are exchanged, and news-leads; places to eat found, beds arranged, transport pooled, moneys borrowed and lent, problems solved in concert: how to get communications across sealed frontiers, ways and means to pry out denied information. Quick briefings are shared, the background of each new situation: the intricacies of power in that place, the significance of misery or desperation, the alignment of troops, guerrilla positions. On each new story groups form and reform, depending upon who is sent where. Each newly reshuffled unit goes off together, to face in new territory whatever are the difficulties or the dangers for as long as there is a "story."

In the twenties to be a foreign correspondent was the glittering prize, the world the newsman's oyster; by the mid-thirties it would become the option for danger and death; and in the early forties, for those who survived, the participation in despair.

Most of that brotherhood of the news had chosen the road that inevitably would lead them through hell, as innocently, as ignorantly, with as little commitment, except to seeing the world, as I had. Edgar Mowrer for one had come to Paris from the Middle West in the last glow of La Belle Époque: Paris, the eye of civilization. In the Rue de Fleurus the Steins spun their web. Inspiration was nurtured *sous les toits de Paris*, especially under Left Bank roofs. Endowed by his father for a year in which to produce the great novel, Edgar settled, blissfully, under the eaves of a skinny house on the Rue Vavin. But before he could get well started, 1914 blew art and the novel right out of his head. He flew into a passion to get at the war, for fear that it would be a short one, and he would have missed the great drama of his lifetime.

Paris was filled with such young men. One hundred young Americans joined the air force. The Champs Élysées rang with the singing of the "Marseillaise" by bands of Spaniards, Scandinavians, Latin-Americans, Russians, Rumanians, all besieging the enlistment offices.

Edgar took the shortest route to the front. His brother was Bureau Chief of the *Chicago Daily News*, but Edgar didn't wait for credentials. From the tower of a ruined belfry, a Stendhalian hero, he counted the opening salvos. Permits, *laissez-passers*, were never to impede him. Nothing, not lack of papers, not jail, not deportation nor threat of death, was ever to keep Edgar Mowrer from seeing for himself and telling it the way he saw it.

The leftover reporters of that war of mud became the first foreign correspondents. Having come close to death with France, they returned to Paris to live; and were heads of bureaus and special correspondents watching over the dollars and the dead their countries invested in the Permanent Peace of Mr. Wilson. It was a mixed company. Girls who'd been ambulance drivers, who'd worked for the Red Cross, the Salvation Army, weren't going home, either, until they'd seen something of the Europe they had helped to succor. They learned to chase the stories of the politics of peace, first on space rates and then salaries; and some, too, settled into capital cities as bureau chiefs. Where there was a shortage of skill, no employer quarreled over a journalist's sex—not if she could do the job, as Anne O'Hare McCormick did, in Rome, and Sigrid Schultz in Vienna.

By the early twenties, a new flock had descended upon Paris, not inspired to produce the American epic—although La Belle Époque enjoyed a short-lived renaissance: Edna Millay, and the Fitzgeralds, Scott and Zelda, and Red Lewis. Hemingway came from the retreat at Caporetto, not yet conceiving of himself as a "foreign correspondent." Dorothy Thompson, daughter of an upper New York State strict Methodist, had scraped a living in New York publicizing a Bible society and freelancing articles for the *Times*, the *Sun, Leslie's Weekly*. Determined to assess the Russian Revolution for herself, she sailed off on the S.S. *Finland* with vague commitments from the *Post* and the *Buffalo Evening News*, a pattern I repeated some fifteen years later. She never got to Russia. Within a short eight years she was Berlin chief of the *Philadelphia Public Ledger*. Red Knickerbocker, he of the flaming hair, who had come to study psychiatry, stayed on as her assistant, and later became her successor.

Vincent Sheean, just out of college, swallowing bitter disappointment that the Armistice had cheated him of the Great War, tired of reporting on scandal, murders, pimps and prostitutes for the *New York Daily News*. His head full of Greenwich Village talk with the intellectuals who gathered at the feet of Louise Bryant (back from Russia with the message of Revolution, the inequities of Versailles), he got together enough money to get himself to Paris, which had always "pre-existed" in his memory; but he was not to stay for long. He was sent into the Riff (he went on camelback, disguised as an Arab in a burnoose that exposed his white Anglo-Saxon ankles) to find the elusive Abd-el-Krim; and then to Persia, and then to China, and then to Russia. . . .

Ed Taylor had covered the hospital beat and the morgue for the *St. Louis Globe Democrat*. He had some French, a small windfall from an aunt, and "an unappeasable curiosity" about the world beyond America's Middle West, "a passion to travel and look on unfamiliar sights, to breathe strange air and think alien thoughts, to accumulate new experiences and to wonder upon it." He, too, took off for Paris; Hank Wales, the tough "ex" of the War Press, put him on a vacant typewriter to fill in for a man gone to Manchuria.

These young escapees from Main Street were not dedicated to Peace nor to Wilson's self-determination of nations, nor his Fourteen Points, nor were they concerned with the risings in China or Russia. They were hungry for adventure. To chase after stories allowed them the freedom that their pockets could never have afforded. "Don't go, you'll be sent," became the password of the newly accredited foreign correspondents. Press cards, train tickets, cars and chauffeurs to drive them, expenses and hotel rooms; credentials authorizing their presence wherever the earth trembled, and interviews with the movers and shakers—all these were their endowment. The world was their natural habitat.

Their press cards were passes to the Ruhr, scene of melancholy adventure. There was no glamor either in the steelworks, or in the occupying French, who could not vomit up their hatred of the Germans. The correspondents went to Lausanne for the conference to bring peace to the Near East after Greek forces had burned Smyrna, and to Geneva where the League adopted the Protocol for the peaceful settlement of international disputes. As the twenties grew older, this new generation of newsmen became sick of the talk, of the politicking over fine wine and too much food; of the interminable conferences over disarmament and Articles of Peace.

In 1932—as John Whitaker reported—Madariaga, the Spanish disarmament expert, told the Geneva Conference a fable: "The lion looked at the eagle, and said gravely, 'We must abolish talons.' The tiger looked at the bull and said, 'We must abolish horns.' The bull looked at the tiger and said, 'We must abolish claws.' And then the bear looked at them all in turn and said, 'Let us abolish everything but the universal embrace.' "

"If you want disarmament," said Mr. Maksim Litvinov, speaking as people's commissar for foreign affairs for the Russians, "Disarm, throw your weapons away!" This was dismissed as a Communist trick.

A year earlier, in 1931, old Aristide Briand, premier of France eleven times and pilgrim of peace, assured an assemblage of journalists, "So long as I live there will be no war, but peace. It is I who say this to you, Aristide Briand who promises you!" Away with cannons! Away with machine guns!

In 1932, in the Palace of the League of Nations in Geneva, Lord Cecil rose up. "No one," he rumbled in all the majesty of upper-class English, "in this vast assemblage will . . . contradict me when I say that war was never more remote nor peace more secure."

The Parliament of Man blithered. The rest followed according to script. At the Disarmament Conference in 1932, there was an assemblage of some five thousand survivors of the First World War,—many blind, deaf, with half-faces or half-bodies, on crutches, in wheelchairs, carried on stretchers—parading through the streets of Geneva, crying: "Don't humanize war! Abolish it! Create a world police force! Punish the Aggressor!"

The reporters were to be connoisseurs of misery before the decade ended. The more they saw, the more furious they became with lies, with the utopian oversimplifications proposed in the Geneva of the "ideal landscape of Rousseau." They were "saturated," as Ed Taylor said of himself, "with token justice and verbal fraternity, symbolic cooperation and paper security." They saw terror growing while the world statesmen argued pacts and protocols, and the world's military planned their next campaign.

In Rome, Mussolini, the new Caesar, turned to zoological language for exhortation. "It is better to live a day as a lion than a year as a lamb!" "Duce! Duce! Duce!" chanted the crowds. But Edgar Mowrer watched the black shirts dragging their victims to the nearest *farmacia* to be dosed by castor oil, "medicine for those who are sick." Not a single member of the Italian Chamber of Deputies resigned in protest. Looting, assassinations, burnings; Edgar refused to describe the Duce's Italy in terms that pleased the censors: "trains that ran on time." He abhorred violence and was never to yield to it. It was a paradox that when his usefulness in Rome was impaired by his disgust he was posted to Berlin. By 1933 he was calling Germany an "insane asylum." His brother Paul began to wonder if he was "breaking under the strain." By the time Hitler had been elected Führer by plebiscite, Edgar had declared war on the Nazis with his book, *Germany Puts the Clock Back.*

The Führer, Edgar was advised, disliked the book.

"That's all right," said Edgar. "I feel the same way about *Mein Kampf*." What can you do with such a man? He was to outlive them both, Mussolini and Hitler, and continued to tell the truth as he saw it.

Dorothy Thompson had had to wrench herself free from her delight in German *Gemütlichkeit* to recognize the evil of the mind that operated beneath the cowlick of the house painter (said to have been originally named Schicklgruber) with the beady eyes and the comic mustache, who denied the rights it had taken man a thousand years to win: a man's home is his castle; he cannot be condemned without trial; he is free to speak his mind, to read any newspaper, and to worship any God he chooses.

She vowed to devote herself "to the destruction of Adolf Hitler and the system of thought and action presented by him to the infinitely deludable German people." She had loved the German people ("to excess" thought Jimmy Sheean). In 1934 when she was escorted out of Germany, Hitler hadn't worried about getting rid of her, as he had worried about the effect of kicking out Edgar Mowrer. Edgar had been chief of foreign correspondents in Berlin, and a man. It had not occurred to Hitler that tossing out a woman would be noticed as anything but a housecleaning gesture. It was a serious error on his part. She was not only a woman but a passionate and handsome one, and the wife of one of the best-known American authors, Sinclair Lewis. Daughter of a preacher, she recognized hellfire when she saw it, even on the streets of her beloved Germany.

The Anglo-American press who came en masse to the Nord-Express station to see her off with honor filled her arms with long-stemmed roses for the journey. She, in turn, would one day send such roses to me, as though they were the Marathon torch.

A German went into a Nazi meeting, as Vincent Sheean discovered aghast, "one sort of man and by means of songs, slogans, cheers, came out another, ready to kill Jews." Meanwhile, in *Mein Kampf* Hitler was declaring that "Skillful and unremitting propaganda can persuade people to believe Heaven or Hell or conversely that the most miserable existence is Paradise," and again, "[The] mass of people in the primitive simplicity of the heart more readily

129

falls victim to a big lie than to a small one." All this Hitler wrote out in his exact plan for the defeat of the world.

The Peace Treaty of Versailles in 1919 to the Fall of France in 1940—the route those newsmen followed was as inevitable as the way to Calvary. From the triumphant landing of our top-hatted, pince-nezed President Wilson, schoolmaster more than savior, with the people kneeling to pray wherever he and his train passed, to the stage from which the Führer shouted to the frenzied crowds, "and Tomorrow the World!": this was a progression which transformed every newsman. Step by step they realized that they were the scouts sent forward to reconnoiter Armageddon; it was clear to them that they were watching the crucial decision in the fate of mankind.

The reporters would have rejected scornfully any imputation that they were the last idealists. They saw themselves as tough-minded skeptics: realists, impatient with political rhetoric, whether in behalf of the powerful or the powerless; zealots of complexities (nothing so dangerous for mankind as the simple solution), knights of the "hard facts." Whatever the cost or the circumstance—punching out the story with two fingers at a typewriter perched on a rock amid the debris of the latest disaster (often enough at risk of their lives), imbedding the evidence of their eyes in enough official-ese to get the piece past the censor—this was their job: to inform, to make possible Walter Lippmann's "educated citizenry." Except they did not believe *quid* is followed by *quo*. Between the Apocalyptic vision and Armageddon lay the almost unbridgeable gap of human experience. Experience not being transferable, whatever the eloquence, there was no way of hurrying mankind to embrace its fate. Journalism was no therapeutic cure for lethargy. For America, it will take the Japanese attack on Pearl Harbor to transform all the shouted warnings into the Writing on the Wall.

Nevertheless, there was nothing to do but shout.

"The more monstrous the evil grew, the wider it spread, the more essential the function appeared, the more difficult and dangerous to be a witness," wrote Ed Taylor. Public relations departments of their newspapers invented glossy phrases for them, like "brave watch-dogs of the truth at the frontier of the news." But "people began to complain," Ed wrote, that "our barking disturbed their sleep, harmed business, made dangerous enemies, gave aid and comfort to political adversaries, endangered peace in our time."

Once home, Dorothy Thompson could not contain her frustration with a country that believed in freedom and would not look to

its defense. She was a Cassandra, a "breast-beating Boadicea." After one explosion on American radio, her friend Alice Longworth,
indulging in a wry phrase, dismissed Dorothy's agonizing attempt
to communicate mortal danger to the country of the deaf: "The only
woman in history who had her menopause in public."

Before the thread of the world's destiny was well spun
out, there came the day in mid-July of 1936 when for me knowledge
turned into action; it began with newsmen dropping into the Flore,
drinks ordered, chaff exchanged. Whose office was it that called to
whisper, "Frontiers of Spain closed!"? Within minutes the café emptied of the press. Blown by the wind, comprehending nothing, I
pelted off down the Rue St. Benoit to the *pension*. Passport! Money!
So little money left! When is the next train for Spain?

chapter ten

"Hang Yourself, Brave Crillon"

Pends-toi, brave Crillon; nous avons
combattu à Arques et tu n'y étais pas.
Henri IV, 1597 (as given by Voltaire)

The train stopped at Hendaye: the end of the line. Across
the river Bidassoa was Spain. Nobody was allowed to pass its closed
frontier. The traffic was one way only; every foreigner caught in
Spain was escorted by the guards, fingers on the triggers of their
loaded guns, bayonets fixed, to the border. In Hendaye, in the little
plaza beneath the plane trees in front of the Hotel Imatz, or
crowded in its lobby, milling about, were newsmen from everywhere in the European compass.

A girl in felt slippers and crisp white apron ran out of the hotel.
She bobbed a curtsy, grinned and grasped my bags. "Je cherche
Monsieur Taylor," I explained to the hotel proprietor.

"Monsieur Taylor? Quelle dommage, Mademoiselle! Il est déjà
parti! Mademoiselle has missed him." I had never thought that I
might get here and find him gone. "He will be back?" The hotel man
shrugged. "He keeps his room. There is mail for him. Mais, qui sait?
Il essaye de passer en Espagne!"

My room was small, the bed big. The windows opened over the
rooftops of the town and looked down upon the blue bay. I sat on
the edge of the bed in my coat, my patent leather hat pushed to the
back of my head. In the long pier glass I saw myself perched, aimless,
coat open and the visor of my hat pointed at the ceiling. "Well?" I
asked of the image in the glass. I had made a wild dash from Paris
and here I was in a quiet room, above the quiet town. Somewhere
near is Spain. There is a war in Spain. The thing to do is to get up
and go find it.

In the lobby were the quick-moving men, the competent, arrogant army who had been taking over the town: swinging off trains, with typewriters for their only baggage; commandeering rooms, cars, telegraphs, telephones; demanding of the proprietor's daughter, drafted into service at the switchboard, "Get me London!" . . . "New York!" . . . "Paris!"

There was no office waiting to hear from me, no sheet held open for my phone call, for my cable.

Everybody in the town was headed for the International Bridge. Family groups sauntered along with little girls holding the hands of their papas; the more independent men moved purposefully, elbowing past those hampered by small children. A few boys rushed by on bicycles. A fast car squealed around a curve and unloaded gay young people with tennis rackets and golf clubs. They had come from Biarritz to find out if there was anything exciting to be seen. I felt a rush of resentment and animosity towards these amateur onlookers, and thrust forward through the crowd to show that it was my *job* to be there. But there was nothing to see. The crowd on the French side stood behind the soldiers at the customs and immigration barrier at the end of the French rail line. Here, normally, passengers would walk across the bridge into Spain, since the Spanish train tracks are another gauge. Today the traffic was one way only—out of Spain.

"What's happening in there?" I asked an evacuee trudging the tracks.

"An' what ain't?" This one was Irish. He took up the bag he had rested on the road. "There's shootin' all over the streets. The Reds have took over the town and got all the blasted aristocrats shut up in the best hotel. They're shooting in the windows. It's the death of you if you come out from under cover. Well, here's luck to them!" The Irishman plodded on.

The Spanish Pyrenees were deceptively near in the clear light. "Go find a smuggler who will take you across the mountains on burro back"—I remembered Mowrer saying that. But how to go about finding a smuggler?

Late afternoon. A dusty car squealed as it came around the square and skidded to a stop before the hotel door. The chauffeur was young and moved quickly. He swung four typewriters to the sidewalk. Ed Taylor got out. He looked dusty and exhausted.

I had the grace to be embarrassed. All during the train ride down I

133

had thought of things to say. Now I knew I had no right to intrude my amateur self upon intensely occupied men.

The two men he was with were arguing furiously. One had black hair that fell across his eyes with his energetic gestures. He was very elegant—in body, not in clothes: old pants, old shirt and no socks on. The other had a military bearing, gave commands to the chauffeur and talked to Ed and to the sockless one at the same time. Everyone from the hotel stared at them. They looked full of secrets.

Ed saw me. He came forward, smiling. "You don't lose any time, do you?" Gratefulness flooded through me; I opened my mouth to answer.

Another man rushed out of the lobby. He had a shock of red-brown hair and a harassed and stubborn look, as though he weren't getting anywhere and was furious about it.

"John!" Taylor called to him. He put a restraining hand on my arm. To me: "This is John Elliott." To him: "When did you get in?" John Elliott! I could see the type in which the *Herald Tribune* set his by-line.

"What have you got, John? Got anything?" I stood with them, included in their talk, their fraternity.

"Not a damn thing," said John. "You've tried getting through down here?" He meant the International Bridge.

Ed shook his head. "You can get across the bridge all right, but there's a Soviet sitting in Irún; they'll run you out of town. They put me back across the border with a military escort. No. We've been up and down the entire frontier today. The only place you may be able to get through is at Dancharinea."

"We're going to try to get to Pamplona through the Dancharinea mountain pass," said Ed, as he pulled a map from his pocket. "Look, here's where the pass is." He scribbled on a bit of paper. "There aren't any proper customs men there and there's a chance you can talk your way through if you meet any soldiers. It's a cowpath of a road, but why don't you come in with us? There's room in the car." Mowrer's smugglers' tracks! Then it was true, not musical comedy.

The conundrum, I began to understand, was this: no one could cross into Spain without a pass, a *salvo conducto* to offer the guards. But *salvo conductos* were issued only where the headquarters of the army was established—in this case, with Mola's army in Pamplona. How do you get to Pamplona to get a pass to get to Pamplona?

"Dazzlers!" I said. Edgar had regaled me once with the details of how he had made his own passes: pictures taken at the local photographer's; gilt paper indecipherably stamped with a vintner's crest;

red ribbon streamers affixed with glue and flair; names inscribed, permit signed in wedding certificate script by the village priest.

"In case," I put in, "that even on a smuggler's trail there are some kind of guards. They might not yet have seen the regular passes. We could make up dazzlers to impress them."

Ed grinned. "We'll do that," he said, well aware of the "we" that included me.

"We" turned out to be a company of six in the big car that the military-looking man, Cardozo, had hired. He was called "Major" by his paper—Northcliffe's arch-reactionary *London Daily Mail*. They all paid their way, but me. Ed Taylor of the *Chicago Tribune*, a paper as reactionary for the United States as the *Mail* was for England; Bertrand de Jouvenel—the elegant sockless one—of *Paris Soir*; John Elliott of the conservative Republican *New York Herald Tribune*. The chauffeur, Antoine, made six. The Major ran the show. It was evident that he was not sure how far he would carry me, but the "dazzler" idea had won me at least the try at Pamplona.

A few miles above Hendaye, the Café Hiribarren overhung the river at its narrowest point. From its terrace you could look across and down on the meadows of Spain and up to the Pyrennean slopes. Here, with a cornfield between them, employing the rocks of the mountain as cover, the two sides skirmished for position, affording a fine spectacle to enjoy in approximate safety. While our "dazzler" papers were in production the Major established a headquarters from which we could see the war from the French side—in the bleachers as it were—with all the comforts of a good café.

Late night: we sat upon the balcony, smoking, finishing the last of the wine as the cold mist began to curl up from the river. Over in Spain, flat on their bellies amid the rustling corn, the sentries listened for danger. The only light in the darkness that filled the valley was the stage set that the balcony made, hanging brightly lit in the night. We drank and talked. Across the river in the impenetrable black, there was death.

A spurt of flame from the darkness, the following crack of a rifle; on the balcony a glass splinters, the red wine spills. Chairs tip over. I am under the table. Ed Taylor reaches the door. Even the Major jerks back his chair. "Jove, what a target we make for those blighters over there! Jove!"

Trembling, I manage to come out from under the table and reseat myself. The wine stain on the tablecloth spreads. The Major digs the bullet out of the wall behind us—a memento.

In the ebb of fear I was aware of shame, expanding, filling up the vacuum in my breast. I saw the waving grain, this Spanish cornfield; and at the Farm the fields of corn, Kit and his cohorts planting and hilling, myself with a basket to be filled for lunch, going in and out the rows, tugging down the tassels to test the ears, the long green fronds rustling to my passing. It was like a small cathedral inside the corn rows under those heads of seed, uniformly nodding, with sun filtering in, green as the light penetrating clear waters. And I saw an inherited vision—the waves of grain of Polly's Russia, the sea that hid the conspirators reading Tolstoy; and Polly, on her belly like a small fish, listening absorbed to forbidden prophecies of brotherhood.

This Spanish corn was inhabited, too, but by men who lay on the chill wet earth alone, hidden to their enemy. Only our box of a balcony was illuminated in the night. How was a man's finger, numb with cold, not to press against the trigger, a little pressure of the finger to see those puppets jump? The man out there, secret in the cornfield, was vulnerable. He and I were one. I was no longer an observer at somebody else's war, on somebody else's planet, I, too, was flesh and bone. I, too, could be shattered by a bullet.

The next morning was fresh and sparkling. Outside the hotel, Antoine was polishing the dust off his beloved car. Equipped with our self-made permits, we were about to try the mountain pass, that unfrequented smugglers' way.

Getting ready for such an expedition takes organizing—the Major's métier. "Well, well, are we all set?" Cardozo looked at the military watch on his wrist. "Antoine! The typewriters." The typewriters were standing on the sidewalk in the sun. Antoine stored them in the boot. "Taylor! Elliott! Ah! here's de Jouvenel." To me: "Got your passport? Got your typewriter? Coming as you are? Get in then." The door slammed. Antoine let the brake out. The car coasted down the hill and shot off onto the river road.

At the foot of the mountain the traveled road wandered a little hopelessly among the low slopes, then lost itself in dust and dried grasses. If you looked hard at the face of the mountain you could make out the ruts, a way that wound in and out behind the grey jagged rock, hid, and reappeared. Here and there were rocky areas upon which the ruts had made no imprint; then a path was visible again, curving upon itself up the mountain side. I traced the corkscrew track all the way up until it dipped over the topmost ridge and was gone. Antoine wriggled himself more surely behind the wheel, and we started up, our grinding passage loosening a slide of rock.

On the outer curves the shoulders had rotted away. Little clouds of dust danced in the air behind our wheels. It was not good either to look up or look down. Smugglers' trails!

Leaping off a rock under a shading tree, soldiers run across the roadway. One is an old man and the others are young boys in blue work pants, with shirts wide open at brown necks; they hold their guns stiffly with the pleasure and the importance of being armed. Antoine pulls up sharply. Below the lip of the road is a cluster of houses. Chickens, pigs, children, and villagers come to join the soldiers. They cluster in the roadway and stare at the foreigners.

The Major, armed with all our beribboned passes, gets out to parley with the guards. They listen with self-conscious gravity, examine one of our theatrical passes upside down. There is a feeling of precarious balance. One too many words from the Major, one grumble from the old man who appears to have taken a dislike to him, and the decision will be against us. We are ordered out of the car and stand at the roadside, saying nothing to upset the equilibrium.

In an unthinking gesture of kinship with any child, and because my head is hot, I take off my patent leather hat and stick it, backside to, on the black curls of the nearest child. The child, recognizing its affinity to the hats of the Guardia Civil, jumps up and down laughing: "Guardia! Guardia!" The soldiers and the villagers smile: a girl going to look at their war is an amusing matter. Relieved, I smile too, dig into a pocket and find a pack of American cigarettes to offer around. We stand and smoke, a pleasant, fragile comradeship established. A wineskin is produced and passes from hand to hand. Its mouth is not to touch the drinker's lip; the stream must be poured at the proper angle directly into the open throat. I get the wine in my eye, down my chin, and hilarity erupts. When the old man has finished his cigarette to the stub, I, having mopped up the wine, hand him the pack. He accepts the gift with dignity, nods his head, and turns away, climbing back onto his rock perch. The boys wave their rifles to indicate that the newsmen are to get back into their car. I snatch my hat. Antoine releases the brake.

"Good girl," says the Major. "Create a diversion. Sound military tactics."

In this preoccupation with how to get into Spain, I had not asked myself who was at war. Few of us knew much about recent Spanish history. The country, a monarchy, had been under the repressive dictatorship of General Miguel Primo de Rivera from 1923 until 1930. Then, after an abortive attempt to set up a new government that would be more moderate, King Alfonso left the country, although without officially abdicating. A provisional government framed a new constitution and Alcalá Zamora was elected first president on December 10, 1931. For five years there was incessant inner turmoil, punctuated by events such as an unsuccessful conservative revolt under Gen. José Sanjurjo, a radical rising of anarchists and syndicalists in Barcelona (a sign that the workers were impatient with the slow tempo of social reform), and enormous tensions between the factions of the Right and of the Left. On February 16, 1936, the Popular Front—a coalition of Left political parties: Centrist Republicans, Socialists, Syndicalists, Communists—won a victory in the elections, decisively defeating the Conservative Republicans, Clericals and Monarchists. The new government was openly against the privileges and the power of the rich and of the Church. Manuel Azaña was chosen prime minister and was then elected president. On July 18, the army chiefs—Generals Sanjurjo, Francisco Franco, and Emilio Mola—in Morocco spearheaded a revolt against the government, which rapidly grew into a civil war. Sanjurjo was killed in an airplane accident and General Franco assumed command of the army of revolt, supported by large contingents of Moorish soldiers. On October 1, the insurgents appointed Franco their "Chief of the Spanish State." His government was quickly recognized by Fascist Italy and Nazi Germany, who lent military support. Soviet Russia supported the Republic. Spain became known as "the battle ground of rival ideologies." By the end of the war, 400,000 lives would be lost in battle, 15,000 in air raids, and 30,000 in executions plus 200,000 dead of starvation, malnutrition, and disease.

In the early days of the war, none of us could know with any certainty whether a given village or surrounding region had gone over to the insurgents or had remained loyal to the Republic. Nor did we know with any certainty just where the battle lines had been drawn, especially in the mountains. The Major was bent on getting to Pamplona, at that time the headquarters of the Generals. He would have been as unwelcome in Madrid as Edgar Mowrer on the Generals' side.

The Generals had decreed that they were to be called the "Patriots." To Madrid they were the "Rebels"—those Generals whose mission was to wipe out decadent democracy in Spain. They were soon to be surrounded by the counsel and matériel of their fellow-kind: generals of Germany, admirals of Italy. And Italian foot soldiers and tanks. And German planes.

The "Loyalists," more logically, were the armies that stayed faithful to the elected republican government of Madrid; the Major called them, as later we were told to, the "Reds"; and it is true that Russians did fight this Civil War in Spain.

What was I, heir to that distant vision of a better world, doing in the country of the Generals? I had been deposited there by the meanderings of a mountain road; by having come to Spain on a train to Hendaye instead of Perpignan, by chasing after Ed Taylor, who was as much a democrat as Edgar, but who was working for Colonel McCormick, who ran the *Chicago Tribune*, a reactionary paper devoted to the state of order (even when imposed by Pinkertons or the police).

A *salvo conducto*, if Pamplona deigned to award it, would accredit me to the war only within that Spain held by the Generals' armies, and on the Generals' roads. Once your passport was stamped with a Patriot place of entry, you, too, were marked for the duration. No changing sides. On the wrong road, behind the wrong lines, these papers would entitle you to be shot.

Sliding, slipping, skidding down the mountain roads, the Major had said little. If the lines of battle had shifted during the night we would have been in the hands of the Reds. He was relieved only by the "Arriba España" of the old man and the boys with the rifles who'd held the road.

Down from the mountain and flying over the way to Pamplona, I, too, swallowed apprehensions. We sped past groups of young exultant soldiers with newly issued arms. "Arriba España!" they cried. "Arriba España!" we called in answer. This exchange with strangers moved and excited de Jouvenel and me. We were caught up in a surge of brotherhood. But I began to realize that sewn to the tunics of these young troops were medallions of Christ crowned with thorns, weeping bloody tears. I shivered. I had never seen faith and blood as one before; innocent that I was, bred in the pallid religion of humanity. Would the cheers that greeted the unexpected appearance of a girl at their war turn ugly with suspicion if they knew my real background? I think they thought of me, because I was olive-skinned and dark-haired and present at their war, as being Spanish, Catholic, and one of themselves, a participant in their crusade.

139

In Pamplona an open touring car was driven around and around the Plaza, filled with young boys sitting upon each other's laps and standing mixed up with each other's legs, carrying rifles with bayonets fixed. Every house in the square had a balcony, from which people watched the street as though it presented a spectacle of fiesta. There were cafés under the arches of the square; wire-legged tables and wire-backed chairs packed the sidewalks. Nowhere was there a vacant chair or empty table top.

Now and again a small detachment of soldiers marched past the cafés. The people at the tables jumped to their feet, saluted, and cried "Arriba España! Arriba España!" Uniforms were everywhere. The soldiers wore bright red berets. "Carlists," pronounced John Elliott, who had been boning up on Spanish history and politics, "active royalists, originally supporters of the claims to the throne by Don Carlos, son of Charles IV, and his successors. Now they are out-and-out monarchists." The red Carlist banners with the big gold crown hung from the balconies; small crown-imprinted red flags were stuck in the radiator caps of the cars. Pamplona's Plaza bloomed red and gold.

The Major ordered the men to come with him. He did not say so, but it was clear that I was to stay out of the way. Antoine and I were left in the car. The men went off, making an inverted *v* like a spearhead which penetrated the crowd, the Major at the apex. A Spaniard with a long aristocratic face, like a Goya knight, came forward to greet him and introduced him to two officers with so much gold on their shoulders and caps that I knew they had to be generals; one had a red sash about his waist. These generals were holding court at the largest table at the head of the square. The Major made the shadow of a bow.

The two generals inclined their heads. They invited the Major to sit at their table. He sat for a moment in courtesy, then went back for Taylor and de Jouvenel and Elliott and presented them. All four newsmen sat down and animation lit up their faces. I watched the Major being deferential and putting questions, the reporters scribbling upon bits of paper. Their faces were tense with concentration.

Abruptly the Generals got up; the audience was over. Bertrand's lock of black hair had fallen across his forehead into his eyes. They all almost bowed again—except John Elliott, who had missed something and was talking to Ed Taylor. The general with the bright red sash moved off. As he passed the tables, men, whether they were in civilian or military dress, jumped to their feet and saluted.

I could not sit still any longer, and got out of the car and stood in

its shadow. A man with white hair and very black eyes who had
been watching me asked, "Periodista? La Señorita es periodista?
You will come to the *Comandancia* with me? I will secure your pass.
Where do you wish to go?"

I was transfixed. If I left the security of the car, the men might
return, fling themselves in, and rush off, and I would be left behind.
But how could I go anywhere without a pass?

I waited in the anteroom of the *Comandancia* standing first on one
foot and then on the other. A shaft of sunlight slanted across the
room and the dust motes danced on the bare floor. It was a hollow-
sounding barn of a place. On a row of hooks along the wall a priest's
hat hung, swaying a little every time a door banged in an adjacent
wall. There was an heraldic emblem above an archway, and on one
wall a torn tapestry; under this, there were three heavily carved
mahogany chairs on whose dusty red plush seats I was too devoured
by impatience to remain seated. The room filled and emptied. Peasants twisted their caps in their hands. Runners smartly saluted the
guards and disappeared behind the door, which closed quickly after
them. There were secret-faced men, arrogant, who were not asked
to wait, for whom the door was opened at once.

The man with the white hair reappeared. Despite his civilian
black suit, the soldiers moved aside at his authority. He nodded at
me.

"Señorita, give me your passport." He passed the document to a
young man at a typewriter. The young man copied from the passport and I was given a paper headed *Salvo Conducto*, already signed.

 "And now," said the man, who had taken it upon himself to do the
honors for this, the first feminine observer at his private war—
these were the first days of patriotic festivity which in all wars are
the prelude to death. The Spaniard had still the leisure to be gallant.
"Now for pleasanter matters," he went on. "You are familiar with
Pamplona? In our crowded city today, have you made plans to
lunch?"

I could only shake my head. My unlikely sponsor picked up the
phone, gave orders and scribbled the name of a street on a bit of
paper. "Your driver will have no difficulty." All the needs of a new-
comer to war having been assuaged by his courtesy, he smiled dis-
missal, "Arriba España, Señorita!"

Overwhelmed, I got to the car only an instant before the conference in which the men had been huddled broke up. Antoine saw the
Major coming back, and leapt to open the car door. But the men
stood in indecision.

"Good morning's work, what?" the Major said. The men were pocketing their notes. "I say, the thing now is to get passes to go to Saragossa. Follow the army. Find the front. But first we eat. Can't do anything at the *Comandancia* now. Too late. Closed up for siesta. Open for business of war at four o'clock. Antoine, do you know where we can eat around here?"

Antoine suggested the Hotel Perla. But everyone who had sat at the café tables was now sitting in the dining room there.

"Oh, I say!" the Major grumbled, as they trailed disconsolately back out of the hotel, "We'll never get anywhere this way." I followed them out, as much in the rear as I had followed them in. I put my hand on John's sleeve to get his attention. "John, I know a place . . . ?"

"That would be fine," said John with equanimity, as though Pamplona and I were previous acquaintances. "Could Antoine find it? Major, she knows a restaurant."

"What?" the Major barked, and his sharp eyes reexamined me. "How? Never mind! Take us there. Tell Antoine."

I gave Antoine my mysterious friend's directions. We drove into the old part of the town, climbed the dark wooden stairs of a house indistinguishable from the others on the street. A waiter greeted us, "Buenos días, Señorita," as if my assortment of men and I were expected. He ushered us into an inside room. At the deal tables soldiers were sitting, men in uniforms and young officers with wings on their lapels. But this was not a restaurant for outsiders; the habituées looked at us with surprise. They belonged to the Falange, the Spanish fascist organization founded in 1933 by José Antonio Primo de Rivera, son of the former dictator.

"Good-o!" The Major gave me a brief congratulatory nod, his black eyes appraising me. There was a little pause, then the Major said, "Here, she's got to have a story. This is what we got this morning. Ready?" I scribbled in such elation that I was later unable to read what I had written.

Over coffee, the Major in gustatory comfort eased his belt, "There! You do make yourself useful, what?" he said to me.

"She can serve in our army. She's a good soldier, isn't she?" de Jouvenel urged.

"Quite," approved the Major and then turned military. "Quite. But how is she to come on with us without proper passes? Can't have her endangering the entire maneuver, can we, what? Hardly can ask for a pass for a *girl*, to go to the front, what? Spaniards won't like it. Think we don't take their damn war seriously, what? Have to find her a ride back to France. Sorry, old girl."

"But Major," I tried to prevent his sweeping over me like an army tank. "But Major, won't this do?" And I put out on the cloth, among the crumbs, the *salvo conducto.*

When the men's laughter subsided and the Major stopped saying "Bloody Spaniards," it was agreed that I was officially the army's private.

There was no air of fiesta in Saragossa. The few civilian men we saw seemed in a hurry to get the task done that had brought them out—to get back in, off the street. Houses were closed and shuttered, women and children invisible. This town was filled with the military, soldiers marching up and down; each square, each alley, head and foot, had its complement. Bertrand quieted. Even Antoine was subdued; he refrained from blaring his horn. The Major looked thoughtful. After Saragossa the villages became fewer, the faces different; no friendliness, no cheering, no singing, no shouting. We had come into a land of infertile valleys, the purple and yellow mountains of another planet, rolling into a sea of distance, fearsome and interminable.

At each new town John thumbed through his guidebook: "Calatayud. From the Arabic, Castle of the Moorish king. This town is said to be carved out of the limestone mountain." "Look," exclaimed Ed Taylor, "They've got apartment houses." Caves had been scooped out of that soft yellow rock, one above the other up the cliff's height—sacking hung in the openings to provide the privacy of a door.

In the next town the car bumped over the cobbled street of the square. We could see into the open doorways, built as wide as they were high to admit the domestic animals. The beasts lived downstairs in the steamy dark, the family in the lofts above. A dust of crumbling limestone lay over all.

"Alhama de Aragón," read John.

"One of the seven birthplaces of Cervantes," the Major teased him. In that town, wherever we looked, white rags hung limp in the heat: from all the balcony railings, from the projections of the houses, and on a pole stuck up in the middle of the square. The Major, veteran of many campaigns, recognized the signs. An unwelcome army had been through here and not very long ago. We were nearing the war now, and the Major rubbed his hands in satisfaction.

"Medinaceli," read John, unperturbed, from the guidebook. "Stronghold of the Dukes of Medinaceli in the wars against the Moors." The road ran up the mountainside and Antoine took the

143

grade very slowly, so not to surprise, not to antagonize. Nevertheless we were stopped abruptly and surrounded by men with guns. We had found our war. The Major, with military escort, went off to parley. The soldiers guarded the remaining occupants of the car.

The whole flat top of the mountain was covered with the rambling brown ruins of a wall and tumbled castle towers. Innumerable doorways opened out upon the cobbled courtyard. There were a few people, a few pigs, a few chickens, and everywhere, soldiers. Far below, the land was flat to the horizon; lime fields lay dazzling white in the sun; the road wove across the plain. From this commanding height, one could see, far in the distance, a dust cloud move. From here the Dukes of Medinaceli had kept watch for the approach of the attacking Moors. "The damn place is impregnable!" I announced, feeling my oats.

"Except from the air," said John, who was calmly putting away his guidebook, his eyes upon the two specks traveling in the sky.

A sea of sound surged up and engulfed us. Bells rang from the ruined towers. Across the cobbles women ran, tugging children after them. "Aviones! Vamos!" A soldier grabbed my arm, jerked open the door of the car and pulled me out. We ran together, hand-in-hand over cobbles, through an opening in the wall, and plunged into a damp, dark doorway. Inside was a whitewashed stairwell. A band of bright sunlight streaming through a slit in the thick stone wall showed stone stairs descending. I took my place in the line going down: soldiers and peasants, children and a cow. The cow had to be pushed. The darkness of the cellars was impenetrable. I wondered where Ed and John were, and accepted a cigarette from a soldier. Then I heard the Major's voice. "Wine cellars. What? Walls must be six feet thick. Excellent shelters from air raids."

The raid over, once again in the sunshine, the Major dusted the whitewash off his beret. "There it is," he proclaimed, "Walked right into it. Good story, what? Very front line. War's first air attack. Light stuff, though. No damage done." And then on another tack, "Splendid chap, the Colonel. Cream off the top, these men of his. Aristocrats, all of them. Must say they need shaves. Good spot, what? Commands all roads. Marched his men out of Saragossa. Went through those villages just as we thought an army did. 'Take prisoners?' I asked him, 'What do you do with your prisoners, Colonel?' Now, John, what do you think he does with his prisoners? Smells their hands. If they smell of gunpowder, pop, pop. Picked off six with his own pistol. Pop, pop. Here we are! There's a room up here he says we can use."

We five climbed the stone stairs to a door above. "Now then, where's Antoine with those typewriters?" In the room was a pool table, its green baize thick in dust. Typewriters were lined up on it. The men took the covers off their machines, found something to sit on, and pounded away.

There was no need for me to pound away. I had no need of pecking out a story in barely legible copy to be read over a telephone to London, or sent by cable to New York. What I had to do was to type out twelve careful copies, one to Springfield, one to Great Barrington, one to Northampton—New England towns whose existence I found it difficult to believe in from this mountain top at Medinaceli—then type out twelve envelopes and address them and put each story in its envelope to go by mail. I desperately longed to have to sit in this fly-thick room on an upended box pounding out a story. The flies crawled over the table and over the men's hands as they typed.

The Major found a pack of old Spanish playing cards. They had cups and saucers instead of diamonds and hearts. "Cut, old man," he demanded of Ed Taylor. "Low card takes the stories back to France. No!" to me. "You cannot draw. I will not have a girl dashing about Spain alone, y'know. Card, Bertrand, John, card! Leaves four of us. Four of us to sit here among these damn flies and wait. Do you think you can play bridge with these damn culinary cards?"

I don't play bridge. If I took the stories, that would be a way of paying for my place in the car. "Let's see your stuff, John, Ed, Bertrand? Major?" I went about collecting the stories. The men gave them up to me without question. They were not thinking about why I asked for them. Each was occupied in hoping he would not have to go. Those who stayed here might see more action; the one who went would lose out. When I had collected the stories, I made a short speech. "Major, I'm going."

Bertrand gestured in irritation, as he had done at the flies. "A girl cannot go alone. One of us will go with her."

But I was talking only to the Major. "You'll have to give me money for phoning. Here, put the phone numbers on your stories, will you?" The Major opened his mouth to sputter. He looked at me and I looked at him. "Major," I said stubbornly, "I'm a private in your army. Don't demote me."

Half a day later, choking in dust, aching from the swings and turns of the car, passing in and out of villages, through country I was uncomfortably aware I had not seen before, we at last climbed into the mountains. The fog came down. From sheer restlessness and unease, with no logical consideration of what I was doing or why, I took the men's stories out of my bag. They had been written on flimsy paper and I folded each very small and tight, unzipped the back of my dress and stuffed them inside my girdle, flat against my skin, then zipped my dress up again. I crackled a bit, but was not noticeably plumper. Not much longer, even in this war, would such naïve tactics be employed.

The car had sharply rounded a mountain shelf. Out of the fog a guard loomed. "Antoine!" I managed to whisper before the guard reached the car, "Antoine, don't show them our papers. Look at the flag!"

The red, yellow, and purple flag of the betrayed Republic fluttered above the barrier. We had crossed the lines. Now I understood that spatter of sound in the mountains, those puffs of cloud. Guns, I realized, somewhat tardily. I prayed that Antoine would keep to himself those damned French Croix de Feu papers he carried.

A man in civilian clothes came out of the customs house. He talked to the guard, looked at me, leafed through the passports and shrugged. "What money have you?" he asked. I tried hard not to breathe or move for fear of crackling. Thank God that at Dancharinea they had as yet no entry stamps to put on the passports. "Will you look, Monsieur?" I handed him my purse with its small hoard, open to be examined.

"A young lady should not travel alone in Spain in such days as these. You have no intention of returning?"

"Oh, no Monsieur! I have been very frightened." I will never, at any rate, return by way of this route.

Suddenly we are out of the fog. The road is clear and wet and shining. Here in France it is raining, dark slivers of rain that dissolve the mist. A bar of light falls across our way and the car's headlights shine on the oilskins of the French *douaniers*. We are out of Spain. We get stiffly out of the car and go into the warmth of the customs house. It smells damp, but I am very grateful for the French faces smiling at me in the poor light.

In Hendaye, Antoine and I rang the night bell of the Hotel Imatz. Upstairs was my bed, the pillows stuffed with down, the comforter light and warm. But I had the four stories of my men to transmit. With difficulty I managed to wake the dozing desk clerk. Now operator woke operator across the sleeping miles of France. "Élysée 1287. Oui. C'est ça." "Herald Trib? I have a story from John Elliott. Are you ready? Dateline Medinaceli—Elliott-Tuesday your correspondent . . ." "Chicatrib? I have a story from Ed Taylor. Are

The author trying to beguile her way across the closed frontier. The French gendarmes were willing enough but the Spaniards were not. The typewriter is set up for a story on refugees fleeing the shooting in Irún.

you ready? Taylor, dateline . . . Advance column rebel army . . ." "Paris Soir? J'ai une histoire de Monsieur de Jouvenel . . ." I worked up a momentum in my reading, while my mind was half asleep and took little part in this. My voice went on monotonously. "The planes swooped down upon us. Colonel Palacios P-Peter A-Apple C-Cain I-Isadore O-Orchard S-Sugar gave the order to separate . . ."

One more, I had still to do London. "Daily Mail? I have a story from the Major. Are you ready?"

The English voice replied primly, "Sorry. Too late. We're not taking any more tonight."

I woke up. "What do you mean you're not taking!" I shouted, furious with the stupidity of that clipped voice. "I came halfway across Spain through hell tonight to give you this story!"

"What's that?" the voice demanded sharply. "What's that? Who is this? How did you get the Major's story? Hold on, will you?" No smugness in the voice now. It vibrated with interest, with effort to

147

hold onto me, that indignant, invisible female somewhere on the other end of a wire.

A new voice came on. "You have a story from Major Cardozo? Go ahead, please. And when you are finished, Miss, don't ring off. We want to talk to you. All right, Miss . . ." Grinning to myself, I began, "Dateline: Cardozo-Medinaceli . . ."

It would seem I had just shut my eyes, yet there was day-light in the room. A knocking on the door had waked me. Even with my eyes open it took me time to recover, find my voice and call "Entrez!" Père Imatz himself was at the door. "Has Mademoiselle yet spoken to London?"

"London?" I sat up. "Non! Did London call me?"

"Ah! London attempts to speak with Mademoiselle. Venez, you are to telephone London and you are to eat. Come with Père Imatz. Things will arrange themselves." I struggled into my trench coat and went down with him. Mademoiselle Imatz connected me with London and I sat where Père Imatz put me, in his private office, with a glass of port for breakfast.

"We've been trying to reach you since seven this morning," said the man from London. "The editor would like to speak with you, Miss. That was a fine story of the Major's. We gave it banner position. Everyone here thinks that was a fine piece of work you did, Miss. Here's the chief, Miss."

"We want to thank you for bringing in the Major's story." A new brisk voice. "Under shot and shell, eh? Excellent!"

"Look," I was sleepy no longer, "look, you may not hear from the Major for a couple of days."

"What's that? What's that?"

"He's in a very dangerous position. Caught between two armies. It'll be a wonderful story when he gets out."

"Jove! You don't say!"

"But it will be a day or so before we can manage a way through the lines, you understand? The . . . the Reds have taken the border passes."

"Jove, yes! Good man, always in the center of it. Well, well . . . you'll cover for us? Right. Only Woman Correspondent with the Patriot army, eh? Keep in touch. Need money? Spend what you need on cars. We'll wire it. What's the hotel you're calling from?"

I put the telephone receiver back and grinned. So I was a war correspondent. I worked for the *London Daily Mail*. No longer excess baggage in a car. No longer a freelancer doing mail columns. The

Daily Mail's Only Woman Correspondent With Patriot Armies at the Front!

In this manner I became an accredited war correspondent. I would acknowledge the complexion of the sheet for which I was to be working. Among all the men in the car the Major and his *Daily Mail* were the least neutral; he was a proud apologist for the Generals. I had hired myself to punch out the words that would call the rebel-Generals "Patriots," and the Loyalist people of Spain "Reds." Had I not been careful to say "Reds" to the editor? But I was too full of the privilege of sharing the mechanics of reporting a war to worry too much over what the war was about.

The winter settled over Spain. The battles moved back from the borders deep into the land. The reporters moved with the armies in the perpetual presence of grief and destruction. Fatigue and apprehension of death were constants.

I lived upon the roads of Spain, only now and then in companionship, usually the solitary courier: Burgos—now fixed headquarters of the Generals—to France; France to Burgos. I had come to accept the tension of my body, taut against terror. I lived with fear. The fear of speed; the sudden slowing of the car, the screech of the brake for a cart and mule on the wrong side of the road; the squeal of the tires as the car barely missed the two old women riding donkeys side by side. Fear of the company of the dead: the bloated corpses of horses lying by the roadside stinking; the bodies of two limp scarecrows against an outhouse wall where they have slipped to the earth; in a field, absurdly peaceful, three old ladies arranged toes to toes in a circle about the crater of a shell, as if for a little dance, their skirts blown up in levity. High against the blue-glazed sky the vultures circled.

There was the never-ending fear of the guards at the roadblocks. It was true they called me "amiga." I was by now an accustomed phenomenon. But they were Spaniards, Spaniards at war, and I was there on sufferance. Who could tell at what word, by what small unconscious action, I would become the enemy? I greeted them with "Arriba España!" and yet I knew that crying "Up Spain!" was a commitment to their cause and was already becoming anathema to me. I was not their friend, ally, comrade-at-arms; I was the enemy.

I flew in my fast car through that land where the people lived in the caves in the soft limestone cliffs, nothing growing, no herb or small green weed. The yellow stone was sufficient for wealth; the Duke of Alba owned the hills and valleys as you would own a potato patch. What need had he to irrigate this land? Limestone grew without water.

Upon the endless road, where horizon to horizon there is no purpose in walking, a man plods. There is nothing where he comes from, nothing where he goes. His face is rock carved by pride. His great, unused hands hang against his sides, like pendulum weights. In this yellow waste there is nothing for him to do with his hands.

I signal my driver to pass slowly. The peasant lifts his eyes. In that brief instant his eyes and mine meet; and I refuse what I see. "No, no, it is not I! I am not your enemy!" Guilt overwhelms me. I have begun to wonder about the price I am paying to report this war; about this license with which I move behind the lines of the army of privilege, whose adversary was the army of the people.

For all his conservative paper's politics, John Elliott will not write "Patriot." He writes "Rebel" and Aguilera, the press chief, in a fury, tells John he won't have it. The Generals *are* rebels, aren't they? insists John. "They 'rebelled,' didn't they?" I know John can't win, but I respect him. I write "Patriot" into my own stories and am ashamed. Even if I wrote "Rebels" the *Daily Mail* would change it to "Patriots."

One day at San Rafael, we watched an attack closing in: the capture of sixty men in a circle of machine-gun fire, the circle tightening around them and running them out of the woods to crowd together in a field like sheep. And when the prisoners were gathered in a herd, the gunners came out of the woods and drove them across the field into the muzzles of the rifles awaiting them. Under that hail of bullets the prisoners ran across the road, their rifles held above their heads. Some were laughing, some were crying—the tears streaming down the seams of their faces—and some were shouting "Madre de Dios! Arriba España!" One was screaming that he went regularly to Mass. Some made no sound and did not weep and would not run; their faces were stubborn and sullen.

"What became of those men you captured at San Rafael?" John asked Aguilera the next day. The press chief's eyes narrowed:

"They are glad to be captured! Y'understand?" He rapped at his boot with his short whip. "They are glad to have the food we give them and are well treated. Y'understand?"

"How about letting us see them?" This time it was Ed Taylor. "Then we can write stories saying we were eyewitnesses that the prisoners were well treated and it is not true that your prisoners are shot."

"We do not shoot prisoners!" spat Aguilera. "I will arrange a visit to the prison." But the visit was postponed and did not come off, and Aguilera was not fonder of Ed and John for asking each day when we were to visit the prison.

"There will be a trip to the front tomorrow," announces Aguilera. "Have your cars ready in front of the Hotel Norte y Londres at seven in the morning. Picked members of the press will be taken to the front under military escort."

"De Jouvenel, Cardozo . . ." He ticks off names of those who are to go. There is hesitation over John's name, but the *Herald Tribune* is an important paper, sympathetic to the right; Aguilera decides on John this one more time. There is never discussion about my name. The stuff I have been sending is fine.

In the morning the cars are lined up in the cobbled square, the chauffeurs walking up and down a little nervously or talking in groups. There is much scurrying in and out of the hotel, the porters and the chauffeurs bringing out the typewriters and paper bags stuffed with rolls and meat and fruit: a picnic at the front. The Spaniards stand and watch as the reporters come out of the hotel, seeking out their cars and chauffeurs. It is cold and damp. All the Spaniards wear scarves and sweaters, wrapped up against the icy penetrating fog. One by one the cars fill and Aguilera goes up and down the line checking again on the passes of those who are allowed to go. Now a man is here whom everybody knows but me, the new cub. This is Knickerbocker of the International News wire service, a legendary figure. The war is now big enough for him to attend it. He has a bright red roadster to match his hair; restless at the delays, he climbs in and out of his fast car, impatient with Aguilera. "Come on, come on, can't you speed it up?"

"Five hundred yards," Aguilera orders, rapping the fender of each car with his stick to emphasize the precision of his words. "You're under military discipline from here on. Y'understand? No crowding. No breaking line. Y'understand? Five hundred yards."

The parade of vehicles moves off following the lead car through

Top: The author, her back to the war, works on her copy at a café lunch at the French border with, from left, a staff photographer, Cardozo (back to camera), Ed Taylor, and John Elliott at right. *Bottom*: A journalistic foray to the front. The author, the only woman correspondent present, stands in front of the tree at left, protected by Cardozo, left, wearing beret. Antoine stands at the extreme right.

the streets out of the town, each keeping its allotted place. We enter the foothills of the Guadarramas, climb until we reach the ridge that splits the two Spains. From this height we look down onto the guns of the other Spaniards, the Loyalists. Fitfully, the sun breaks through a cloud and pours down upon the bronzed plain. There is going to be a storm. Above the mountains the clouds are black and thick. In the fields the bodies of long-dead beasts stink. The vultures, disturbed by the convoy, rise and circle, and settle again when we have passed. The cars ahead appear and disappear, winding deeper into the mountains. Knickerbocker's roadster swings around a curve and into view; he drives as if irritated at having to keep his allotted place behind the lead car. "This," pronounces Cardozo, "is a damned stupid business. A convoy to the front! We'll have the whole damned Red aviation thinking we're the whole damned G.H.Q. Damned lucky for us it's clouding over. Damned stupid. Y'understand?" We all grin a little at the Major's mimicry of Aguilera.

Three of the cars have turned about and are coming back along the other side of the road. "Clutch trouble," laughs de Jouvenel, "half these drivers get clutch trouble every time they smell the front!"

"From the Alto de Los Leones pass," John reads from his Baedecker, "Madrid is visible on a clear day."

By the time we reach the battery positions a thundershower has passed over. I sit upon the wet ground behind the guns like a camper behind a campfire. Knickerbocker and the Major stand under the hill's crest, field glasses to their eyes. Every time the guns fire they fix their glasses upon the village in the ravine, noting the position of the hit. I can stand the noise of the great guns better if I am prepared for it, and stay where I can watch the men pack the gun, slam true the shell, and step back. Then I clap my hands tight over my ears. The gun draws in its breath, slides back, lurches forward. Before each salvo I pull my head into my shoulders like a turtle.

To stand erect is to draw fire. I bend my knees and crouch down to make myself small. It makes me feel better to see the men do this too. The men laugh at me. "Listen," they say, "you, down there, if we were your height we wouldn't have to duck. You're only half our size anyhow!"

A soldier looks at the sky; "Aviones," he remarks conversationally.

"He means," John predicts, "that now the storm is past the planes will probably come over to search out this battery. We're doing some damage." John waves a freckled hand down at the village. On the slope below the crest a cow grazes. I watch, grateful for its bucolic presence; the cow disappears in a spout of smoke.

The Major comes back up the crest to the gunnery captain. "Getting our range, eh?" he says in English, and as it always is with the Major, the gunnery captain nods, understanding him.

After that, there are puffs of smoke to watch on two fronts: the fire from our battery hitting in the valley; and on our hillside the hits from the guns of the enemy.

Knick comes up the slope. "We'd better be getting out of this," he says, and goes off. I pray that the others will think so too. Heads bunched in and knees bent, we trot in single file down the path that recrosses the road to the cars. The bullets make a little whistling sound, splitting the air above us. Now and again a twig snaps off. When we reach the road we break cover and run for it.

A half-burned, half-demolished house, with no wall to its upper story and Christ in Gethsemane hanging crooked over the unmade brass bed, is used as headquarters. The commanding officer stands on the steps of the house, one foot resting on an upper step to make of his bended knee a table for a map. His face is pitted as though by smallpox; in some other war he'd gotten a faceful of shrapnel. One hand holds a heel of bread, from which he takes great bites; with the other he is pointing out the positions on the map to the Major and Knickerbocker. There is an instant when they lift their heads. They listen. The scene dissolves. Everybody runs. Planes!

The soldiers run, the officers run, the newspapermen run. Aguilera's voice rises in English, "Break it up there! You're making targets. Get under cover! Break it up, y'understand?" A furious popping of rifles. Behind the rocks and the tree stumps, the soldiers crouch, taking pot-shots at the planes. Bullets ping in every direction.

A flat-topped rock. I am possessed to get on the other side of it. I clamber up and skid down. And then I am on my feet again, running, spurning the earth . . . to get away from there! If I had touched that thing, it would have burst! Under the rock lies what had been a man, burnt, crisped, fried; his arms stuck up to embrace my descent, the skin across his chest tanned tight as leather, his teeth grinning ear to ear. If I had grazed that leather flesh, it would have crumbled and the gas of the putrid insides would have risen and engulfed me.

I find myself with Ed. We run together. Between the onslaughts of each wave of planes, everybody scrambles up and runs for the cars; scattering, flinging themselves flat when the planes are overhead; getting up, scrambling, running, when the planes have passed. Each time nearer the cars. We lie in a shell hole, flat on our backs. I have a fan of pine branch with which to cover my face. From what I cannot see, I am hidden. Again I am wedged into the *v* of a rock. Ed has thrust me into the *v*. It is a great slab of rock, and if a bomb should land not even on it, but nearby, the rock will tip and tilt and flatten us. There is not quite room in the *v* to shelter both of us. His arm is out. I struggle to get tighter into the *v* so that he can get his arm in. The soldiers are sniping at the planes above. The spent bullets ping against the rock. Here it comes! Here it comes! I squeeze my eyes tight closed, and stay my breath. The planes are gone again.

Each group reaches its car, scrambles in, slams the doors; the driver yanks the car out of its place and shoots off down the road. I can see Knickerbocker's roadster heading down the straightaway. Tires squeal as we hit the curve. John observes, "There they are again, over to the left!" The Major swivels his head to the left. We all look to the left and search the sky. Except the driver, who never takes his eyes off the road. "Brake!" shouts the Major. I hear the planes scream, diving.

"We can't make it, Major! We can't make it!" Ed is on the edge of his seat, his hand on the door handle. Now we shout in chorus, "Brake! Brake!" The car, pinned in flight by the brakes, swerves in a semicircle. Ed has the door open and is out, running with the still-skidding car, using the half-open door to keep his balance.

There is a stone wall. There is a field. I press my face to the earth. "Open earth, open and hide me!" And then cry nothing, and think nothing, and feel nothing, suspended in the scream of the diving planes.

The road is pock-marked where the machine-gun bullets spattered. Two bombs fall close, tearing great wounds. But the car is untouched. The driver, his hand shaking, smoothes the fenders. We get back in.

"That should be all for the day." The Major is settling himself, putting his beret back on. "We should be through with that for the day, y'know. Sun's setting." I put my hand to my head. I am whole, but I have lost my lucky hat.

chapter eleven

The Face of the Enemy

Burgos: Perhaps, say I to myself in the icy morning, I should stay in bed. As sure as I go to bed something will happen . . .

It is increasingly hard for me to turn myself out of bed for the day. Sometimes the job of getting dressed makes me weep, clumsily struggling with clothes and hating the dark, damp-smelling room. I must be sick, I think. Spanish Flu. That would make me ache like this. I have a shell sliver wound under my knee. The wound will not heal and I can not often find clean bandages. The crusty bandage and the pain of the wound make me limp. And, somehow, I have lost all voice but a croak.

The city at night is blacked-out for fear of marauding planes. A small group of newsmen, I among them, comes for a late drink with the press officer. We cross the cobbled square to the *Comandancia* in the Hotel Norte y Londres, our heels ringing on the uneven cobbles.

On a wooden bench outside the hotel the guards sit, their backs against the wall. In the pitch dark, no crack of light escapes at window-frame or door. Occasionally a face is briefly illuminated by the glow of a cigarette; sometimes the sharp edge of a bayonet glints, leaning in a comradely fashion against a shoulder. One of the guards is singing a flamenco. The darkness in the square quivers to the vibrations of the notes pulsing from his throat. There is occasional stamping and the cry "Olé!"

From the darkness we reporters emerge into the light of the lobby, into a confusion of sound, a crush of people. Young men stand about pushing and laughing. They wear blue denim overalls zipped up the front and belted at the middle, decorations sewn to the denim. They carry revolvers in their shoulder holsters and poignards stuck in their belts. And they wear elegant pointed beards in homage to Spain's Philip II, the symbol of their allegiances. These are the pilots in from the airfields, the rich young men of Spain, heirs of tradition, sworn not to shave until Spain is cleansed again and pure, as in the age of Philip.

There are preoccupied groups of civilians, wearing berets and sweaters, suits baggy at the knees and elbows from overmuch traveling, surrounded by redundant luggage: dukes, marquises, who have come by train, by plane, by fast car, from banking houses in London and Paris and Berlin, from villas in Biarritz and Juan-les-Pins and Nice and Cannes—home to Spain. These are the men behind the Generals who run the war. They are waiting now for the soldiers to clean up their country so that they can reestablish possession. Occasionally there is a monk amid them, brown-robed, with bare feet in sandals; he is treated with ceremony.

There are the Generals. Near us, with rows of medals pinned across his tunic, stands he of the one eye, one arm, one leg, who commands the Moors. Why should the Moors die for a General of Spain? He despises them with cold, pitiless distaste because they are Moors. He is a cruel man, and a brave man, whittled down to essentials. For the women in the lobby he exudes the fascination of a hypnotic python.

And there are the soldiers—in torn uniforms, with stains of blood on their tunics—who have just come in from the front; suddenly propelled into the bright lobby, they blink in the unaccustomed light. These fighting men are immediately swallowed up by those who belong to them; fathers throw their arms about sons and they kiss each other and tears run down their cheeks. Others, wounded—an arm or a leg or a head wrapped in clean bandages—sit in the chairs about the wall, their faces drawn with the patient endurance of pain, and with their weariness.

The women who are the spectators of the war sit here: women in black with coal black hair, who never weep. Some wear widows' veils, eyes vigilant behind the thin film of black. They knit and watch and listen to the never-silent radio, to the news of victory and the news of defeat and to the casualty lists. They listen to the news of air raids on Madrid, on Seville, on Barcelona, the cities where they have homes, where many still have families, mothers, sisters, children.

Everybody in the hotel lobby is waiting. Everybody stares at the door and at those who come in and out. The reporters alone are intruders, strangers at the deathbed, the uninvited at the funeral, welcome only for any news they may carry.

We, the reporters, go through the lobby to the empty dining room where we are to rendezvous with the press chief. We dispose ourselves about a small table: Ed Taylor with his chair drawn up close and his elbows on the cloth, Knickerbocker with his chair tilted on its back legs, holding it from going over backwards by his heels upon the floor.

The center of attention is the same Aguilera, the press chief who had directed our convoy to Alto de Los Leones. He is of an old Spanish family of landowners. His face is thin, colorless; his hair is straw; his light eyes, too, seem to have no color. He wears a white silk scarf in the neck of his tunic, for he is a sensuous man and likes to feel the cool silk; and it is also a badge of his arrogance. He wears boots of very fine, soft leather and carries a little whip. He himself is above all law, discipline and regulation. Educated in England, he is very proud of his clipped Oxford speech, of the facility with which he uses the language. "I've got the gift of gab," he says. "Right? Eh?" He picks up his glass and tosses the wine down his throat and the light catches in the single, clear diamond of the ring he wears. He raps his whip against his boot for our attention, and makes a little speech.

"You know what's wrong with Spain? Modern plumbing. In healthier times—I mean spiritually healthier, y'understand— plague, pestilence could be counted on to thin down the Spanish masses; hold them down to manageable proportions. Now, with modern sewage systems, they multiply too fast.

"The masses are no better than animals, y'understand? You can't expect them not to become infected with the virus of 'liberty' and 'independence.' After all, rats and lice carry the plague. Y'understand what I mean by the regeneration of Spain? It is our program to exterminate one-third of the male population. That will purge the country. Sound economically, too. No more unemployment in Spain.

"Age of Reason! Rights of Man! The masses aren't fit to reason! Rights! Does a pig have rights?

"We've got to kill, kill . . . y'understand?"

I sit tightly on my chair. Except for my ears I am numb. My eyes are fixed upon the tablecloth. I am terrified to look up at the press chief for fear he might see through the orifices of my eyes into my head. If he could see into me he would shoot me too. "Masses," the word repeats itself inside my head. "Are not the masses people? 'If you prick us, do not we bleed?' Philip who fought for a living wage for all who labor; Polly who fought for clean toilets, clean milk for the children. Philip who organized unions, Polly who was jailed as a striker. All the people who came to the Farm and to the Hill, who lived and worked for the masses? Dear God, what am I doing here!" I get the shivers and stumble out of the hotel across the square; I cannot make my body cease trembling with fatigue and fear.

I am often with the press chief, eat with him, ride with him, stand beside him at battles. But I know him for my enemy, and I am his. Everything that has made me is death to him; everything that has made him is death to me. "Perhaps it's because I feel so rotted with sickness," I tell myself.

Cold winter months later, the Rue de la Paix, Paris: having escaped once again from Spain and the mountains, I am on my way to see Edgar Mowrer. That newly arrived would-be foreign correspondent of two years ago, out to conquer the world, is not recognizable in this morose girl, her body moving stiffly with fatigue, and something else, some illness in her flesh. That other one had been barely able to contain herself for sheer delight. They have nothing in common: not even the patent leather hat.

I have made my decision of what is tolerable and what is not. I can survive as a reporter in the country of my enemy as long as I have a valuable role as a gatherer of information behind the lines. In Italy, Germany, reporters have played out that role until their presence no longer has been permitted. I, too, am on the wrong side by the mischance of that descent of smugglers' tracks into Franco territory. I am in the position of all reporters in countries under a dictatorship, where the government and the army have imposed strict censorship. Under these conditions, either you write each story as the censors want, in effect to spread their propaganda, or you become *persona non grata* and are escorted to the frontier—not to come back without being jailed or shot. Not only were the dispatches which we sent out checked by the Spanish censors and unfavorable portions deleted, but the censors even kept track of the stories as published in the major newspapers, in order to see whether or not the printed versions still corresponded to the censor's version of what was going on. For a reporter like me, to whom the principles and actions of the Franco government were anathema, it was a question of staying on to see for myself what was going on, to store it up, and eventually to be able to tell all I knew about the actual events and true conditions and then never be able to go back again.

As a reporter in these circumstances, you develop, consciously or unconsciously, a set of rules of conduct. Whatever you see, whatever you hear, whatever you learn, and however much you detest it—what you write must be tempered and balanced against the value of your continued presence. You wait until your time is up, until you can come out and be free; or until you have been put out. And sometimes you haven't even that luck and you disappear and apologies are tendered; or you are jailed without apology. When, and if, you get out, that is the time for you to spew up the terror of having eaten, drunk, functioned, in the presence of inhumanity.

What I can sustain no longer is to be cast as an advocate. I will ask Mowrer to send me back for the *Chicago Daily News*, a great liberal paper, with the *Daily Mail* as cover. He himself is *persona* very much *non grata* with the Franco side. He and Richard Mowrer, his nephew, can report from Madrid, but no Mowrer can get in or out of Burgos. He has been in Spain on the other side. We have checked up together, he and I, and have found that on this day and on that, we have been opposite one another, his guns firing upon my guns. I want to go back for him, as long as I have credit with Aguilera and his kind, to spend it where it will serve the purpose I believe in.

We are in Mowrer's office; he looks at me and explodes. "My god! Can't you talk? How are you going to get along with that squawk? What are you doing about it? Are you sick? Should you be in bed? Why do you walk stiff-legged? What's that bandage on your leg? Have you got a doctor? Are you taking care of it?"

"I'm OK. Just a cold." He dislikes straining to hear faint voices.

"You don't look it. But you ought to know. What do you want to do?"

"Work."

"Look here. It's slow in Spain, yes? And likely to be for a month or more, yes? You look as though you could use some sun. Yes?"

"Yes."

"Go shut that door." I shut it.

"Nobody knows just what the Italians are doing in the Balearics. Nobody knows what the Germans are up to in Spanish Morocco. Nobody knows the extent of Portuguese cooperation in this business. Nobody knows just how this blockade of Franco's works or where its strength lies. Balearics . . . Spanish Morocco . . . Lisbon . . . Ferrol . . . Complete picture of Spain from the sea. Don't try to send anything. Just go and look and come back when you can. Maybe there's a story in it." He glances up at me to see how I like it. It's quite a plum of an assignment.

It will be one of the best stories of the war and next to impossible to accomplish, without being caught. "Wonderful," I squawk. Something more than a cold must be wrong with my throat.

"When?" And then I remind myself, "But look, I don't want your name on any of my credentials."

"I suppose you don't," Mowrer agrees with seriousness, and calls his secretary. "You'd better sign these credentials. Dress it up!" Mowrer orders his secretary. "Put seals on it and get in a flourish in the signature. Make it look like a peace treaty." At this, I smile but even as my smile fades, I am thinking about the dusty press offices in the *Comandancia*, wondering if there really is a blacklist of papers. Will I find that the access that was open to "La señorita del Daily Mail de Londres" is closed to "La señorita del Chicago Daily News"? There is a file, somewhere, of Mowrer's stories.

Mowrer is saying to his secretary, "Take a memorandum to sign all wires sent to her in Mallorca yourself. Be careful to keep my name off any wires sent into the country. And advise Chicago not to change the wording in the stories they get. Tell them that's dangerous."

"That's right. Anyone whose stories in print don't duplicate the copy in the censor's files goes out—like that—pffut! y'understand?" I grin to myself without laughter, mimicking Aguilera.

"You might try to get a rowboat and row over to Minorca," Mowrer says as an afterthought to me. Minorca is still a Loyalist holdout.

"My passport is covered with Dancharinea stamps!" I protest in a croak. Dancharinea is now one of the main entrances to Franco's Spain.

"You won't show your own passport in Minorca. We'll get you Loyalist papers for Minorca." Even if the papers were good, what if I were to be searched, thoroughly, by either side? "Put 'em in your shoe." I didn't like it. Papers openly carried can sometimes be explained. Papers hidden and found . . . But you don't make involved fusses with Mowrer. You go or you don't go.

The S.S. *Lepine* was a small boat, its saloon close, dank, and uninhabited. I tried a chair, found no comfort, poked among the magazines on the reading table: a *London Sketch*, a *La Vie Parisienne*, both ancient, tattered, forlorn. I looked out of a streaked window: the last of the string of lights on the Marseilles shore twinkled and disappeared.

Wind's blowing up, I thought, grimly. Already the S.S. *Lepine* bucketed about in nervous anticipation. We'll get it. Just as soon as we're out from behind the land's arm—we'll get it. In the blackness the mistral lay in wait for its prey.

A sailor was piling the chairs upon the tables. There would be no friendliness in the little saloon that night. Weren't there any passengers on this damned boat but me?

Few enough passengers these days, and they had shut themselves in their cabins. "Tonight the crossing will be bad," the sailor prophesied. "But Mademoiselle will find the sun again at Algiers."

Mademoiselle was not going to Algiers. "Tiens!" exclaimed the sailor, a chair arrested in midair. "Where was Mademoiselle going if not to Algiers?" Mademoiselle will get off the boat at Palma de Mallorca.

"Sacré!" expostulated the sailor and he set the chair down again upon the floor. "Mademoiselle is Spanish? Mademoiselle lives, most unfortunately, in Palma de Mallorca? Why does not Mademoiselle refuge herself? Quelle horreur, votre guerre! Comme elle est sauvage!"

"Pas Espagnole," corrected Mademoiselle. "Américaine."

"Américaine? Américaine!" The sailor stared, shrugged, and dismissed Americans. That explained everything. It is well known that Americans are mad. He picked up the chair and set it with precision in its place.

The next day was leaden, the sea turgid, the sky forbidding. The island rose out of the sea, a mountain top stranded by receding floods, its crags washed clean of living things. My sailor friend banged out of the saloon door. He grabbed my arm and rushed me to the offshore rail. Grey as the seas, its knife prow slicing a foam-edged wound, slid a destroyer. Italian, by the green and white flag fluttering above her propeller, intent upon business. We bobbed about in her wake, the S.S. *Lepine* a flat and wallowing nobody. At that instant the sun cast off its shroud. In a golden semicircle the terra-cotta town of Palma de Mallorca rose from the bay.

The island of Mallorca was a microcosm of the Europe so soon-to-be: a world cut off from communications, shut in by censorship; base for bombers; secret hideaway of fleet raiders; training ground for conscripts; concentration camp for prisoners; storehouse of slave labor; torture chamber for those who carried secrets in their minds. All the mechanism of terror was there, in the sun. The people who lived in those green hills rising out of the sun-lit sea went through their days as though there were still continuity in small tasks. Yet each man lived in isolation, in fear of those he loved the most, and of his neighbor, and in fear of himself—of what his mind might contain that could betray him. He slept, woke, ate, talked, in the sun; and was never free of the weight of fear. The clear air and the blue sea, the warm sun and the golden town were treachery.

The island was a prison. The little boats in the bay were metal-clad, guarding each cove and inlet. There was no escape.

In the warmth of the sun on my balcony, I looked up to the ancient Bellver Castle and knew that those walls enclosed a tomb: the galleries divided off into cells, each a little space for rats, for damp, for mold, for dark—and for a living man. The surrounding woods were deep with light and shadow. I knew that rusted strands of wire interlaced the greenery. There stood the guards with bayonets. Passage along the street to the castle was forbidden under penalty of death.

At night I woke in the blackness of my cold room to hear the ssrush, ssrush, of rope-soled feet marching from the inland hills, past the window, to the sea. "Under penalty of fine all shutters closed at night. Precaution against raiding planes."

But I dragged my protesting body from the warm bed and crossed the floor, icy to bare feet. My shutters creaked as I pushed them back a little to peek out and down upon the sea. When my eyes were intimate with the dark, I could see, out there in the harbor, another Italian destroyer, a black shape against a lightening sky, taking on a shipload of newly trained men bound for Spain. In the morning the destroyer will be gone, will never have been.

A young officer of the Spanish navy, a lieutenant commander, his gold braid shining, pointed to the mound of books flung on the cold stone floor, backs broken, boards bent, pages crumpled and torn, lying as they had fallen. Some were books I had known at the Farm. The young lieutenant commander took pride in their shame. From the top of the heap he picked a book at random, an expression of distaste on his face. He smacked the covers together to clear the book of dust. *J'Accuse*. "Trash!" He flung the book back on the heap by one cover and dusted off his hands. "Liberalism! We will cleanse the world of the contamination of all this 'liberalism.' " He moved an index finger close to my face. "This war, do you know what it is? It is the American Revolution and the French Revolution that we finish off! We have inherited that struggle. It is our destiny. You think you have won, you Americans. You think it is over, done with, old history, those Revolutions of yours? Pah!" He gave another dusting to his hands and dropped the subject. He and I walked off together down the stone corridor.

Another morning an air force officer, with pride and a fine un-concern, showed me the underground hangers, Italian built, this mole for Franco's ships, and that for the Italian Navy's. In all those warm, bright days I became gravid with dangerous information. I wondered why I was allowed to know so much. Under Mallorca's Mediterranean sun I was cold.

Thirty and one mornings later, I woke and threw back the shutters. The sun was gone, the island was shrouded in fog. Below me in the harbor there was the S.S. *Lepine* tugging at her lines. Who knew when she would come again? For thirty and one days we had been officially polite to one another, the Island and I, watching each other. Today was the thirty-first and the Island was done with enchanting me. I dressed in a scramble, stuffing oddments into my bag. I must leave, now, this morning, or the evil in this place will stretch out its claw and destroy me.

My bags were packed; the taxi waited at the door. I held my small black notebook above the fire that burned in the stove. And then pulled my hand back and riffled its pages. I'll try it. It's such good stuff, what if I forgot? " . . . crews of captured ships do road work in hills . . . German officer, who learned in the 1914 war how to run prison camps, organizes discipline . . . at the battle of Málaga, two Italian ships are disguised to look like the two 20,000-ton cruis-ers, the *Baleares* and the *Canarias* (the most modern ships in Franco's navy—which had been in the last days of construction at the begin-ning of the Civil War) in order to lure the Republican fleet away from the besieged town . . . the *Baleares* later sunk by torpedoes from Republican destroyers off Cartagena . . . new harbor forti-fications, Italian built . . . airfield with underground hangars . . . thus and thus is the total of new bought planes . . . liberal Mayor walked into market place, demanded—pointing to newly hung pig—a leg of General Franco . . . public execution . . ."

I wore a man's coat, tailored for me by a man's tailor with such practical places for wallets and notebooks as a secret pocket slit in the lining. As I dressed I thought of stuffing the small book in the girdle next to my skin. But the girdle trick is well known . . . I should have memorized these notes and burnt them . . . I stuffed the small book into the pocket hidden in the lining of my coat.

The taxi bore bag, typewriter, and me down the sea road to the harbor. Along that way there were places where the houses fell back and, briefly, I looked out upon the ships riding in the bay. It made me ill with impatience to see the *Lepine* and not be able to go straight to her. Each time there was an alley between the houses I strained to catch another glimpse. The ship looked nervy, tugging in the spank of the wind against her anchor chains, and I was frantic for fear that she would back, turn, and steam off without me. Now that this thing was almost finished, how could I stand it until it was over?

"Can't you drive faster?" As I squirmed in the taxi, the notebook nudged my ribs. What else could I have done with it? They'll search my bags . . . they'll probably search me.

In the dock shed the customs men went through my bags with a thoroughness that froze me. The thing was to look entirely unconcerned. I was not doing that very well. The customs guard nodded; I was to pack my bag again. I beckoned to a dock hand to take it down from the counter. The docker carried my bag and typewriter onto the open jetty. He handed them down one by one to the man in the small boat bobbing below. The police officials stamped my passport. Passed. I went out onto the open pier.

"The señorita is ready?" "Yes, the señorita is ready." A hand was thrust up to help me down into the *Lepine*'s tender. But the shed door opened, slammed, and a guardia ran across the pier. "That one," he said, pointing at me.

It had come.

The policewoman and I were shut together in the windowless room . . . I've got to stop this trembling. Perhaps she thinks it's the cold. Her hand would make anyone shiver. The hand patted my body, standing in underclothes. There was still the bandage under my knee from the wound, which had suppurated. It was removed. I wrapped the wound again. The rough fingers did a professional job, moving rapidly over my girdle. If I had tried that simple-minded trick! "Dress!"

I stepped back into my shoes . . . What a job I am making of hooking this skirt . . . Does that harridan see my hands shaking? But the policewoman was going through my purse. She was not concerned whether I trembled or not. The policewoman bent to pick up the coat. As if politely, I held it open for her, my left hand clutching the slit in the lining. There were four pockets on the outside. The policewoman went through the four pockets, nothing: she looked at me with cold black eyes. I was free to go.

When the policewoman turned her back, I struggled into the coat. Not until I was securely in it did I loosen my grip upon the pocket in the lining. Then I buttoned the coat tightly around me, walked out of the dock shed again, and was helped down to the boat. The immigration inspector got in, nodded to the boat man, and the tender headed across the swell for the *Lepine*.

The immigration inspector spoke a little English. Sitting next to me on the wet seat, he turned, smiled the warm smile of the Spaniard.

He said, "Your papers are very good. We think perhaps your papers are too much good. It is always the Reds who have papers as good as that!"

chapter twelve

The Worst of Two Worlds

Paris in the spring of 1939 was a city desperately disbelieving the inevitable. It was beyond comprehension that the slaughter of the 1914 World War could be required twice in the same lifetime. "What a contradiction in terms," Simone de Beauvoir cried, "to condemn a million Frenchmen to death for the sake of humanity!" But Sartre shook his head, "It is not a matter of moral abstraction. We are ourselves in peril."

The French, anguished, continued to demand, "Was not *anything* preferable to war!" "No, not anything," denied Sartre. What is not faced, he insisted implacably, is that there is no choice. Those who do not fight against Hitler will be made to fight for him.

For a few months more, until Hitler ended all argument, France lived an unreal life consumed with the delusion that it could cling to peace. At each crisis in the years preceding the inevitable, the French had rejected involvement. "What have we to do with the Ethiopians?" "The Spaniards?" "Must we die for the Czechs?" Now it was: "Must we die for Danzig?" (The question of whether any people were to die for the Jews was not raised.) Hitler himself had denied the cowering nations the possibility of hope: "Each country will imagine that it alone will escape. I shall not even need to destroy them one by one. Selfishness and lack of foresight will prevent each one fighting until it is too late." Yet nothing could shake the passion to will away the war. The French dreamed of the German Army flinging itself to destruction against the impregnable Maginot Line.

"The Palace of Nations has become a mausoleum haunted by the ghosts of braver men," Edgar Mowrer cabled the *Chicago Daily News.*

Madrid had fallen to Franco. The Spanish story was finished. The momentum of the past three years, which had kept me in motion, slowed, finally stopped. Looking at me, unsound under Mallorquin tan, Mowrer said, "There's the real war coming. Get home first and get well." But for me it was already too late.

As you are turning these pages, you are breathing. No thought for the miracle of your lungs as they pump the good air in and out, in and out. You sleep, move, talk, and the thought of breathing does not impinge on your consciousness. What if you couldn't get your breath? What if your lungs ached to fill and could not? What if you pulled with all your blood and could not get a lungful of air? Some are able to suffer great pain and retain integrity. No one, whatever his courage, but is reduced to a frantic organism in the fight for air. There is one fixed intolerable in human life: to realize that you cannot breathe, that at any moment you will not get the next breath.

In my bed in the Hotel Atala in Paris, I lie between sleeping and waking. The door is opened. That will be Gaston, the fourteen-year-old "buttons" with the coffee and the paper. I unfix one eye, nod at Gaston, renounce sleep and pull myself up into a position enabling the small waiter to deposit tray and paper on my anatomy. Then I manage the other eye and focus on the headlines. Abruptly I come full awake. How heavy the air is! How hard it is to breathe! What weight on my chest! Coffee will help. I use both hands to raise my cup.

I cough and choke. In an instant the world changes. I cannot breathe.

These are the things I remember, registered in my mind by volition of their own: the tray clattering to the floor; the burn of hot coffee spilling down one leg; Gaston's voice shrill: "Mademoiselle, Mademoiselle, qu'est-ce qu'il arrive? Mademoiselle!" In the open door a chambermaid, broom in hand; a waiter with a napkin on his arm. "Qu'est-ce-que c-est?"

A portion of my mind remains aware of spectators, instructs me to clutch a sheet as I spring from bed. Modesty is a habitude in a world from which I have severed contact.

I carry out of that time the distinct picture of the concrete courtyard below the room, its grey walls and a bare tree. I have no recollection of reaching the window. Only of determination to shatter the frozen, fixed, immobility of my lungs by shattering the shell of my body. Gaston, the chambermaid, and the waiter bar the window.

I throw myself back across the bed aching for a sliver of air, aching for lungs to fill. Tears run out of my eyes, my head wags in automatic No, No, of disbelief. I spend precious air on whispered repetition: "I can't breathe, I can't breathe."

A seedy-looking doctor found by the hotel had been waiting upon me during this long weekend I had spent in bed, swabbing my throat; cleansing the wound under my knee with alcohol. Now he reappears, sits beside me, overcoat on, hat on, the emptied hypodermic in his hand, saying, "Rien, ma petite, c'est l'asthme."

By night it is obvious that the hotel can tolerate me no longer. Each time I breathe, the entire population of the corridor breathes with me; the man next door has to be assured that it is not diphtheria. I think of him, sitting on the other side of the wall, his own day destroyed; he must either leave his room or breathe with me— in . . . , out . . . , slowly, in . . . and . . . out.

At the American hospital in Neuilly I was put to bed in the ward, a great, bright room. The patients in their beds were lying quietly. But I made a great deal of noise breathing. I, intruder, tried to smile apology for the disturbance. I was still wrapped in my own dressing robe; a pair of gloves, slippers, a woolen scarf and my pocketbook piled beside me, incongruous upon the sterile bed; we have lost meaning and are now ridiculous, my possessions and I.

A nurse began professionally to undress me. "Have you ever had asthma before?" "No," I shook my head, stubbornly insistent that this was not asthma. The nurse pulled off one stocking, uncovered the bandage protecting the infected wound. She undid the bandage, looked at the wound. "Is there anything else?" she finally asked, straightening up and looking sharply at me. I shook my head.

She pulled the sheet over me and went off. When she came back it was with another nurse. Together they tugged at my bed, sliding it out of its place in the row. Bed and all, I was removed from the ward and put off by myself in a tiny room.

"If it's diphtheria the first twenty-four hours are important," the senior intern pronounced. "We can't be sure until we see the culture tomorrow. But if it's OK with you we'll give you the injections anyhow. On the chance."

At intervals during the long night a junior intern searched my arm for a vein, and finding it, jabbed in his needle. Between times he slept in a chair beside the bed, his white coat became more and more rumpled, his head tousled. I sat and breathed and waited. In the early hours of the morning the veins were harder to find, the needle less true, the junior intern's eyes bleary and bloodshot.

169

Sunlight slid through the venetian blinds and moved in horizontal stripes across the floor and bed. Everyone who entered the room wore a mask over chin and mouth, but by the middle of the morning the masks were given up. It was not diphtheria. My arms, from shoulder to waist, were purple with antitoxin marks.

Six doctors filled the room. They removed the clean bandages from my leg, looked at that, talked, and rebandaged the leg. They spoke in French. In my weariness I could not follow them. One sat on the edge of my bed, questioned me about Spain without expecting an answer and looked down my throat.

Because I neither ate nor slept there was no division between day and night, except that the daylight ebbed and flooded in again like an ocean tide: late afternoon, a minutely measured retreat across the bed, across the floor and from the room entirely; early morning, a barely perceptible advance from window sill across the bed.

I longed to lie down, to lie flat, to stretch full length. Now with each breath I drew, there was the pain in my ribs, in my chest. Now and again I held my breath to find an instant's rest.

The middle of the night: I wake from a doze, suffocating. It has come again. I cannot breathe.

By the side of the bed stands a bowl of ice. I plunge my hands into it. I grasp the bowl to empty the ice over my head. The shock of cold will break me loose. I struggle to get up. I must get out of there. Something must be done, some action to break this vacuum, my chest must move again, my nostrils must draw air; I am locked, clamped, in a vise.

The senior intern holds me down, shoulders pinned against the pillows. "Quiet. Don't fight. Be quiet. Don't struggle against me. Breathe. You can breathe. Breathe with me. Be quiet and breathe with me. In—out—in—out—." I feel his concern. The senior intern and the nurse are beside me on the bed; very still, we three practice breathing together.

Abruptly, I am shaken with convulsions, gag desperately, struggle upright. The door opens. I catch an impression of instruments on a table by the door, shining in the light.

Someone is tying something at the base of my neck. I am breathing. I take a deep, luxurious purchase on the air, spew blood but regardless smile, and slide into sleep.

Morning: The doctors came in. They stood grouped in sunlight at the foot of the bed. At the sight of me smiling, they smiled too. "How are you? No! No talking. Write. You mustn't talk. In fact, you can't talk. Write everything. She must have paper. Get her a pencil. A lot of paper and pencils."

"In here? She wants something in the drawer. Notebooks. This is what she wants. Good. Give her the notebook."

I wrote as though it were a miracle, that statement—"I'm breathing!" At that they laugh.

In my neck, bypassing my throat, a tube has been fixed, in that soft-fleshed place where the pulse beats between the body bones. I imagined that it looks like a brooch, a pin, a clumsy ornament lying against the bandage. I could feel the tube move when my breathing moved it, pulse with the beat of my pulse.

"Just stopped breathing on us. Abscess, general septicemia. Blood poisoning. You nearly lost that leg as well. Anyhow, the leg wouldn't have mattered to you. You were gone like a light turned off. Like that!" The senior intern illustrated his account by snapping his fingers. "We were sure you were finished. I thought you were finished! The way Dr. de Vaux worked! He had the table in here and the tube in, and *then* you didn't breathe. And just when we think it's no use, that you're flat dead, you breathe!"

Was that being dead? There was nothing to that! One moment you're there, and then you aren't. It was being alive that was hell. I felt an absurd relief in the discovery of how simple it was to be dead.

From the notebook: "Could someone phone my boss for me? Edgar Mowrer. *Chicago Daily News.* He doesn't know where I am!"

The senior intern and I had become good friends. "So he doesn't even know where you are, eh?" The intern, conversationally inclined, leaned on the rail at the bed's foot. "Only spent that whole night walking the corridors, looking as though he was going to cry. Funny guy—your boss. Know what he kept saying? He'd say, 'Best girl reporter I've had my hands on! And she goes and dies on me!' You don't believe me? Ask the nurses."

A dozen long-stemmed roses are brought in by the nurse. FROM ONE NEWSPAPER WOMAN TO ANOTHER WHO ENORMOUSLY ADMIRES YOUR COURAGE AND GALLANTRY. DOROTHY THOMPSON. What in hell am I crying about? I have a job to do. I have a story to write.

I mustered up what strength I could. I took out the notebook of figures on Italian ships and German planes and wrote up the results of my findings in Mallorca. Soon the story was out and on the wires. By this act I had made it impossible for me ever to go back into Franco's Spain. But now the news was out, in facts and figures, about the actual extent of Italy's naval participation in Franco's war and also of Nazi Germany's air support. Here was proof for all to see of the Italian and German collaboration on the sea and in the air. My mission was accomplished.

I must get well quickly, I told myself. I wasn't going to miss this war. I experimented with the new apparatus, that intrusive little whistle, putting my finger over it, and discovered that I could make a nearly intelligible word. "Come on!" I wrote in my notebook to my convention of doctors. "Now that I can breathe, fix up the rest of me. I have to get out of here. There'll be a war on while I lie around here." The doctors looked as though I had lapsed into insanity.

"Have you seen that leg of yours?" asked the orthopedic surgeon, looking very cross. "You deserve to know. It's time you faced reality. I think we should take that leg off. You're hung up with a Dakin's drip. Well, it did some good in the 1914 war, but my bet is you'll have gangrene unless we get at it. I've seen these in the French field hospitals, more of them than these young squirts." He shrugged in the direction of the young doctors. "But they want to give you time. Anyhow, if they don't get that abcess in your throat lanced, you might as well die with two legs as one. You've got septicemia. Your body is a banquet for bacteria." He stalked out.

I don't think my face showed any expression. I flatly disbelieved I would ever have only one leg.

"That guy!" said a young American intern of Dr. de Vaux, the throat man. "You wait and see. All that pus will slough off your leg, and then we'll clean up your throat. You'll be as good as new." The old banality.

"A convocation of medical pals of yours in New York tied up the trans-Atlantic wires, trying to get the big shakes around here to at least give a whirl to that stuff they're beginning to use, the sulphonamides—sulfa drugs. But the chiefs here thought that to remove one leg was a neater solution. Well, it might have helped, but we'll show 'em. Wait until tomorrow when we clean out all that muck in your throat."

I waited. What else was possible? A "whistle." Crutches. I seem to be threatened with more mechanisms than I could handle. It was a long night.

And the next day's process was not much better, though the leg seemed to be saving itself. The orthopedist thought it might be clearing and took down the Dakin's drip and bandage, though somewhat grudgingly. Now all the attention was on a complex of mirrors in the effort to reflect up what was going on in my throat. It was decided that they could not depend upon the mirrors to give my throat a clean bill of health. I was to be sent to the Salpetrière. The young doctors told me that it was Charcot's old hospital and that the young Freud had once worked there. It turned out to be a huge early nineteenth-century hospital which—either as a result of my fright or an expertise in recording—I still see as a combination of railroad station and cathedral, with wet mops puddling the floor and with patients lined up like victims in confessional booths of a sort along the walls.

There I was cocainized; "You will feel nothing." Accompanied by four pleasant young men, I climbed the curly iron stair to a huge operating room with what seemed to be at least fifty tables. We met Dr. de Vaux, and the young men tossed me up on a plain metal table, such as veterinarians use for dogs. Today, a bronchoscopy is no longer the end of the world, thanks to voyages to the moon, miniaturization, and tubes (as thin and flexible as parachute cords) using fiber optics. But then the tubes were like plumber's tools. And the purpose of the four young charmers was to hold me down, each to a limb. I am still haunted by that session.

But I was pronounced capable of being returned to my own charge. Dr. de Vaux slid the tracheotomy tube out before a cheering audience and stitched up the wound. The boys thought it would be lovely to have a red bow at the top. Now I could once again breathe normally through my throat.

When I arrived at Edgar's for a new session of work, he turned me out, as not yet equipped for war. I was to go home for six months and a job would be awaiting me when I returned. My guess is that he was going to keep me behind the lines. He hadn't liked that whole episode.

Before leaving Paris, I stopped off at the INS office. I still had some things that belonged to Knick. It would be safer if I left them there for him.

The International News Service was moving. It had just been relocated. People were wandering through the rooms carrying books and files; pushing furniture about to try positions. On an emptied desk near the door, a young man in a battered felt hat sat smoking.

"Look," I said, my voice barely audible in the din. "I'm Frances Davis. You don't know me. But I've got some stuff for . . ."

"Sure I know you," replied the young man at the desk, grinning.

He got off the desk and found a wastebasket filled with "flimsies." He scattered the flimsies and came upon the one he wanted. He got back up on the desk and read it.

"Frances Davis. Boston, Mass. Aged 28. First woman corr. credited Franco's armies. Began news career *Medford Mercury* printer's devil aged thirteen . . ."

"Hey! What's going on?"

He grinned up at me from under the brim of his hat. "Sure I know you, I was writing your obit. Good story you spoiled!"

"Oh!" I grinned too. "Sorry." And then on second thought, "File it. Maybe I'll give you a break yet."

We both laugh.

"Look, about Knick . . ."

I went off to find Dr. de Vaux, by whose devotion I had escaped death. I was to meet him, not in the antiseptic corridors of the Neuilly Hospital, but for the first time in his own orbit, his offices in the entresol of his apartment in a small street on the Left Bank. The concierge pointed out the doctor's office across the cobbled court, one of those private courtyards, large enough to turn a coach and four, around which the eighteenth-century French built their "hotels particuliers." I rang and was admitted to the reception room. The chairs were carefully placed along three walls, not in order to leave the center free for the usual publication-piled table of a medical waiting room, but because the floor space was taken up by an exhibit. Four brass posts marked off a square formed by the red velvet ropes that museums require to prevent the public from touching exhibits. Inside posed a population of dolls, some upright upon doll chairs, sitting at tea in genteel groups, some reclining upon doll divans, some stretched out in doll beds, some without the luxury of their own furniture, propped for support against the brass posts of the cordoning rope or against other dolls. They were all lady dolls, sumptuously dressed, with china-heads set precariously on their stuffed bodies. Each doll was broken at the neck, so that not one of the dolls' shoulders upheld the neck and head. There was a contradiction between the two parts of each doll, the limp bodies attired in rich silks and satins and the painted, wobbling heads.

The dolls were somehow nightmare repetitions of myself in a hospital bed: myself in two parts—separate head and its swathed and wounded neck unrelated to the body that could not be independent of it.

I had been eager to see Dr. de Vaux again. We'd had a comradeship through hours in the presence of death. I would not have survived alone. We had accomplished life together, and I expected to resume, at the sight of him, that intimacy. But de Vaux gave no indication of special relationship. He greeted me perfunctorily, examined me perfunctorily, advised me perfunctorily: neither was I healthy nor was Paris a healthy place for me. I had better go back where I belonged and see my own doctors. Generalized septicemia was a shock from which the system did not lightly recover. I was only temporarily rescued. I was not to play the fool. When I opened my mouth to argue that I must stay to cover the coming war, "Manque la guerre! Vous avez presque manqué la vie!" Dr. de Vaux cut across my expostulations, got up, escorted me to his office door, his face shut against me, one hand in his pocket jingling change. He gave me no choice but to leave. Then for a moment he relented in this eviction, shrugged weary shoulders, "Life is ironic, is it not? You, a small stranger, I could save; but in her room my daughter lies waiting for the paralysis that will reach her lungs; I shall not be able to save her." And then he was suddenly fierce, "If for a few short months more she lives, how can I care for her in a Paris at war? May death take her before the Germans come!" Eyes blind with tears, I stumbled across the cobbles to the street.

And went home.

chapter thirteen

The Messenger Denied

Summer, 1939. While crossing the Merrimack bridge I looked downriver; from here you can see the Farm. There is an old custom in the Farm family when we have been away, whether for years or for an afternoon of shopping: you come this far across the bridge, turn your head and look downriver. There where the deep curves of the river enfold the wooded hills, at the last bend where the trees give way to a clearing, there on the bank, the glimpse of white—that's the Farm.

Everything was as it had always been. No one had patched the mortar washing away between the fieldstones of the gateposts. The clambering net of vines held the stones in place. The juniper and sweet fern tumbled down the hillside. From the rock pile the maples marched along the lane towards the house. The lane had fallen in where the culvert ran; the car bounced in and out of old ruts.

Who will be here? I wondered, returning to the childhood game of counting over the tally. Hazel. It wouldn't be the Farm if Hazel weren't here. And Laurie and Kit, and Donny and Debby—the twins will have sprung up like weeds. Not Dutchie, production boss in an airplane factory; nor Jude, picking over news pictures in the New York office of *Life*. Not Brian, breeding selected bulls; nor Timmy, the voice of a late-night radio show. Nor my sister Phyllis, gone away to college at Antioch. But Kathy—a zephyr of affection stirred me and I smiled to myself—Kathy would be here. And Raymie will still be here, in the background, the whole weight of his body upon his crutches. I had a sudden vision of the blaze of fury I had once seen in his eyes when the others had boasted of how they were going off to conquer the world.

Roney the Second, the horse Kit had bought from the gypsies, lifted his dark head, flicked his mane, and trotted off. Valdean, the honey-colored mare, wheeled at his flank, always a little late, always a little behind, dependent upon the lead of the small black stallion. Incurious, the cows Daisy Mae the Third and Babe regarded the car as it went by, no pause in their steady munching. The ducks walked Indian file beside the lane. There was old Luke, the big white Pekin, still in the lead of his family, and the little wild duck, Lucille, in the rear—each year's family marshalled in between, the big mallards with emerald necks and the small brown females. Luke, hearing the car coming, seeing it almost upon him, ordered his household across the road. They strung out, diagonally, wings slapping, scolding, refusing to be hurried. Polly slowed, then stopped to let the parade by.

The Farm heard the horn and the outraged chorus of the ducks. From house and barn, the family erupted. Across the grass ran Hazel, her hair, now cropped short, lifting off her face in silver wings. She clapped her hands as she came, her voice ascending: "Look who has come home at last!" The front door banged. Laurie in dungarees flew across the intervening space, yelling "Hi! Hi!" From the tailboard of the truck drawn up in the barnyard Debby vaulted, her legs and arms caked in garden dirt. On the embankment by the barnyard, his shirt flapping on his hips, Donny, skinny and lengthened out, set down the buckets he'd been lugging to the pigs. In the woodshed door Kathy stood smiling, undecided whether or not to retreat from all this hurly-burly. Around the side of the house the dogs came pell-mell; Jock, small grey cannonball, traveling close to the ground, Bing in a cavalry charge, thundering onward. Clumsily, my leg still not healed, I got out of the car.

Nothing was changed. In the house I saw where, on the north window, Hazel's initials had been cut on the pane: "H.H.A. '18," Hazel Hammond Albertson, 1918. The winter wind howling out of the north had not loosened the glass. I'd died, been resurrected, but nothing had happened to crack or break a pane of glass. The bearded Whitman continued to smile on the room, daisies in the basket vase under his picture. The room endured the same jumble of interests that had always been left there: a pair of shoes on the stairs waiting to be remembered, books laid down for a moment and then forgotten, piles of mail, Jock's mouse on the rug, a clock taken apart on the lamp table, a hammer and chisel never put back in the tool cupboard. I breathed the remembered smell of the house, and limped slowly up the stairs.

But after the excitement of arrival had subsided—when I was

resettled and left at last to shake down—I found myself reduced to what I once had been. Not hero nor messenger, returning wounded, bearing urgent news. No one stopped haying, cultivating, shopping, dishwashing, picking crops, canning, or even gave over the games they'd been playing, to gather around and ask, "Tell us now, tell us of the world you've seen. Tell us what's to come."

The voyage across the sea from Le Havre had been a week of grey seas and cold rain. I kept myself inside myself, struggling with my defeat. I alone had been sent home while the others waited for the crucial battle. I told myself it was for a few weeks only. I would get back. But I was benumbed by apathy. I made no effort to talk with other passengers, closed my ears and heard nothing of what America "would" or "should" do if the war came closer. As I covered the last few miles by train to Boston I rehearsed my message to Philip, to the Farm, to my world. I would tell them all of the significance for them of the war in Spain, that trying-ground for the great war for Europe, as though I had been elected to go out and discover fate. My return would decide their lives. But when I opened the door to the little apartment where Polly and Philip now lived, Polly's love overwhelmed me. It was her child who concerned Polly, not oracular prophecies of war.

All the brass in the apartment, the heavy Russian candlesticks, the dough mixing bowl, the samovar with the Czar's seal—all shone in welcome. The sun flooded through her windows, her flowers bloomed in welcome, as only Polly could persuade them, in celebration of my homecoming. From the kitchen came the savory steamings and smells of Polly's familiar necromancy of love. Who would bring specters to such a feast?

After the first effusion of love, daily life closed over me like waters over a pebble. When the ripples subsided it was as though I had never been away. There was no war anywhere. Yet I carried within me an air of latent fury, which frightened Philip into leaving unspoken the questions he would have asked. Once he did sit down beside me and began: "Now tell me, what was it like in Spain?" only to trigger off a terrible barrage, delivered in the squeak that was all that remained of my voice, a forecast of violence, not just in Spain but in all Europe and Asia, even spreading to his own American

Home at the Farm for a brief time between hospitals in Paris and New York, the author sits on Hazel's log and works on a story.

world. He limited himself to immediate matters after that. He didn't ask again.

"Six weeks! You think you're going to go back in six weeks?" exclaimed the family doctor, another medic looking at me as though I were mad. "Closer to six months, maybe six years."

"Nonsense," said I, "there isn't time." "From the looks of *you*," the doctor insisted, "you may just have to take time. And for you, it may be never." I wrote him off as a political imbecile. I would spend a few weeks at the Farm, and then get back, via New York, to where I belonged, to Europe and the road of history.

At the Farm, Hazel told me about the war in Spain: the great idealism of the men of the Abraham-Lincoln Battalion (one of the International Brigades), and the persuasion—her own—by which she'd induced the women's club to make up a subscription for an ambulance. Hadn't they been an *inspiration*, all those courageous young men! I could not convey to her that her young men, her ambulances, had not been on the roads I knew—Franco's roads. How could the war have been lost with such young men in the ranks!

I struggled with the shred of voice I had left to insist that it had not been like that, and finally retorted furiously that there was nothing very pure even amongst Hazel's beloved "Loyalists." They too had fought a more complicated war than would fit the frame of simple morality. Communists who fought Franco in the morning shot the anarchists in front of the fresh-dug graves before dinner. Hazel, hurt, turned away from the subject and warned the others that I mustn't talk about the war. I must get strong here in the lovely sun!

Donny was difficult for Hazel to control; he was consumed with excitement to hear what war was like. "What was shooting like? Did you ever seen anyone dead?" But Hazel scolded him: "She *must* want to forget all that! We must *help* her to forget!" I gave up. I hadn't the strength to take a stand that would catch and hold Hazel (whoever had?), and force her to look at war in Spain as preliminary struggle in the war for all her beliefs, her Better World. Hazel grieved for the defeat of the poor Spaniards—such a dreadful tragedy; but meantime there were squash to be gathered, apples to be picked. My war was a nightmare of which Hazel was convinced the Farm would cure me in time.

It did not. I gave over trying to knit those two worlds: Franco possessing Madrid and with it, all Spain; and the Farm on the riverbank. It was only amidst Europe's agonies that I would not have been an alien.

September, 1939: now that Hitler and Stalin have signed a non-aggression pact, the Germans invade Poland and take Danzig. The Russians invade Poland from the East. France and Britain, forced, declare war. The H.M.S. *Courageous* is sunk. October: the *Royal Oak* is sunk. Polish Jews are rounded up and herded into the Lublin corral. November: 60,000 tons of shipping go down in one week.

America in that fall of '39 engaged in frenzied argument. Each side could not hear the other for its own shouting. At those who warned "Stop Hitler now" the America First-ers cried "Warmongers!" "Tell them the Yanks are NOT coming!"

The air over the country was full of words—the words men die for: "Freedom," "Democracy," "Our Way of Life." At night, alone in my room, from across the differences in time, from all over the country, my little radio brought me the voices of Americans talking it over. The voice of an orator in Texas, haranguing: "Do you folks think this man Hitler would dare to invade Texas! Go ahead, folks, laugh, that's right. Why, do you know what we'd say to him? We'd say," fist thudded, water pitcher rattled, "Remember the Alamo!" Safe behind the adobe walls of the Alamo? Suspended by myth in some safe space while the rest of the planet hurtles into the void.

From Connecticut a veteran of the First World War shouted, "Do we have to go and clean up their messes for them every time? Can't they settle things themselves?"

I heard men talking from all parts of the country, a forum in the middle west, an orator in Seattle: the democratic process hashing it over—the battle will rock back and forth, while FDR cautiously will move his country from the spiritual sin of neutrality, through "cash and carry," through "lend-lease," to "all measures short of war."

But people go on talking long after they have come, without acknowledging it, to decision. The War had invaded the barn cellar. In the morning when Kit went out to the barn and switched on the light, the radio that Donny had hooked up for him warmed up before he'd got to the bottom of the barn stairs. It said in a loud voice coming up out of the cellar, "RAF planes rain leaflets on Germany during the night . . ." The ducks gobbled the grain on the cellar floor, their beaks clacking steadily. Kit walked among them and they set up a furious scolding. It distracted him from the news. "Damn steam shovels," said Kit. "Bunch of old biddies. Shut up your gobbling." The horses chewed and turned their heads. Daisy Mae the Third stretched her neck round in her stanchion and swished her tail. The barn cats skittered across the floor, tails in the air, impatient for the warm milk. Kit set down his pail, drew up his milking box, nudged Daisy Mae over and began squirting. The milk hit the pail with a rhythmic ping. "Adolph Hitler" began the radio, but it was Kit who overrode the announcer. "That guy Hitler!" Kit exhaled the rage pent up in his breast, "I'd like to get that guy Hitler alone behind the barn, for just five minutes. And another minute for the fat one with the medals."

One afternoon towards the end of October, my last weekend before going back to the war, a young man came out to the Farm, his arrival much heralded by Hazel and Laurie. Adam was one of the new Harvard generation who had become members of the Farm family in the years I had been away. Late in that Indian summer afternoon he walked down the lane, stirring up the dust; over his shoulder was slung, like his turn-of-the-century predecessors, a misshapen green bag crammed with books.

Hazel, Laurie, and I in desultory fashion, had been picking the late beans. Our feet were bare and caked with earth and our bare legs and arms and backs were brown with the sun. We sat on the porch floor under the awning, tipping and tailing the beans for supper, watching the figure slowly approaching and speculating on who it would be. When Hazel and Laurie saw it was Adam, they ran to greet him, escorting him, one on each side, across the lawn, both at once talking to him of where he'd been and how glad they were to see him and had he brought the books he'd promised?

I looked at him as he mounted the porch steps, and refused to smile. There had been too much talk about him. I was jealous of this young man, stranger to me; resented Hazel's eulogies of his virtues; the respect with which Hazel and Laurie quoted everything he had to say about the world, my private domain. I would not be impressed. Who was he, but a young man teaching science, that incomprehensible way of explaining the universe, to the Navy.

Like the Harvard men in the earlier years, Adam had found the Farm, and especially Hazel, an absorbed audience for his ideas. And like them, he was to learn that it was devotion she offered him, not comprehension.

I was irritated by the excitement of Hazel and Laurie at Adam's coming. I had returned home full of the importance of my new role; and was about to go off again—to be present at War, but the Farm family went on treating me as they always had done—loving, accepting, teasing me. I dumped my share of beans into the pot and, in disdainful withdrawal, retreated to the railing, prickly with consciousness of my new sophistication, stepping backwards into a band of sunlight which poured down through a rent in the awning. Adam, to greet me, walked forward into that same area of brightness. We two were caught in such a glow of light that we could not see each other's faces. Nor when he spoke did I hear his words. I heard the vibrations of his voice. I heard a profound gentleness, concern for the vulnerability of living things. Later I was to find myself watching his hands, not seeing what they were doing, but seeing the solicitude with which he handled even the inanimate. I was moved; and furious with myself for that swift response.

That night I lay awake in the moonlight that filled my room. A waste to sleep. In the morning I was up early, got myself from bed, dressed, and downstairs, went through the rooms without acknowledging to myself what I was looking for, then out onto the porch. At the corner we collided, Adam intently bound upon this same errand. Urgency dropped from both, like cloaks. There we stood and were going nowhere and had nothing to say.

It was like that all day. Whatever room he was in drew me as if I had pressing business there and the room he left became intolerably vacant. If I was not in the room he sought me out, and as soon as we were in the same room together the purpose of having come there was satisfied.

Towards sunset, the family off on its own concerns, Adam and I were left alone. He took my hand and led me away from the house. I did not ask him where we were going or why, but followed. We went down the lane, climbed over the pasture fence and slowly up the side of Brake Hill, brushed by the tall grasses.

His presence was a magic that heightened all my senses. I saw how the sun glinted off the shining stalks of grass, how the stalks stood out separately like woven linen thread. I bent to feel the prickly texture of the silver reindeer moss; crushed and smelled the juniper leaves. All this had always been here. I knew the smell and feel and color of what grew here, yet it seemed as though I had never been aware of the miracle in each blade's separate existence.

My hand in his I followed his steps, intoxicated by submission. Where was that independent girl? Where was commitment to the war? Was I now content to be led, to receive destiny through him?

We came to the crown of Brake Hill and in the little grove walled by the trees, sat down to rest. Through the trembling leaves the late sunlight made a moving pattern over us. I watched the dappling of light and shadow on his bare wrist. He, murmuring as much to himself as to me, repeated:

> Where, like a pillow on a bed,
> A Pregnant banke swell'd up, to rest
> The violets reclining head . . .

There was never again to be loneliness. His thoughts would be my thoughts and we would communicate without words.

Adam put his hand out, touched my hand and he said, very softly, out of his dream, "I will study and you will read all my papers and darn my socks, and someday when the world is again at Peace I will take you off to Spain. Stay."

Stay! Stay? Put a stop to all the built-up momentum that was to carry me off tomorrow? Stay? The word in all its implication spun me and turned me about. To give the heart in this one gesture, hedged about with no reticence, not waiting upon time, to fling away all protection of one's vulnerable self? I did not dare, and where was there time for knowing? Tormented, I jumped up and cried out the first words that leaped into my head: "Socks? Socks! And what about the war! There will be war, it will be our war—you know it, even if Hazel does not! How can I stay if there is to be a war! Socks!"

Adam, still prone upon the hillside grasses, looked up at me. "Yes," he spoke soberly. "I do know it and when the time comes it will be my turn to go off. And I will come back to wherever you are. But if you don't stay—you will destroy yourself. You will have flung yourself away." Adam paused and began again, more gently, "You are consumed by what you have seen and what you believe. You come from the war like an emissary—but look at yourself. How much more can that body of yours take? Stay where you are and grow strong for me. Let the others go off now. Wait for me . . ."

"I *can't!*" I had clapped my hands over my ears, as if I could listen to no more. "I can't! How can I wait—*here*—in this unreal place? With Hazel every day denying that there's any world beyond the Farm gates? *I* know what my body can take; it will do what I tell it to do. And how do we know what *this* is?" I made a wild gesture toward him, encompassing his long recumbent shape. "We've known each other only a day. Twenty-four hours! How can we *know* what we feel?" I stopped gesturing and looked hard at him. "I know one thing. My job is to cover this war. How could I deny that fact for the dream of a private life?"

Adam got up, dusted himself off, and we walked down the hill. The next day we both went away.

I was not to get very far. Mary, a childhood friend and now a New York doctor, gave me a camp bed in her New York apartment as a base. I went out and began to take care of the delightful necessaries of travel: arranging passage, getting French money, extending my passport, wiring Edgar of my advent. But all the time I was not in my usual traveling state of euphoria, but sitting down—in an unaccountable manner for me—on every bench and taking deep breaths. I had begun to feel a tightness in my throat. I said to myself, "I don't believe it. I'm tired. Tomorrow I'll wake up and breathe as easily as ever." Mary was off-duty that night in New York, and we were to have been together. When I came in, she gave me that sharp look, which I had come to recognize from my experience with other doctors. Mary had known me since childhood. She knew that I was stubborn as a goat, that I would not allow my body to deflect my will.

In the middle of the night she got up to make a phone call. She couldn't have had any sleep. My breathing had become noisier and noisier. She didn't tell me whom she'd called nor did she ask me any questions. At almost the same instant I felt I couldn't pull in the next breath, a knock came at the door, and there in white suits were two ambulance men with their stretcher. I didn't refuse them.

We shot up Fifth Avenue and over to the George Washington Bridge with all sirens going. We reached the emergency ward of the Presbyterian Hospital. There was only the barest thread of space by which I was able to drag air into my lungs. My face grew purple with the gigantic effort of forcing in whatever air I could; tears streamed down my face, from agony and from fear.

Two of the interns called out, "Get her up to the operating room and get Dr. Brighton." I was taken up in an elevator to the operating room, where a pleasant-faced man stood partly-masked in the swinging door. "Now what have we got?" he said. The interns were stripping my clothes off. "Oh, you've had one of these before. Do they know what's blocking your throat?" I managed to say, "No, and I've had a bronchoscopy too." Dr. Brighton said, "Well, look, this time we'll find out. I'll do a tracheotomy and you can breathe. Later on we'll see what you have there."

The rest of the night I slept in the ward, choking now and again on my own blood, but breathing between the spasms. In the morning when I opened my eyes, Mary was standing there. She had been there all night, I suppose. "You sap," she said, "but I was a little slow on that one."

One day a week or so later, after morning rounds, Dr. Brighton, who was the chief of surgical staff in the Ear, Nose, and Throat division, took my week's accumulation of newspapers off the chair next to my bed and drew it up beside me. "This makes no sense," he said, "you can't go through life with your airway closing up every time you get a cold. That's no way for you to be anything, much less a reporter, until we find out what's wrong. I know they had a good look with the bronchoscope. I've had a report from Paris from de Vaux. He saw nothing to account for these repeated collapses. I'm going to open you up, chin to wishbone, and see what kind of structure you have in there."

Pain is suffered not in the aggregate, an entirety; but broken up, instant by instant, into fragments. I crawled from each moment to the following. The one just past had never been, the next would never be; all my awareness was concentrated on the present, the mind its own merciful protector; to what was beyond its strength it turned a blank self; like life, pain is an ebb and flow and no intensity maintains its level.

For Philip and for Polly, my pain was too awful to be contemplated. But it was their vicarious suffering that was intolerable. Polly's sleepless anxiety was inflamed by the night; by the distance between herself and the hospital; by the scraps of information of which she could make so little—the professional jargon of the doctors.

Philip, who could not look on and do nothing, retreated, "to take care of things at home." But Polly was not to be induced away from the proximity of the room containing my bed. The doctors, the nurses, even the woman with the pail and mop, all had rights where she was trespasser. The door which swung behind them shut her out. She would not leave that door, stretched her plump, short self upon tiptoe, in the attempt to see over the rim of the small glass pane set high in the door. She searched the faces of the professionals going in, coming out, asked them nothing, apologized for getting in the way, then in the instant before the door swung shut again, tried to catch a single glimpse, to see for herself. She would not be detached from the area of that door. If she went out of the range of what was going on in that room, something might change. It might be different when she came back. Who dares to say she accomplished nothing there?

Inside the room, propped straight up in the white bed, under the pitiless glare of light, there came a night when the issue was simple: to continue the battle was too wearisome. Hidden within myself like a small animal in the earth, I wanted only to escape the intrusions by which the doctors and the nurses tried to catch and to hold me. They awakened me, summoned me, tormented me, thrusting ice under my burning armpits, never letting me be. I wanted only to slide away, down into the darkness. It would be so easy to slide down, to slip away, to escape them.

In that night of decision, even across the barrier of light and shining steel, the murmuring of voices, and the crackling of uniforms, I knew of Polly's compact figure exiled outside the door and of its vulnerability. Far inside my burrow came final perception: I could not hurt her, and I turned from death.

When I finally saw Dr. Brighton again my neck was bandaged round and round; my head looked as insecurely attached as those of Dr. de Vaux's dolls. Dr. Brighton no longer looked perplexed; his eyes had only compassion.

"That septicemia you wouldn't let kill you has corrupted the entire structure of your throat," he said. "You don't have any proper cartilage left. Nothing to hold, no cracoid rings to hold back the walls of your throat against swelling." He paused.

"And no voice box. No vocal chords. Well, you do have secondary vocal chords. Maybe you could learn to use them. It's not often done. You had better make a firm friend of that little tube that insults you so. What do you call it? Your whistle? It's the only route for air to your lungs. The big thing now is to get rid of your general infection. You are still a very sick girl. We'll be reading your damned newspapers here for a long time. We may even have to give you a room and let you write a book." And then he gave me a pat and left. I suppose he thought I was going to cry.

I didn't. I wouldn't have, and I couldn't. I could no longer speak. I was alive only by way of my eyes. I winked. The wink was an old signal between Polly and me. Polly had never learned to wink with one eye but blinked them both; now my wink was meant as reassurance.

Later, I was shipped from hospital to hospital, ripped out of context, reduced to a voiceless body in a flat white bed with no will of my own, no capacity to organize even the minute details of my own life, dependent wholly upon others, to be washed, fed, and to be made whole again.

We are familiars of war, you, I, and the lot of us upon the planet. Past war, present war, future war. War immediate, war in the middle distance, and war, remote. War, capable at any instant of obliterating us.

The quick, who return, and the dead, are the lucky ones. Those who will never be whole again draw the short straws. A chasm divides their lives; on one side what they had been and the war and that brief issue of living or dying; on the other whatever existence is to be made out of what is left; their discovery of the irreducible, of that core of which neither war nor any trick of life could beggar them.

Between one existence and the next they live, for a shorter or a longer time, in a state of hiatus, usually in hospital. There they wait. The day and the night is a state of waiting. Each, entering that sterile world, is stripped of anything that makes him separate, unique—an individual. Each is allotted a bed, a bleached gown, shuffling slippers that, fitting all, fit none. Thus paupered, each clings to some small identifying scrap, a comb, a small book, a picture. His body now belongs to the organized routines, the nurses and the doctors.

Those for whom living is temporarily in suspension are cut off from the world where there is volition, jurisdiction, role, and work. They are a community of their own, with its own rules.

Since they are in some valid part reduced, each draws from the common pool what he lacks. The armless are fed by the lame, the blind hear for the deaf. Yet each in his secret belief rejects in horror his kinship with the others. In his dreams he is always whole. Who knows which is the waking? Which the dream?

We wake; wash, eat, and return again to sleep, heavy with the weight of hours, and with the shame of a day in which washing and eating can become the purpose of waking. It grows difficult to remember anything but this; to remember having been passionately alive; what effort feels like, and satisfaction, and despair; difficult to believe in a day lived otherwise than this: inexorable routine, and the imperceptible movement of the hands around the face of the wall clock.

In the end, for all their aseptic routines, for all the shining complicated instruments, for all the formulae of drugs, the doctors can do little for us. Our bodies are returned to our own dominion; we are informed that we are now "as good as new." We go out, single, isolated, a newcomer in the world each to work out his own accommodation.

Spring, 1940. The first restlessness of life returned, I exhibited an incomprehensible compulsion. I would not lie back and release my hold on the existence from which I had been expelled. The further the bed and I were removed from the cataclysm, the more desperate my clutch upon events, my effort to coerce the people about me to look up from their preoccupations and accept the auguries. I was a mute and mini-Cassandra in a frenzy. My own immediate disaster dismissed, my voicelessness transcended by my purpose. First things first, and first the fate of man. Perhaps this was how I kept alive, gave myself, in that ruined shell, identity and value.

My hospital bed was submerged in a sea of newspapers. The newsboys stopped the carts, snapped out the fresh editions, smacked them double and piled them up wherever place could be found, on the bedclothes, on top of books, on chair and table. Nurses complained that there was no room for trays. Doctors complained that there was no room for instruments.

April 9, 1940: Norway and Denmark are invaded. May 10: I scribbled to the resident. "Look," making the pencil dig and the lead snap with passion, "I can't go up to the O.R. tomorrow! Churchill's going to speak!"

The resident read the message and, astonished, looked at me. Then he took up the pad and with unconscious mimicry began writing in return. But I seized the paper out of his hand and scratched in fury, "I can *hear*! *You* don't have to write!" And under that wrote out, "I've got to listen!" meaning the Churchill speech. This will be known as Churchill's "blood, sweat and toil" speech.

"*She* has to listen!" The resident threw up his hands. "The Prime Minister of England addresses Parliament and here in New York City, United States of America, we should change the O.R. schedule because she has to listen!"

Only the refugee doctor, standing at my bedside, has the same stricken look upon her face. She has forgotten her pipettes and the blood samples she came for, the slow patching up of individuals again reduced to futility. It is clear to her that the world is round. You cannot go on escaping. You come back to what you fled from—unless, somewhere, you take a stand.

May 14: the French are defeated at Sédan. The Dutch army surrenders. Belgium capitulates. From Dunkirk the British evacuate what is left of their army by a huge flotilla of naval ships, yachts, and small boats.

June 14: the morning's papers lie open under my hand. I have read the headlines and the dropheads: "Germans Enter Paris . . ." and then I came to "Knickerbocker: dateline Paris," and put the paper down to stare at the ceiling.

My neighbors in our row of beds have come to accept the fact that I cannot speak. It does not hinder them from speaking to me in one-sided conversations. Addie, next bed to mine, sighs and looks at the clock.

"Iss long, No?" she says, and I come back to the present and nod.

"Iss long," goes on Addie, "when no visitors come in the afternoon." This is a set piece of information. Addie never fails to comment on it. Addie says, "Here, is nothing to do. By my house I am busy all day. By my house I cook, I clean. All day I am busy with the kids. Here I get nervous." I nod in sympathy.

"You like papers with no pictures, yes? I seen you like those papers. I like papers with pictures. I like to look at pictures." I smile at her.

An intern pauses at my bed to look at the headlines. "Gosh! This Hitler guy, there's no stopping him." And then he turns to the sports section to get the final scores of the ball game.

The charge nurse stands by my bed, order book in her hand. She is near the radio. Seeing her there, Miss Stein, at the other end of the ward, remembers that this is the night for "Burns and Allen," and calls across the room, "Get Gracie Allen, Nurse. Time for Gracie Allen."

The charge nurse twirls the dial. "We take you now to Bordeaux, France . . ."

"That's not it!" objects Miss Stein. "We don't wanna listen to no more war. We got our own troubles."

". . . correspondent Ed Taylor. Go ahead Bordeaux . . ."

But I had leaned out of my bed, grabbed the nurse's arm to keep her from touching the dial and annihilating this miracle. I scribble furiously on my pad, "Leave him, please! It won't be long. He's a friend."

A flick of the dial, there was Ed's voice, there on J ward!

"Wait a minute, Miss Stein," the nurse says, patiently. "This is a friend of hers." Shame creeps up my neck. "Besides, you can have Gracie Allen any time."

I was concentrated into a listening instrument, fixed upon the voice that came from the box. In an instant now, I'll feel the lift in my heart. I'll recognize the inflections of Ed's voice. At that instant J ward will collapse like a pack of cards. I dreamed the smell of stale ether. I dreamed the six of us down one side, the six up the other, sitting in our identical gowns in our identical beds. I dreamed Miss Stein . . . I'll hear Ed's voice and I'll know there's still a thread that holds me to another world, that I belong to it, and will regain it.

A moment of pause. Then the voice came out of the box. I could hear the waves of space like the waves of the sea. The voice was borne to me across the distances of night.

It was not immediately recognizable, space and airwaves change a voice. But as I listened, fixed partly upon the words and partly upon the sound, Ed came alive in my mind.

The newsmen of Europe struggling back over the roads from the rout at Sédan, from the awful night at Dunkirk, had come into Paris in time to see the ministers cramming their brief cases with state papers, cars waiting below, engines running. The newsmen followed the ministers from Paris to Bordeaux. They watched the rich, the men with paunches and the women in furs, eating well in the best hotels. The reporters lost their own appetites. The government went to Tours. The reporters went to Tours: The rich stayed on, eating at Bordeaux.

"We spent the night," Ed Taylor is saying, "sleeping on newspapers on the floor of a loft across the street from the hotel where the ministers established themselves. In the morning Knickerbocker threw open the door and said, 'It's over. I've just been across the street. They've given up!' Mowrer, said Knickerbocker, went pale as death. 'I will not believe it!' he cried, 'It can't end this way. They will go on fighting. They must fight from North Africa. I've got to go see for myself.' "

In my mind, I could picture Ed speaking into the microphone, and I could anticipate what would come next. Once the fact was established, the newsmen had to think quickly of themselves. The door of the fortress of Europe was clanging shut. The continent would be closed to them. They had to get out. Through Spain to Lisbon. For some it would have to be done quickly, before Franco's government knew whose passports their frontier guards were stamping. They who had fought in the advance guard, been beaten back from country to country, must now retreat off the continent of Europe itself—to move in again only when they came with the ranks of a reconquering army.

I looked at the beds across the aisle and at the lights in the nursing station and did not see what I looked at.

"Good night, America!" says Ed Taylor.

Good night, Ed . . .

"And now," called Miss Stein, "*Now* we can have Gracie Allen?"

chapter fourteen

Thanksgiving

Midsummer, 1940. When the hospitals could think of nothing more to be done to me, Polly reclaimed me. Wrapped like fragile china in a cocoon of quilts, I was carefully stored in a corner of the car, and taken back to the Farm. The rampant life at the Farm, Polly had decided, would entice me back within reach, back from that pit into which I had fallen.

This time the family had been warned they must not smother me in welcome. On my arrival they stood like a game of statues, each frozen in the attitude, on the spot in which the coming of the car surprised them. Only Kit moved forward. He walked out of the shadow of the barn, wiping his hands on a rag. "We gotcha this time," he said, reached into the car, plucked me out, carried me in his arms into the house, up the stairs, and kicked open the door of the River Room. Polly, Hazel, and Laurie crowded through the doorway after him, all talking at once. Hazel had given up her own room—the River Room was always hers—and even her big bed was to be mine. The sun flooded through the south windows. The big bed was set square under the river window, clean-sheeted and turned back, ready. The Farm, Hazel's tone implied, had been waiting for me, everything else suspended until I was returnable.

Then, as ever, Polly began to pull one way, Hazel the other, and Laurie to arbitrate. Kit had laid me upon the bed.

"In the back of the car, Kit dear," Polly was at her most beguiling. "Will you be a nice man? I knew she'd need it if she had to have this big old bed." Hazel, taking off my shoes, held one suspended in her hand and looked up suspiciously. "Need what?"

I wanted everyone to go away, I wanted to have my clothes off and slide between the sheets and lie there.

"I don't know what she needs such a big bed for anyhow," Polly persisted, disregarding Hazel's anxiety. "If she took my advice she'd have a nice small bed that wouldn't be an elephant on her."

"Oh Polly!" Laurie tried to come between the two, "the elephant isn't on her. She's on the elephant. And besides, the bed is her castle. Like an Englishman's home."

Hazel looked offended and forgot about my second shoe. "But she always *liked* this bed. I planned it especially for her. I moved all my things back out to the bungalow just so she could have it."

Kit returned, a hammer under his arm, positioning the nails in his mouth ready for use. He was lugging a mahogany-colored, scrollwork headboard. He squatted on his heels, took a nail from his mouth, and set the headboard in position. Polly, who had taken over my undressing, forsook me in her turn. She pointed out to Kit where he was to drive the first nail.

"Now Polly," Kit said, "you want this hammer or you want me to use it? What did you want me for anyhow? Hold the hammer for you? Let a man drive his own nails." He drew back the hammer to strike.

But Hazel had found her voice. "Polly! you can't put that awful thing on this wonderful bed. You'll spoil all the lines." Kit held the hammer blow.

Polly said, "It's a perfectly good headboard. What's awful about it? What lines are there about that big square box of a bed?"

Kit eased his weight back on his heels and relaxed his hammer arm, still holding the headboard in place with the other hand. My eyelids had grown too heavy to hold open. "If you don't want the headboard," Polly said, "you don't have to have it. My feelings won't be hurt. Why don't you just put the top of the bed up against the wall?"

"Polly," Hazel cried, "she has to see the river!"

"You women make up your minds," Kit announced. "I didn't come up here to hold a hammer. You better catch me while you can. Don't get me and a hammer together often."

"Then why don't we get a smaller bed?" persisted Polly; perhaps she still could win. Kit to me, "You want this bed? I'm not gonna put a headboard on this bed and then come up and take it off and lug this bed out and lug you up a small bed. *You're* sleepin' in it. You have the say. You want this bed?"

I wanted only to get into the bed, and nodded. Kit brought the hammer down on the nailhead. "Laurie, you get that girl's clothes off," he said. "You women will have her kilt' by the time you get her fixed the way you want her."

When I was at last alone, I lay sunk among the pillows of the big bed and looked out of the window up into the heart of the maple. Its boughs embraced the roof and the walls of the house, leaves flickering and pattering in incessant caressing.

"I used to lie here and watch the river," I thought, "when I was small." My remembering eye saw the sunbrowned children. Of all of them, why was I the one now in ruins? Why? Why had I thrown away so golden a beginning to be brought back, deposited in the middle of the square bed, bankrupt, stripped of everything except fear? I who had gone off so splendidly to be chronicler of wars, now forever maimed. What I had been, finished, the body that had been my instrument now the prison of my defective being. Nothing "could conquer in me," I quoted harshly to myself, "the ardor that I had to gain experience of the world and human vice and worth." The choice had been mine alone. Was it from no common destiny but one willfully embraced—a private sortie—that I was now returned home, destroyed? Or so I charged myself, in my despair, yet knew that my fate and I were only forerunners. The time was yet to come when even this Farm would be engaged and I merely the family's earliest casualty.

In those first days of my return the door of my room was kept firmly shut. I dropped out of sight like a stone thrown into the waters. Of all the family only Hazel and Laurie went in and out of my room, and sometimes Polly, who would suddenly drive up the lane, drawn because she "had an instinct." Yet the lives of the rest of the family were changed by my unseen presence, their habits adapted to include my separate existence under the same roof, the atmosphere of the house altered for my being in it.

The door of the River Room had always stood wide open, so that the sun would penetrate the corridor, each day regilding the tarnished frame of the picture that hung in the hall. Now the family, passing the blank, closed door, became accustomed to the hall grown dark and chill. They grew accustomed to being displaced from the center of Laurie's attention; to Kit grumbling where the hell were his clean shirts. For whole sections of the day Laurie was inaccessible. The family shifted for itself.

In the evenings Laurie no longer sat by the fire. Dishes done, she would come slowly up the stairs drying her hands, looking backward like Lot's wife, torn between the solitary watch in my room, and the convivial family below.

Signals telegraphed the news, upstairs, downstairs, outside, I was worse again. Laurie's voice was low so as not to convey fear,

"Polly? Mo-ther! Where are you two? Shouldn't we call the doctor?"; footsteps running too quickly down the stairs; the jangle as the call was rung in. Get the doctor! He'll know what to do!

In bitter negation I would shake my head from side to side on the hot pillow. What good was the doctor? He would come and stand and look at me and he and I would know there had been no use calling him. There was nothing he could do. I lay alone and think of the many-windowed hospitals rising against the sky: the endless corridors gleam, nurses rustling in starched aprons, doctors going by in their white coats, stretchers wheeled in soundless passage to the operating rooms, metal of the intricate machines and instruments glinting under the lights, chemicals promising miracles—so much to do with and so little that can be done.

Waiting, like a fog, settled over the household. In the barn cellar Kit waited. Kathy walked about the kitchen with only half a mind to pots and mixing bowls. In his room in the "Crack," Donny whispered to his little dog that they must be very quiet, listened to his radio turned low, and waited.

In the bed I lay as if the world were fallen away. The room, the bed, vanished, nothing remaining but an airless universe. These were terrible times, the times against which every cell in my blood froze. I applied myself to the discipline of drawing in and then expelling every breath. I pulled at the air, through my whistle, forcing it into all the passages, into all the hollow treelike limbs of the bronchia. My pulse leaped up thudding; leaping, demanded more air and pounded for lack of it; fear and lack, each augmenting the other, grew until airlessness locked about me like a shell, and I was caught, again and ever again, in an intolerable vacuum.

Polly, Hazel, and Laurie, each in her own way, in desperation, tried to drive the terror out of my eyes. Polly, who would not admit her powerlessness, tiptoed to the bed table, seized the water pitcher and took it down to scald it and refill it with cool water. She emptied the wastebaskets. I wanted the world to be utterly still, no action anywhere, rebellious tears rolled down my cheeks. When Polly saw my tears she would go out quickly, close the door behind her and retreat to the kitchen to squeeze orange juice.

Hazel came up and sat in the big chair by the river window. She would exorcise my demon; with the tremendous force of her spirit she would cast it into disbelief, deprive it of existence. She would summon peace to that fear-filled room as if weaving a spell. "How I love the river!" Hazel would say in a voice determined to transport me. "It winds down from the hill and flows out to sea; it carries away all my troubles." But I refused transportation. Between Hazel and myself there was a silent, unyielding struggle. Her voice, insisting on supremacy, went on saying, "Trust yourself to life as if it were the river, let it carry you to the sea. 'As the marsh hen builds in the watery sod,' " quoted Hazel, " 'so I will rest myself in the bosom of God.' " But I could rout fear only by meeting it in combat.

When Hazel allowed herself to look at me and saw the furious resistance in my eyes, she would be so shocked and hurt that she could not go on. "Look, look, I'll pull the blind up and you can see the first star . . ."

Home for the weekend the new Farm family got out of their town clothes, took up old habits as if they had never been away. The house was filled with the signs of their right to occupancy: mail that had accumulated in the letter box, an old sweater rescued from where it had been left in the East Room closet, books with their owners' names on the flyleaves; this one sat on the chair she had upholstered, that one examined the clock he had oiled to see if it was keeping proper time, another took up interrupted knitting. Norah investigated the state of her garden; she was the schoolteacher who with her young brother Walt, orphans, found their first home at the Farm when we were still young and wild. Brian was off to the barn; Timmy looked over the newly acquired music.

Listening from my bed, the door now more often standing ajar that I might miss nothing, I knew who was here before the family took count. The wooden doorlatch of the fireplace room clattered. "Hello? Anybody home?" Jock yipped welcome. "I know, Jockie," said the voice. "*You're* home." Pierce. "Guess this is as good a time as any to shave," the voice went on, still addressing its only audience, the little grey Scotsman of a dog. "What do you think, Jock? I'll never get an empty room again, will I, old man?" Whenever the army released him, Pierce came home to the Farm, walked down the lane with his toothbrush and an electric razor in his pocket, and settled himself among the books he had left unread on his last leave.

A car hurtled down the lane; a hand leaning on the horn; outraged quacking of ducks, Jock's excited yip, Bing's deep woof, squeal of brakes, explosion of laughter, voices calling "Hi! Here we are! Beans, Kathy?" Walt had driven the girls from Boston. Only Walt would begin to blow the horn at the gate.

There was the sound of another car and Polly's voice announcing, "I've brought my sheets!" On weekends Polly deserted Philip,

Top: A new and smaller Farm family at a summer lunch. Hazel shouts from head of table to Kathy, who pours coffee at the other end. *Bottom*: Coming up the lane from the fields, Laurie on the left and Debbie on the right. The line of maples edging the lane from the house to the gate was planted by Rory soon after he bought the Farm.

who didn't like the Farm when it was noisy. Polly's excuse was that she was sure I'd be forgotten in all the excitement. She appeared in the door of my room with a clothesbasket loaded with fresh linen, fresh oranges tumbling over the sheets.

And so the house filled up, distended. Nobody knew where he was going to sleep or if there were enough beds or sheets or whether Laurie had bought enough meat to go around. Beds were rearranged as in a game of musical chairs. The "Crack" ceased to be Donny's room and was usurped by feminine gigglings. Donny, radio under one arm and Jockie under the other, evacuated from the Crack, retreated to the men's side of the attic. Three folding cots were carried down the precipitous attic stairway. I watched them being maneuvered around the corner, the boys backing into my doorway. In the hall I could see the increasing collection of belongings on the old chest: briefcase, shoes, Nell's feathered bonnet, Norah's best suit. Those who didn't know yet where they were going to be put, left the appurtenances of their city selves at this convenient terminal.

Another weekend, and still he had not come. Now there was nothing more to wait for. The new week would begin, empty. And yet by Wednesday expectation was there again like a persistent weed sprouting up again in my mind. What on Monday I forswore, by Friday woke me with a spring of joy; the time had arrived again when he might come. To burnish that recurrent hope, I would take from under the pillow a small book of Donne, its pages opened to a marker, and read first the lines:

All day the same our postures were
And we said nothing all the day . . .

And then I would lay the book down and examine the marker: a postcard. The card was a print of St. Jerome—the lion at his feet, book open upon his table, the instruments of knowledge hung up on the desk and walls beside him. On the reverse in a calligraphic script, there was written, in Latin, "How can we sing the songs of the Lord in an alien land?" In the first days, when I was again able to engage in expectation, I listened for the sound of his footfall on the stairs. But for that listening the days stretched on, one into the other.

During all the hospital time I hadn't dared to consider his continuing presence in my mind. There had been, sent to the hospital, only the book of Donne; inscribed with a date—not of the sending day, but of a summer now a lifetime past. The book, the card of St. Jerome; and a note on a round robin letter the whole Farm wrote: he and Laurie had been up on Brake Hill looking at the stars and he had shown Laurie where Orion stood. The friendly message made me, in my hospital bed, furiously jealous. To what was I clinging? With what pregnancy had I filled so brief an encounter—now a lifetime past?

On a Saturday afternoon, at a moment when the house was still, I heard his voice, "Hello, Jockie. Where's everybody?"

I heard him come up the stairs, hesitate as if he looked into the open doorway of Hazel's new room, into the One-Step-Down Room, into the East Room, and then, before my door, closed now only during my midday rest, I heard him stop. The boards of the floor creaked under his weight, and I remembered with a sharply in-drawn breath how tall he was and broad across the shoulders.

A gentle rap on the door. I could make no sound for struggling so to breathe, and was in fear that he, hearing nothing, would go away. I pursed my lips—no whistle came. Yet the door handle turned. That door always stuck. Everyone else pushed it irritably; but Adam eased it, and the door opened.

The young man in the doorway and the ravaged girl against the pillows of the bed—we looked at each other and said nothing. I had thought of him always with the brittle appearance that young men have, as if from hip to waist they were so thinned out, so sparsely shaped as to be breakable. He was solid now, a tall, firm man, and pervading all his bearing, was the remembered tenderness. I heard his voice as if it lived inside my head, resonant and compassionate— "So, you're back."

The visit was a short one; Adam was afraid he might tire me. He had seen what soon enough I could no longer deny: that there would never be true strength again in my spent body. Was this the end, then, to all domestic dreaming?

When he closed the door again the tears trickled down my face. After a while I got clumsily out of bed and on bare feet went across the floor to the dresser mirror and looked into it, trying to see what Adam had seen. And when I went back to bed I took with me the hand mirror, and the comb, and rearranged my hair upon the pillow, and smoothed my covers and rumpled jacket. This perhaps was the first tendril my female self sent out, to take grip, reroot, and participate in living. Then I hid the mirror and the comb under the pillows.

By the week of Thanksgiving an increasing ecstasy of preparation seized the household. The vacuum cleaner buzzed in a transport of cleanliness. Donny no longer found even my room sanctuary against the rugs that had to be beaten. The china shelves were stripped of the dishes to be rewashed, the silver was out for repolishing, the floors had been rescrubbed. Kit skidded on the new coat of wax on the kitchen linoleum.

"What's the matter with women anyhow?" he growled. "If they got one job to do, they back up into it by doing all the other jobs in the house first. They'll be all wore out by the time they get themselves round to cook that turkey." But Laurie, deaf, was laying papers on the newly washed floors and had stopped on her hands and knees to read an overlooked funny sheet.

Hazel hung fresh pine boughs over the doorways and framed the special pictures with ground pine. In the basket under the portrait of Whitman she arranged the last pin oak leaves. She fixed to my door a bouquet of red and yellow dried corn ears tied up together with juniper sprigs thick with green-blue berries.

The tang of the huge pot of cranberries simmering on the back of the stove floated through the house. Day by day new aromas were added. Kathy made mince and pumpkin pies—'tis mince and 'tain't mince, all marked "T.M." Debby brought me a spoon of mincemeat to lick. The dogs, exiled from the house, lay just outside the door where everyone who came in or went out had to step over them, but even the woods could no longer lure them from the tantalizing smells.

To torture me, and himself, Donny read aloud the poetry of the shopping list: celery, raisins, poultry dressing, oranges, apples, nuts, mushrooms; then, in horror, rushed out the door and through the house yelling, "Hey, Kathy, you forgot turkey!"

Thanksgiving morning the family gathered—singly, in pairs, and in flocks. The girls got into aprons and began on the vegetables. Laurie stuffed three turkeys. Kit and Raymie and Donny had the bathroom to themselves all morning. Polly and Philip brought Adam; he came most weekends now and sat in my room to read Lorca aloud.

Philip called out, "Hullo, hullo, when do we eat?" before he was well into the house, and was promptly exiled with his newspapers to my room, away from the temptation of the nuts and celery and olives that already decorated the table. Hazel and Polly went into the woods for more ground pine for the table centerpiece. Adam came up to my room but, finding his place in my chair preempted, went back downstairs. Philip, unaware that he had driven Adam out, was full of the latest stories about Polly. Straining to hear Adam's voice, I half listened.

"We were in the kitchen arguing about something," Philip was saying. "You know the way we do. I got good and angry and I said to Polly, 'You go miles out of your way to insult me.' And what do you think Polly said? 'There,' she said, 'that just shows you. I haven't moved from this spot and he says I go miles out of my way.' " Philip went off into a great guffaw of laughter. Distracted by Adam's being here but not with me, I was a poor audience.

Laurie paused at my door to report that the turkeys were the most beautiful golden brown she ever saw. "You ought to smell my room." The back bedroom, directly over the kitchen, that once was Kit's alone, was now theirs. "It has so many heavenly smells I just like to go there and lie down and smell them!"

Hazel ran upstairs the hundredth time, and before she ran down again came to the door. "Darling, we'll sing loudly so you'll hear us; and we'll pretend you are right down there with us."

Polly came up for a last time. "Now just as soon as Kit carves, I'll bring yours up to you. I've told him to save you the drumstick."

Why couldn't I respond with the pleasure that would give them joy? Pretend that sitting up here alone gnawing away in undisturbed and solitary splendor at a huge turkey leg would make me entirely happy! Ingrate that I was, to return such love with a grudging bob of the head.

From downstairs: Debby: There are SIX punkin' pies and five mince. I KNOW! I counted!

Norah: Aren't we ever going to eat?

Polly: Oh, Tim, just keep carrying that yellow chair. It looks so beautiful against your green shirt!

Chorus: Chairs! Donny! Chairs!

The ship's bell rang. For once there came from all parts of the house the thuddings, bangings of a concerted rush upon the dining room. I heard the scraping of all the chairs and benches.

"No room! No room on this bench!"

"I can't get my hands up to eat with!"

"Where's Kit? He's got to carve. We can't start without Kit!"

"Oh, dear, I hope we've counted right!"

"You can't get *in* that way, you'll have to go 'round!"

"You mean I have to go out of the house and come back in the kitchen door? Somebody else'll be sitting here by then! Why can't I crawl under the table?" The front door slammed behind the irate Donny.

Only Adam had not joined the crowd. He appeared at my door with his armload of student exams. I had been listening so hard to the voices that I was taken by surprise and had not time to try to rearrange my woebegone face. He glanced at me once quickly, then looked away, "This is the only place they'll be safe," piling the blue-books on the chair.

For my frustration in communicating, I held the little whistle in the soft flesh of my throat guilty, that fragile instrument by which I was capable of breathing. If I could barely articulate the words that raged in my mind, could not bridge the gap between myself and another, I blamed the whistle as if it were my adversary and not the means by which I continued alive; without it I would suffocate. But I had learned at last to produce a semblance of sound.

Now I dared not trust my thread of voice for fear I would only weep. "They're going to bring you everything you want?" Adam asked. Then, too distressed to stay, he retreated.

Kit was late to table. He came out of the bathroom, his newly shaven face shining and pink. He poked his head in at my door to give me greeting.

"Aw, Toots, what is it? Tough to be up here alone when they're all eatin' to bust downstairs?"

Petulant as a child, I nodded. "I'm going down too!"

"I don't see why in tarnation you shouldn't," he decided. "You gotta eat. Might just as well eat down there as up here. Come on. Let's wrap something warm around you.

"See who's coming!" he announced and presented me in the doorway of the dining room. Whistling, clapping, cheers, shiny eyes: my return to the table was a gift to all the family.

Hazel made a throne beside her at the table head, wreathing the chair with pine. Laurie ran to bring me a pillow and a jacket; Polly, her eyes twinkling with pride as if she had herself performed the miracle, had personally to see to it that I was snug and warm and the quilt tucked in to keep out any drafts. Philip could only repeat, "Well, well." And then Hazel lifted up her voice and the family, that diverse family, offered thanks as one: "Praise God from whom all blessings flow"; and when the "Amen" was reached, Hazel, in the overflow of joy, threw her arms about my shoulders and cried, "Oh, darling! aren't you wonderful? How happy you've made us all!" Across the board Adam smiled at me.

Kit speared the first big bird with a long fork. The golden skin burst, the fragrant steam rose upwards. Hazel and Laurie dished out the orange-yellow squash, the white potatoes and the sweet, and the onions with butter melting down their sides. The gravy bowl went up one side of the table and met its twin coming down the other way. Donny dickered with Debby, "I'll give you my onions for your squash." "Give me your turkey, too?" The songs continued as the plates went by, with Hazel's resonant voice holding those about her faithful to the proper hymns, but Timmy beyond her reach, at the table's foot, had begun "MacNamara's Band."

"Children, children," Hazel rapped with her big serving spoon, "you are all getting a little crazy." The family was bound together by her love, transformed into an entity by her capacity to love them all and call them all her children. "We don't feel any pain," announced Brian, whose plate had just arrived.

There fell the moment of hush; all conversation collapsed. Everyone now had been bounteously served, and the family, in concert, attacked the heaped-up plates. And then, after the first few mouthfuls, the talk, the clatter, the laughter, broke out again.

Hazel had made me her special care. If she saw me move to speak, she quietened the table until I had a chance to ask, please the salt, or yes, I'd like the gravy. It was then that I discovered what I would too soon misuse, the weight given to what I had to say by the silence created for it. The family, hushing instantly, to let the slender thread of my new voice be heard, gave me the prerogative which no one at the Farm had enjoyed before.

When the plates went up for seconds, Philip pushed back his chair. "We feel better now," he announced, and surveyed this excellent audience. "Hazel," he began, clearing his throat—speaker addressing the chairman—"I have a fine new Polly story to tell you. This is the best yet."

"Tell them about the peace offensive." Adam incited him, playing on Philip's side of the game that Polly and Philip had been waging for forty years of marriage.

"Now that!" cried Polly, jubilantly, "is one on him!"

"On me!" Philip laughed so hard he couldn't start the story.

"Those two!" deplored Polly, wiping the tears of laughter from her eyes. "They have a game. Adam laughs at anything Philip tells him about me. Even if he knows he's heard it before. I have to come out in the car with those two laughing like hyenas all the way. And don't any of you believe them!" Polly subsided in indignation, "They're making it all up!"

"What are we making up?" Philip demanded. "You haven't heard it yet, how do you know we made it up? I couldn't make it up," he announced to the table. "Nobody could make this one up but Polly." He took a breath. "Now this morning Polly was listening to the news. 'Hitler' said the newsman, 'is planning a new peace offensive.' And what do you think Polly said? She said, 'What a crazy man! What's so offensive about peace?' Now how could I make that up?"

No one laughed harder than Polly, but not at Philip's joke. "What IS so offensive about peace?" she asked, but she laughed with us for the delicious companionship of laughing.

This uproar shook down the turkey. The plates, as if by conveyor belt, moved hand to hand out to the kitchen; the pies were lined up in front of Hazel.

Timmy, in a final burst of accomplishment by which he had both 'tis mince and 'tain't mince in front of him, broke into the "Marseillaise." All the table joined; though no sound came from me, I too was singing. It seemed to me in that moment I sang for the French and for the family and for all men marching together. The last "Marchons! Marchons!" died away and the family fell upon the pies.

It was then that I heard Norah say in a conversational aside, "Only I hope this time we'll have the sense to let them 'Marchons' by themselves. Walt's trying to get into a flying school. Next thing we know he'll be a pilot and then he'll go off and join up with the Canadians—just because he likes the uniforms! Why don't people keep their wars at home?" She attacked her pie as if it were the enemy. "What's the good of my raising him, of the government wasting its money on schools; of my wasting ten years of patience at the blackboard stuffing the empty heads of kids, so that he can go off to get himself killed!"

Laurie looked first where Donny sat and then at Kathy who was carefully not looking at Timmy and Brian. I thought suddenly of that month's tally of air raids over Britain: thousands killed by the German blitz. Joy in Thanksgiving vanished. Hazel, seeing my eyes blazing, tried to hush the table. "Children . . . give her a chance."

In the stillness, in the turning towards me of all attention, I gathered myself up and hurled my creak of a voice, shrill with passion, at them like a missile. "*Their* war! It's Walt's war and Brian's and Timmy's war and Donny's war and everybody else's war, or you'll never sit down to another Thanksgiving like this again! There are things worse than war, worse than death."

Kathy left the table. For an instant the rest were stunned. Then from all sides voices broke out. Hazel, horrified at the intrusion of death and destruction in this moment of thanks and joy, rapped on the table with the pie server. "Children!" she pleaded. "This is Thanksgiving. Let us think of all the things to be thankful for. Our family, the Farm, the river . . ."

But Norah, enraged, would no longer cede me special privilege. She cried out indignantly. "She started this! We ought to have a chance to be heard, too. It's not fair to keep us quiet just because we *can* talk!" Out of the rising clamor, Hazel's voice ascended, saying to me, "Sometimes, dear, I don't think your faith is strong enough. Don't you remember the marsh hen? 'As the marsh hen builds in the watery sod,' " her voice, sweet and insistent, soared above the others, " 'I will build me a nest—.' " But the marsh hen was the last straw. I would not let her finish.

"Marsh hen!" I gasped, "Marsh hen!" That one unoffending waterfowl had become a symbol for all Hazel's capacity to pretend reality out of existence. A seizure of coughing ripped at my body. Kit put an end to calamity by picking me up in his arms and carrying me up to bed.

"You shouldn't go picking fights, Toots," he said gently, "until you can finish 'em," and slid me back under the covers.

Late in the afternoon when even Polly and Philip had left, Adam, who was staying over and would ride in with Raymie in the morning, came up to my deserted room and settled in the big chair. When he had sat there some time, he took a small book from his pocket and read a little Dante. The walls of imprisonment fell away. Then Adam observed, as though of a phenomenon, "Too bad you fight it so. I suppose you can't accept it?"

I was able to say, "You mean their not understanding?"

"I mean facts, I suppose; you yourself are just what you cannot forgive them for being—a refuser of reality," said Adam. "The reality is that you are spending yourself trying to convey to others by words an experience which they have not shared. You cannot force them to accept knowledge that will be theirs soon enough."

chapter fifteen

Of Eagles

Winter, 1940–41. The soft, repeated snows began. Not the stinging, hissing, storm-driven flakes, but fat, lazy crystals that float down lingeringly, each keeping separate intricate design. It snowed silently, steadily. At four in the morning the commissioner called Kit, and he took the snowplow out on the town roads.

By morning every twig had its burden. The wires were encased, the syringa bush out by the barn had swelled to twice its size, the roofs of all the outbuildings had risen like loaves of bread overflowing their pans. The river disappeared. The snow over the ice made a continuous field from bank to bank. The world shrank. The eye's radius marked off the white circumference, and nothing was there beyond.

At night, shut in this shrouded universe, I listened to another planet. "London," said an English voice speaking close to me in the darkness of my room. "London blitzed again. A total of 4,558 persons killed in Britain in November in air raids."

And what of Paris? England communicated her agony, but what of France? France was silent. Silent were Belgium and Holland; Poland, Norway, Denmark, Greece and Czechoslovakia before them. Fallen out of the orbit of my radio as completely as though they had been excised from this globe, the earth, and gone hurtling into space.

Tacked up on my walls were the maps of the world. In the dim green light of my radio's single eye, I could make out the outlines of the continents. Onto the map I projected the shape of France. Where the voice of France had been, there was nothing. From that dead place on the earth's surface came no waves that carry sound. Were the grey stones of Paris still pink in the evening light? Did the first rays of the morning sun still unveil the dome of Sacré Coeur? Did the bells of St. Germain sound the hours? What had become of the little monkey who used to tip his gold braided hat from the windowsill across the alley behind the Pension de l' Abbaye?

And the students of the law at the *pension* where I once had my plate and weekly napkin, with their elbows and pipes upon the red and white checked cloth as they sang naughty French songs over the last bottle of vin d'Anjou; which ones were dead, who had lost leg, or arm, or eyes? Who were in prison camps, who in labor gangs? Who has disappeared underground? Are there any who deal with the enemy?

The silence of France was impenetrable. The horror was not that the occupied countries were dead, but that they lived and were mute—it has taken this land two months to argue FDR's Lend-Lease. "When they arrested my neighbour I did not protest. When they arrested the men and women in the opposite house I did not protest. And when they finally came for me, there was nobody left to protest," Pastor Niemoeller cried.

To reassure me that the world that so obsessed me still existed out there beyond the gates of the Farm, Adam sometimes brought out political friends of his. In particular, there were Italians to whom life was a state of exile. One of them, Giorgio, Marquis de Santillana, scientist and philosopher, trained in history, a witty and acerb political analyst, spat at Black Shirts and left Italy. Then there was Gaetano Salvemini, who would not remain a senator in an Italian Senate that disgraced itself in cowardice. He was a vocal and uncompromising foe of Italian Fascism in all its aspects. Edgar Mowrer had once told me that so powerful was Salvemini's voice in exile that Mussolini hated and feared him more than all the others. Bruno Zevi, who often came out to the Farm with Adam, was a young exile from Fascist Italy, a design student; his artistic and intellectual gifts presaged his career as a great architect, historian, and critic. He was an idealistic socialist with a philosophical point of view. "Freedom," Bruno echoed, "is the recognition of necessity." Adam also brought out his friend, the Russian professor of philosophy. And once there was a great conspiracy between Adam and Laurie to kidnap Edgar Mowrer, who was speaking in Boston. They missed him. (Oh! He would certainly have come. His daughter, that golden girl who was now an undergraduate at Radcliffe, did come.) To compensate for their failure in bringing my old boss to the Farm, Adam and Laurie brought me a live duck. He joined the Farm company of animals and was promptly named "Edgar." Often, Adam would bring out Lennie Bernstein, who would play endlessly at the still untuned piano; in honor of Spain, and of me, Lennie played the *Malagueña*. Adam and Lennie delighted in performing skits for all the Farm, especially a series of satirical political dialogues and songs which they had learned from Adolf Green.

Spring, 1941. "This is London," intones the voice on the radio, "April 11th. Coventry blitzed. The cathedral destroyed. Father forgive." By early spring, I could get outside the door. This was considered a great victory. But I knew what the family did not: that I was tied to a small area circumscribed within the boundaries of the Farm, not only by weakness, but by fear. The extent of my freedom was the diameter of an imprisoning circle about the house, as though I were tethered, as a calf is. I dared not allow myself to be drawn too far from the house: room, bed, held all security. If I were to attenuate that safety, stretch too far the distance between myself and sanctuary, I might never again reach it.

I was frightened of everything. A sudden flight of blackbirds from the bare limbs of the maples by the lane startled my heart into frantic pounding. From every side life leaped out at me, attacked; I started this way and that. I sneaked out of the house, shame-faced, bones with no marrow in them, moving only under the compulsion of the shame of not moving; until it was too much to go another step and I fled back to the house.

Never mind, I consoled my pounding heart, I will yet walk that path in the wood which Adam and I had taken in another lifetime, and climb the hill, unbelievable feat, and gain the grove. I will! I will!—one persistent purpose that I would not allow to be driven out by fear.

The dogs, since they had discovered that I alone of the members of the household could be counted on to make the circuit to the woods' wall and back, had become my devoted companions. We established a regular walk, Jock, Bing and I: down the river path, across the still frozen furrows of the lower pasture, and as far as the woods' wall. Jock stuck his nose close to the loose earth and rushed here and there, sniffing. He was a burrowing creature, his gum line shiny black, his teeth small, white and sharp for tearing; when he found a good smell his coat bristled. Bing, a big, loose, undulating, larrumphing puppy, rushed up and down the field, in bounds and flying leaps. He watched Jock smelling busily and pretended to smell, promptly forgot, galloped in an ecstatic raid in the opposite direction, and returned at full charge. But I went slowly across the field, from furrow to furrow. Beyond the wall the path ran into the woods. The stones of the wall were smooth, fine for sitting on.

Jock studied my progress with his bright, unblinking eyes, judging whether this was to be a long pause on the wall or a short one. And then he curled up to wait. Bing crashed about in the underbrush.

Across the river in the pine hills a pair of eagles regularly made their spring return. The Farm was very proud of their presence, now and again catching a glimpse of one soaring in the distance. I did not join in this ornithological delight. Laurie had assured me that the eagles had never been seen on this side of the river. Nevertheless, I kept a wary eye upon the big birds' gymnastics; now one of them was circling, a tiny spot in the high sky.

In Spain the hawks and their heavy-bellied kin, the vultures, had swept round and round above the valleys. The dead upon those Pyrennean slopes were found first by the sharp eyes of those gliding birds. Sometimes the flying specks proved to be not birds but metallic creatures great of wing, heavy of body, full of threat, shooting across the sky with undeviating directness. Sitting upon a New England wall, I saw again, like a camera image, the clouds of black smoke billowing, heard the tearing as the earth rose up. I remembered the cow who was grazing there, and then was not there. I remembered the rain of rock and sod and bits of steel, the bits of flesh and bone and cloth, when the planes made a direct hit.

I had not taken my eyes from the eagle. Without seeming to move a wing, he had sailed across the distance and, now ponderous, portentous as the plane carrying bombs, he soared above the river. The sweat of an old fear sprang out on my skin, my palms were cold and moist.

The land betrays you, the land that speaks of continuity. You cannot bring yourself to believe in the interruption to living that the plane carries, the irrelevant death. The rise and fall of the land is gentle, formed and reformed in timeless erosion. The roots of the trees spread wide and deep. The river works in its bed on the way to the sea. Not in any way are you warned of danger. If any sign were to foretell: if the wind were suddenly to hush; if the light were, by a flicker, to warn the sight; if the clouds were to scud; if the trees were to bend. The air rends. The earth rocks. The wound in the bosom of the land spews smoke: earth, rock, steel. The birds, like you, unsuspecting, rise screaming. The hills echo, and smoke clings about the pit.

I sat upon that New England wall waiting for the sickness to pass. Jock looked up at me with a curious eye. Why does she sit there smelling of fear, when there is no danger his wiggling nose warns him of? But Jock, an old philosopher, shrugs; since it is obvious the girl will stay there for some time, quivering and sweating, he growls once to scare off anything he might have overlooked, then shuts the lid over the one inquisitive eye he had opened, and dozes.

A late March freeze: the dogs were waiting in the fireplace room—Jock with his head on a pillow on the couch, ear twitching and one beady eye snapping open at the least creak of the stairboard; Bing, on the floor on his back, his paws bent at the hinge in an ungainly flap, like the Mock Turtle's flippers in *Alice*. To their mutual disgust, I lingered to watch Kathy and Laurie bring the laundry in from the line, the sheets stiff as boards, dungarees and pajama pants standing up by themselves. The basket was useless; the clothes had to be carried through the doors like so much lumber. Kathy and Laurie bent the frozen sheets into big squares to maneuver them through the doorways. Their woolen gloves stuck to the iced cloth. Noses and cheeks and chins flamed. They put the stiff wash on the rack or stood the pieces over the register, where slowly they wilted.

When I made the first, tentative move to the door, the dogs flung themselves upon me. "All right," I said, pushed into going. "Hey you two, we can't all three go through this door at once." I was wrong, we did, and were simultaneously ejected.

This time, this extraordinary first time, I crossed the wall and penetrated into the wood, keeping myself in a state of somnambulistic balance. I knew the significance of what I was doing, but I knew, as well, that if I let myself respond, quicken, even to the emotion of relief, of victory, the numbness that allowed this miracle to occur would vanish and fear would rush in and rule again. I tried not to think, tried not, by even a change in rate of breathing, to prejudice the progress which I made with each forward step.

And so I came steadily to the place where the path opened out, and into the swamp where stood the hollow broken skeleton of the old pin oak. That I had come as far as this without a thud of terror acted as an opiate; and although I was not until now aware of it, the tension with which I had been holding my arms and neck relaxed. I drew a breath.

The dead trunk of the oak was silver, its bark long since peeled. The eagle, too, was silver, so warped and ungainly, his head hunched between his huge shoulder blades, that at first I did not see him separately from the tree. I was trying to move smoothly so that my cracklings and treadings over the underbrush would not disturb my tenuous equilibrium. Until this moment I had not disturbed the eagle. But now, with a thrust of his feet, with a flap of the vast spread of his wings, he sprang up from the hollow of the oak tree. His ugly neck hung down, his beak curved in a dreadful sharpness. Also hanging, curled in predatory readiness, were the talons, so huge that they seemed to belong not to a bird, but to a winged half-monster. The only sound he made was the heavy flap, flap, flap of those enormous wings. I turned to stone.

To gain altitude the eagle flapped in circles, the size of his circles limited by the swamp clearing, too small a space for that appalling spread of wing. *Wheresoever the carcass is, there will the eagles be gathered together.*

Adam found me in the snow, half-hidden under the scrub of a blueberry bush. He might have passed by, had not I, at the sound of the crunching of his purposeful footsteps, raised a tear-begrimed face. When he saw me, he squatted on his heels and said sharply, "You're all right?"

I always took Adam's appearance for granted. When he was there things were right; wrong only when he was not there. I moved now to sit up. He saw that there was nothing to hold me there: nothing broken, and I didn't seem ill. He took out his handkerchief and wiped the tears.

"Damn fool," he said, very cross with the fright I'd given him. "Sitting in the snow. Here. Blow."

"It's the eagle!" I exclaimed. "He was right here with me in the swamp."

"Well," said Adam, brushing me off and finding my scarf and lost glove and putting me together again. "What eagle?"

I looked up, as I had not dared to do before. Far, far above in the sky, the great bird was still spiraling.

"Come along." Adam, having looked, started me back down the path, propelling me in the direction of home. "It's a bald eagle. Ben Franklin used to say he didn't see why the bald eagle had been chosen the symbol of his country. The bird's a vulture." We had come to the wall. The eagle's circles now included the open field. "It's a myth," Adam stopped at the wall. "There's not much truth about eagles carrying off babies and lambs. And besides, you'd be a little heavy, even for an eagle. Is that what you were doing under the bush?" He had put his arm about me and his voice was less serious.

Still sniffling, I became aware that the panic at finding the eagle and myself together had faded. I began wondering what I'd been afraid of; I'd met the eagle face to face and he was only a bird. I was not afraid of a bird. It was not fear of a bird that had, all that late winter and spring, tied me to my small circle of safety.

Adam had been watching the eagle's high circling. "He looks like a bombing plane," he said. "Is it the planes you're afraid of? The planes that came over and you ran from, ran for cover—in Spain?" I remembered lying at the bottom of a shell hole with Ed Taylor, how I'd thrust a branch of pine, as if it were a shield, between us and the machine-gun in the nose of the diving plane. Remembering still more, a different image came in my mind, and suddenly I spun around and pounded on Adam's chest.

"Aguilera!" I cried. "The press chief!"

"And Spanish for 'eagle,' " mused Adam and picked me up and sat me on the wall. He got over the wall himself and I slid down into his arms, my heart pounding as he held me close. He kissed me, took my hand, and we walked across the open field together.

He had come only for a brief hour's visit, then went away again.

It was after this that I began to uncover, not all at once but as one peels the layers of an onion, the sources of fear—the unreal fear of the eagle, the old fear of the plane and the true fear I had so long suppressed: fear of the enemy.

There came a day of thaw and freeze and thaw. Everything threw back the bright sun; the world glittered: the wet fields, the ice still drifting on the river and the ice cakes piled against the shore; the thin glaze of ice on the tree trunks, on each separate twig, on the wires strung between the telegraph poles; the icicles melting at the roof gutters; the ice casing the porch railing, the frost on the panes. As the sun grew warm everything melted and dripped; everywhere there were noises of melting and dripping. The air was full of restlessness. The firs that had been bent, caught and trapped, as the snow settling down had frozen, snapped up again, shaking themselves. Twigs crackled. Water dripped onto beds of brown leaves. The river current worked ceaselessly against the ice from below, and the sun worked from above; between the two the ice creaked and cracked, grinding and breaking.

The dogs, filled with excitement, ran through the woods smelling new scents unfrozen in the melting world, their ears pricked up by the incessant noises.

I was intolerably restless, until, as gently and gradually as the changes surrounding me, I began to understand the changes within me. The ice was breaking up inside me, too. The persistent and at first imperceptible warmth had penetrated through layer after layer of feelings that had been wrapped up in fear for so long. That cold numbness was breaking up. It is the same for emotions as for a leg or an arm into which circulation returns. I did not know that I had

213

been iced in fear. You do not feel a frozen limb; the pain becomes unendurable only when feeling returns. Now I recognized the unease, the stirring within me, for what it was. I was coming alive again.

One day in early April, Kit rode the tractor down to the lower meadow and turned that land over to get the sun. The furrows were deep and clearly cut. The earth smelled rich with life. And out of the past I saw a meaning that had all this time been buried under my fear. The furrows would be turned again and again, this year and the next and who knew how long after that. I remembered with such terrifying clarity the shell holes which, ugly and barren, had showed their open wounds to the sky; they would grow green again, just as this earth would, and grass would spring up again. The cycle would not stop, could not be stopped. In my terror I had come to credit the planes with more power than they possessed. Whatever the bomb load, those planes did not have the power to damage life itself but only some part of it and only for that instant in time. Season unto season, seed unto tree unto seed, the process continued. Ever and forever the resistless progression went on, a cycle of which I, too, my living and my dying, were part. When I knew this, I was no longer mesmerized. The fear melted.

Early summer, 1941. Each weekend Norah fussed because they hadn't got the peas in yet; there never would be peas for the Fourth of July. Kit was figuring on how much land he was going to plant with potatoes and on putting down an onion crop. He'd give Norah her danged peas, but first the family'd got to get them potatoes cut and laid in. Take them a couple of weekends before they got round to peas.

All over the house the windows and doors were thrown open. More and more often now, as each day passed, they were not shut again; house and family were turned inside out.

December, 1941. The fall that year was exceptionally long and dry. Days succeeded each other without the sharp contrast of the wild northeasters which leave a changed landscape. The autumn coloring faded by unobservable degrees. Grasses dried up, grew brittle. Leaves trembled with sheer weariness and fell one by one. There was an illusion of timelessness. In New England, days such as these are known as weather breeders; yet the weather did not change.

A still, bright day, as warm as if it were Indian summer though this was already early December, the family sat about the big front room after Sunday dinner. The door to the porch stood open and the wasps, still full of vitality, were buzzing. Some of the family listened to the Sunday concert. Laurie and Debby and Brian on the floor were reading the funnies, Timmy and Norah playing cards and half hearing the music. Kathy off in a corner, not apart, yet not too close, was knitting. Donny had swiped the car and gone off to the village.

On that Sunday of the 7th of December the radio announcer's voice began the war:

"We interrupt . . . fifty to a hundred planes in a raid over Hawaii. Two shot down carry the emblem of the Rising Sun . . ."

I did not at first take in the significance of the word Hawaii. And then suddenly I spun about: "Listen!"

Hazel rushed in calling, "Children, the Japanese have bombed Hawaii!" The announcer went on, " . . . return you now to our regular program. We will interrupt the program . . ." A sigh of held breath released went through the room.

"The waiting is finished now!" I walked round and round in fury. "We're all in it."

"All except the Irish," Kathy tossed her head. Hazel had been standing by the window looking out at the river shining under the warm December sky. "But the Japanese said they wanted to go on talking," she protested. "Why, it's so DISHONEST!"

Kit had been out on the tractor all day, over on the back fields of town. He'd been doing a lot of the fall plowing for the farmers around. He'd heard the news but none of the details. First off, he wanted something hot to eat. Then he got the stiffness worked out of his hands, dry and cracked. He sat himself in his chair and stretched out his long legs, careful not to shake the mud that caked his boots onto the rug. Now he was ready for the radio: "We take you to Manila. Go ahead, Manila." Laurie sat at her special table with the solitaire cards spread out in front of her, not noticing whether the game was coming out. "Go ahead, Manila," she urged, "Come in Manila, what's the trouble with you, Manila? We haven't been able to get Manila all day," she complained to Kit.

Back and forth across the dial they traveled, picking out the news roundups and the broadcasters in whom Kit had the most confidence. He sat and listened and said nothing, getting the picture complete in his mind, his face grim at the casualties and the ships lost and the rumored landing at Wake.

When all the news on the air had been sponged up and there was nothing left but Sunday night entertainment, Kit stood up, "Well," he said, "it was coming. We're in it. Some say as how we were caught off balance. But the ones that will holler loudest, they're the ones said this country couldn't ever be attacked."

Donny came back from town full of the boys' plans. "Joe and I have decided to join up tomorrow," he announced. Laurie's heart stared out of her eyes. "All you can get into at seventeen is trouble," she said. But Kit denied this as a matter of truth, "You can get into the Navy." That was all Donny needed: "Can I join the Navy, Father? I want to be a captain so I can make Bilson swab the decks." Bilson was his English teacher. "Come on, Pop, can't I join up with the Navy?" Kit didn't answer and Donny, looking at Laurie, dropped the subject. Debby ran in, breathless, to demand, "What'll we do, Daddy Kit, if a German plane comes over?" "Turn off the lights and go to sleep." Kit went off to bed. But Donny promised her, "I'll take my .22 and go out and pop at him." He picked up his little dog and went off to his own room, talking to Jock, "Poor Jockie can't go into the Army. Jockie's got flat feet."

From the radio floated the strains of the "Star Spangled Banner."

When all the family had gone to bed, I could not settle down. My past was now their present. It had come. And yet nothing had changed. Laurie would make the war a new game. "Come in, Manila! Kit! Manila won't come in." And Hazel would scold the forces of immorality.

I, observer, sat down and wrote out what everyone had said, as though these bits and pieces of family chatter would some day constitute a historical document. At least it gave me something to do. In the midst of writing I went into the hall and stood looking at the phone in order to make it ring. If it rang, Adam's voice would mark the significance I demanded for this moment in time. But the phone remained a telephone, a black receiver on its cradle.

The letter Adam had been writing while I stared at the telephone arrived a day or so later.

"The danger is," he wrote,

that you will confuse this war with your war; the danger is that you will have the absurd idea that now everyone will understand what you have been talking about.

You, too, are a child of the Millenium, no less than Polly and Hazel! You believed it necessary only for this moment to come, for the war to be declared, for the price in suffering to be underwritten—and all the world, in a revelation no less spontaneous or mystical than Rory's social gospel, would see the truth: that the purposeful perversion of the individual, toward whatever ends, whether that end be considered for their common good or to protect the privilege of the few—this is the great and final evil. The evil that destroys victim and inquisitor alike.

You and I believe that this is the great lesson of our time: the use of evil means for whatever end is sin whether practiced for the freedom of the worker or for the rights of the rich!

But you are bound for great heartbreak if you persist in deluding yourself that here in this single contest the issue will be settled forever. You have been convinced that once the war was joined and each man went off soldiering, he would understand that he is his brother's keeper. You thought then Brian would stop being Brian, and become a philosopher. Walt and Donny and Timmy would rise up and drive the wicked from the earth because they knew them by their acts. From now on everyone would practice brotherhood and there would be an approximate peace on earth, good will to men!

On the contrary, at the moment of its starting the war has already lost the qualities with which you endow it. The moment it started it ceased to be the great moral issue, the battle for the rights of the individual soul—which is the war you fight, the war you are urging the Farm to fight. Now the generals take over. You have given over your battle into the hands of the professionals, who are concerned with winning the war, not with Brotherhood or the dignity of the individual.

What each man will bring home from the war will be the particular knowledge of his own segment of experience. Brian will come home full of how to build bridges under shell fire, and Walt will come home talking about airplanes and Donny will come home clever in the techniques of radio communication (that is, if they come home)—and Hazel will think that her boys have conquered and that evil is dead.

You must not let yourself be distracted. You must keep your eyes on what is truth to you. You saw the truth in Spain and heard it in the voice of Aguilera who called the masses "pigs!" You knew him as your mortal enemy. Enemy of everything that has gone to make you; the people of the Farm, whether they know it or not.

P.S. I have never written so long or so passionate a letter in my life. I sound like you. I must be upset. Because I am in the world—you can never be alone again. Because you are in the world I am no longer alone. This is true whatever becomes of you, or of me. You know it, and you must never forget it. Only then will you never be afraid again.

I used to be frightened of dying. Not because I was afraid of death; but because I wanted to leave something behind to show that I had been. Something I had touched.

When he came on Saturday he was, for all his wisdom, as wretched, torn, as I. The dusk settled by pulse beats, darkening my room. Adam was a black shape moving about; sitting down, getting up, too edgy for chair, stool, or bed. For the first time I saw him bitter. "I'm as great a fool as you are! I don't want to stay in my laboratory, behind my books. Why must I stay while they go out? To teach the Navy? They need teaching, but must it be I? I too want to be part of the action, to risk what I am, for what I believe!"

chapter sixteen

A Castle Is Not a Home

Spring, 1942. A lean and wretched season.

The Farm no longer nourished me. I no longer wanted to share its life; I resisted its blandishments. The house could no longer hold me. I would take an armful of books and go off with them to my private place in the dell. The bluettes made a carpet on the grasses. There I threw myself down and longed for Adam to appear and berated myself for longing.

When he did come, one weekend late in May, he diagnosed what ailed me.

It happened once again that I had spent the nights of that weekend sitting up against my pillows. I had learned that release was always to be only a probation; that not weakness, but strength was transient; well-being, a phenomenon never to be trusted. In the night, jailed in my body, battered at, beaten at, convulsed with coughing, I cursed myself and acknowledged the semblance of freedom of my good days as illusion. I was nurturing a dream.

The moon, sliding through the watery clouds, shone into the room. I could see on the big chair the ungainly pyramid of Adam's luggage, his camera and tripod. Among the combs and brushes on the bureau was a pile of his books. His hat sat jauntily on a candlestick. The room was full of his presence. If you love the man, how can you bind him to such a burden as you will always be? A fine strong wife you'd make a man, half-tied to a bed!

But when on that Sunday night he turned to leave, all innocent of storm (or was he?), he got no further than the stairs before a hail of slippers showered down upon him. It is significant that though the books were handier—I threw none. He would never have come back if I had mistreated a book. He picked up the slippers, set his bookbag down upon the stairs, and came back. "Well, now," he said, entirely puzzled, "what was that?"

"Oh, you damned and utter fool . . . why don't you *say* something!" came muffled from the bed, I curled up in a heap, face down.

"Say something? What shall I say?" He sat beside me.

"Never mind! If you don't *know*, then there isn't anything to say anyhow."

Adam, in measured commentary: "I just don't understand women." If I had not been quite so gone in pity for myself and had looked up and seen his face, I might have taken comfort.

A few days later there arrived, without any word for what the sending meant, the ring he always wore. And on the next weekend Adam came back to the Farm with a decision made.

"What's wrong with you," Adam pronounced, "is that it's time for you to have a life of your own. You can't live forever on other people's lives, however full of love they are. We'll begin by building you a house of your own. Then you can get away from all the distraction of Laurie living her day and Hazel living hers and can work out your own day. We'll rebuild the Castle for you."

The men who were at home set to work with him, sometimes Kit and old Mr. Brown, sometimes on Sundays Raymie too. Now and then Donny would help. Donny and Adam sank the posts for a new fence around the Castle. Donny would sink one and then lie down and rest. But when they'd put the stove in and tarred the roof, and Adam had covered the whitewashed walls with maps, installed my typewriter and hauled down all the musty-smelling books on Humanity from the shelves in the big front room, it was Donny who saw to it that I had a flag to run up on a pole in the front yard I shared with the chickens. That done, he went back to the house to rest, the tools scattered in the grass.

Adam and I were alone in the Castle, planning and building. We chose maps for papering the walls. The bookcases found their places. I picked the color I wanted for the outside trim. If I had once paused long enough to think things through, I might have recognized that my delight in rebuilding the Castle sprang from a misbegotten source. The house was being built so that I could live a life apart from the Farm. It never occurred to me that I would not be sharing it with Adam.

Adam had painted the rocking chair blue; now he tested it for dryness and then sat in it and faced me. "Do you like your house?" I nodded. Adam looked curiously hurt as though he had used the pronoun *your* to test me, and my pleasure now excluded him. "Well, it's all yours," he said and got up and went to the screen door and put himself on the other side of it. "Now latch it," he said. "See, you're all safe and secure."

I was inside, Adam out; we stood on the opposite sides of the door. "I won't latch it," I said. "Why, you'd have to knock to get in!"

"Look," he said, talking to me through the screen, "I've got to tell you something; I'm going away. I can't tell you what it is or where or for how long and you're not to ask questions but instead to stay in your little house and write a book."

The Castle of the moment before abruptly returned to being an old chicken house.

Adam was aware how utterly crestfallen I was. "Hey," he said, "I'm ashamed of you. Just because you're on that side of the door and I'm here outside, about to go off and do what I'm best trained for in this rotten war, you weep as though you were deserted and had nothing to give unless—like Kathy—you learn to knit. Well, no one needs your knitting. You have a very important job to do, one that has never been done and needs to be done now more than ever. Don't you know that? You weep because you were not successful as a prophet. Well, whoever was? Your Dorothy Thompson?

"You're a reporter, not a prophet. You're the one who compiles the record, the story that will make it clear why some will have died, and that story will be what honors them. You're sitting right on top of one of the great stories, right here, the story of the Farm—of Rory and Hazel and of Philip and Polly, and of all their generation, of the ideals and disappointments of their lives. Right now the world is tearing itself apart in its effort to reject their simple or even simplistic utopian view of life. But still, don't you see, still, they implanted values of human existence and coexistence that have grown into a permanent legacy to all of us. Anyone who has the time and the energy could compile the factual record, Frances, that's easy enough, just facts and figures. But only someone with your insight and experience could bring out the significance of it all, can sift through those cold facts and reveal their meaning to the next generation. That's your job. That's what you can contribute. That's what you *have* to contribute."

He paused, looking at me steadily through the screen while his words sank into me, slowly. Then he went on. "The books that tell the story are all there, dusty and never read, hidden behind the sofa in the big Front Room. Whether anyone ever reads them or not, they contain the commandments under which all of you have lived.

Rory is still alive. You're strong enough to get to New York now; go to him, find out what he has to say of this final testing of his great beliefs. Others are in New York, too: Walter Binger, Carl Binger, and all of those who were nourished on the ideals of the early Farm. They can tell you what you need to know."

Adam ran his fingers across the screen separating us. His voice had lowered with intensity. "If a world without the obligations of brotherhood is anathema to your soul, tell us why. Speak for the Farm, through all the Farm documents and accounts of life. You *have* a voice. Use it. Speak and prove finally why we fight this war. That's your true purpose. If you don't accomplish this goal, only then will you really have been defeated."

In that vacant world, I sat all summer within the Castle in which Adam had closed me up. From the ideas fixed in print on the pages of the old books in front of me, I would lift my head and look blindly out of the windows, staring through today, back to the Farm peopled by another time. If I willed hard enough, I felt as if I were summoning the youth of the men and women who now had gone on somewhere else, grown plump, successful; or lean and beaten; or neither, but comfortable and commonplace. Here their forgotten selves were still alive, disciples of the gospel of those dusty books.

Everyone at the Farm became part of the team in the new game. Donny carried piles of dusty books and browning magazines from the living room and the attic to my Castle. Laurie told me about her life in Pittsburgh and about the family's early life; Hazel about her days with Rory, and the Farm idyll. There came a day when, after much internal wrestling, she turned over to me that precious box of letters from the "boys" of the Farm. "Here," she said. "These are for you. I want you to have them. They're part of the Farm's story and that's what you're writing. They're now yours." This treasured gift was a moving one, for I knew what it meant to Hazel to part with these symbolic evocations of the great days of the Farm. Three days later she gave me a second gift, Rory's carbon copy of his history of the Christian Commonwealth. Now that everyone had begun to open drawers, trunks, and boxes in the attic in the search for the materials of history, she had found the true account of the community whose principles still governed us. Later Rory himself would give me a copy of his unpublished autobiography. These are the documents with which—staying as close to the story as love allows—I have attempted to reconstruct this history.

221

Polly, who was usually delighted when anyone cleaned out anything and who usually wanted then and there to make a bonfire, now, contrary to her nature, searched the attic for collections of curled and fading photographs and shoeboxes stuffed with letters and carried those off down the lane to me in the Castle. She was contributing to Research.

She left the letters to my deciphering, but the pictures enchanted her. She promptly sat down on the hooked rug, which floated like a small flat island on the painted blue of the Castle floor, and dumped the pictures into her lap. From that heap Polly took them up one by one. It was as if the first era of the Farm had continued to exist for her somewhere in time and space and now she had only to show me a faded snapshot to attest the idyll. "There," she said, offering a photograph of a ring of women in bloomers lying on the grass about a young man declaiming with one arm outthrust, "You see! The Farm was never like this again! They used to be the most wonderful people." I grinned. She meant that all who had come since she had grown up were ordinary human beings.

The world spun. The Farm family, like actors assigned to a new play, took up their roles.

The town paper carried two full pages of draft numbers. Debby flopped down on the couch with one page and Kathy bent over the other. When they came to the names of boys in the town, they read them out loud and called their numbers.

"Brad and Henry Swap . . . that meant both Swap boys. There won't be any men left at home in that family." "Roger Fulke," read Debby. Hazel protested, "He can't be old enough. Why, he was a small boy with a runny nose last time I saw him."

Kathy said, "Brian O'Donoghue . . ." There was dead silence, and then the children made a sudden rush. "Where? Where?" Debby demanded. "Show me." The kids crowded round. Donny said, "I want to see Brian's number. Where?" "Oh!" said Hazel. Kit came in and all the family, except Kathy, announced in concert, "Brian's number's there, Kit, Kathy found it."

"There it is." Kathy pointed to the small line of print as if it were an enemy.

Hazel went into the attic and brought down the instructions from which she and Kathy had knitted helmet-liners and socks for that other war. There were pictures to go by that showed the finished garment, old-fashioned, bulky, clumsy. It would be difficult for a man to move quickly in that stuff. "It's not much the same, is it?" said Hazel nostalgically.

222

"It was all right in those days as long as it was warm," grumbled Kathy. "It wasn't complicated like this new stuff is. They didn't need little doors in their helmets in that war."

Another few months and Donny would be gone, too. Laurie had watched the day approach on the calendar. But whatever life cost it was never to bankrupt Laurie. She had raised one family. Before Donny left, in uniform, there would be a new baby.

Raymie had gone away from us, too, but his place was in the little graveyard above the bank of the river under the gnarled and stubborn pine, so like his own spirit. He had killed himself by overwork at the lathe in the mill to prove that he, whom the world thought less than a man, could do the work of two.

I could not stay inside the gates of the Farm any longer. Like the young men of the years of the idyll, who one by one gave up the poetry of this place to embrace reality, I, too, had to leave. There was nothing more for me here. Life was outside these gates. Here I would starve from malnutrition; would atrophy for lack of the exercise that comes only with struggle. And I had to display that I was no patient hen who sat and waited. At least I could go off to New York and take down the testimony of those who had once been part of that early idyll of the Farm, and from them hear their evaluation of the past. Rory's should be the final word. I sent him the first draft I had banged out in the Castle, with all the recollections of the old days.

Polly and Hazel each reacted to this announcement according to her nature. Polly aided and abetted me. If I went off again to conquer the world, any world, I would restore to Polly vicarious adventure. Hazel was aghast—it was too soon, and I might not come back! Nevertheless, between them, they got me to the station.

The train ate up the track. I sat closed into the compartment and watched the countryside slide by the window, I stayed just as I had been deposited, tangled up in the clothes that imprisoned me; not wearing them, the clothes wearing me. Mostly I was involved with the fatigue and pain already locked about me though the journey had just begun. Clickety-clack, clickety-clack, the train sang over its rails. Once there had been a time when that metronome of speed and I were in perfect harmony. Now I was shut into a compartment, and trammelled up by my unaccustomed city clothes as the train rushed off with me. I might be sitting there still but for the porter. He knocked, and since he could not hear me tell him to come in, came in and took command.

Once there had been, between porters and me, the comradeship of initiates adventuring together. They in their sphere and I in mine, complementing each other, delighting in the element we shared. Now I wandered into a strange world, beyond my strength and capabilities. The porter told me what would be good for me and did it as well: took off my coat, put my hat on the rack, brought a pillow, and by his blandishments reduced me from a crusader setting off on her mission to a charge that must be gently returned to the bed from which it had been allowed to escape. And even if I had summoned the will, I could not have protested. I discovered, but only as the train started, that this thin voice of mine, which could barely accommodate itself to normal conversation in a quiet room, could not be heard above the steel on steel of the wheels and the rails. The porter clucked sympathy and encouragement and instructions not to try to talk. He too had once suffered from laryngitis, lost his voice. You see, now he had a voice again! Honey and lemon—hot—that's what I needed.

Thus my self-esteem was diminished by him, the first stranger I met; I was something to be cared for, a responsibility. At Grand Central I was put into a cab, the redcap and the taxi driver handling me like something fragile and without volition. Fine reporter I was! But the achievement of being back in the turbulent city gave me new animation; I sat up and looked out of the window, to take in with hungry eyes the life in the city of which I had once been such a cock-a-hoop part. At the signal, the traffic flowed and halted; all those separate wills regulated by mechanical *stop* and *go*.

There had been a time when I, on these sidewalks, had been victorious over all the turmoil of the city. When I, too, had swung along, fulfilling my own ends within this complex organism. Now the noise shut me in; the movement was too swift a current. In this maelstrom I would never make myself heard or felt: the speed and clamor that had once been my delight, dizzied, buffeted, submerged me. How to make a reporter again of one who cannot control her own body, to say nothing of the element she had been sent out to report? The city moved on with the lights.

In the days that followed I found that even the kinship was gone that I once had had with elevator men and clerks and doormen, with taxi drivers and telephone operators and police, with all the people who, at their posts, personalize the machinery of the city—that too was gone. An urgent voice, breeding the contagion of excitement and exuberant energy, had been my means of contact. By a smile, a touch of the hand, by a word in passing, I had once expressed a kinship with strangers, with all who went on their way around me. I had not even known that I had done these things until now that I was deprived of them. I had never known until now, that such easy exchange was magic. Now, when I lifted up the telephone, my recollection of the voice that once had been mine was so strong that I was astonished to hear the squeak of the voice itself; the operator and I were equally surprised each time the operator said, "I can't hear you, ma'am." Everywhere I went someone had to exert himself to hear, to help.

I would learn that there were many means of contact and that it was not necessary to conquer the world in order to live in it. I could rely upon its kindliness.

Men and women who had once been young at the Farm came to talk with me. This one was now a successful psychiatrist, that one a great artist; one a poet long since disenchanted. One came by cab, one by subway, and one left his car and chauffeur at the curb. They were all harassed by affairs, but each paid his hour, in tribute to the idealism of his youth.

They all spoke of the Farm as if it were no more, as if their Farm had died with the death of belief in their own hearts. At this I smiled; they didn't know that what they had left behind them at the Farm lived independently of them. They had believed in "community," in refusing no one. Now the Farm, without all the words, principles, and ideals, was, in fact, that disparate family, by practice, and by habit.

At the very last I saw Rory. He came in a rush, in a great hurry to waste no time, hugging to his bosom a clipboard with some sheets upon it. His hair was white, his body had settled down into the short, stocky comfortableness of an old man, but energy radiated from him as ever. He was still trying to force life to correspond to his philosophy.

He plumped himself down in the most comfortable chair. "We coddled ourselves," he announced as he leafed through his typed pages, scolding a self who had once been, "with the firm belief that the thing we were doing had great social significance. We were not doing it for ourselves. We were not seeking even spiritual benefit. We were not dominantly conscious of the ambition for personal development. We did not love ourselves; we loved the world. We loved Society. We loved our brothers and sisters everywhere. We gave our lives and with that we gave our property and our labor, to the dictates of this love for our brothers and to our hopes for Society. If you could ask a dozen of the people who went to the Christian Commonwealth or even those who came out to the Farm, what attracted them, I think they would tell you it was the pursuit of universal brotherhood. I remember one morning somebody had gone around chalking the words 'Universal Brotherhood' all over the place! But what we got out of it was personal development. It was a good investment to us as individuals. We would have been heartbroken if you had told us then that that's what it would all amount to, but, if I were a young man, I would do it all over again!" I laughed.

"I'll tell you something," he said: "The Farm was a very considerable expense to me. There was always a big crowd there to be fed and there was great wastefulness. Worse expense of all, however, was the farming activities. We kept from six to eight cows and three to five horses. For years we sold no milk. Gave it away. Then when Hazel finally found it 'necessary' to charge for it, she sold it to people who could not pay. No butter was made. The horses never earned a cent. Everything had to be fed. A hired man was kept the year round. Sometimes two. The products of the Farm up to the time that Laurie was married cost probably more than twice as much as they could have been purchased for in the open market. Sometimes ten times as much. Hazel finally charged her guests ten cents a meal, at least some of them, reluctantly, apologetically.

"One day I took William E. Butler, with whom I was engaged in business, out to the Farm. He was fascinated by the place, by Hazel, by the happy-go-lucky-nobody-worry atmosphere. 'Albertson's Free-for-all,' he called it once, but then—seriously—he said to me that everybody ought to live that way, with no cares or worries. Well, cares and worries came even to Hazel."

I had listened to Rory without comment. I couldn't have stopped him if I tried. But now he had temporarily run out of steam and it was my turn. "You think," I told him, "that just because your version of the millennium, the particular shape in which you conceived it, fell apart, the whole thing was for nothing. Except, as you say, what each of you has gained as a human being. But it isn't true, you know. What you left behind at the Farm has gone on. We who grew up at the Farm were taken in because of your ideas of the larger Family. We aren't as interesting a crew today as those of the early days. Today those of us who come to the Farm do so out of another kind of need, but we are more than ever testament to your 'universal brotherhood.' What you advocated then is now the unconsidered premise of our lives together. We live it at the Farm. Rory, you ought to come and see for yourself."

Rory, much moved as a man dislikes to be, took a clean white handkerchief, and blew his nose hard. "I must go back and see what the Farm looks like. You tell Hazel that I'll be back for a visit one of these days.

"You give me new heart," he said at last. Looking down at his typescript, he went on to its final paragraph: "I have now completed my eightieth trip around the sun, quite without understanding why and particularly without consciousness on my part, yet let me make bold to reaffirm my existence and my heretical faith. I shall soon be freed from Time and Space and Gravitation, but for what, deponent sayeth not. In the meantime, persistently and buoyantly and basically, I believe that good overcomes evil and that the relatively right conquers the relatively wrong."

And then as if to return from such heights to the practical, immediate world in which he better liked to dwell, he put down the clipboard he had been grasping all this time; he had been reading the words he declaimed for my sake from an autobiography. He handed it over to me, a precious document, his autobiography, including—as major events in his life—the Christian Commonwealth and the early days of the Farm. "I want you to have this," he said. "I want you to be able to document your story with real evidence." Then, the air of preacher deserted him; his face turned pink with an old fury, "But the screwdriver, screwdriver! Hazel never understood. She told you it was a screwdriver! It was *not* a screwdriver. It was a very expensive drill! Can you conceive of such carelessness? There was always too much life around that place!"

Of such is the Kingdom of Heaven.

chapter seventeen

The World Is a Wedding

Spring, 1943. One day there came to me in New York an envelope addressed in Adam's script. There was no word, only a photograph of the Castle, no longer a castle, but a little shack adrift before the March winds on the early spring waste of mud, looking indescribably deserted. I knew that Adam, having come back, had gone to the Farm, found the barred, tenant-less Castle, and taken its picture to tell me this.

I packed and went straight home, riding in the train with some of my old sense of fulfilling destiny; at the end of this trip there waited a decision.

Adam met me. He neither took me in his arms nor conveyed in his acknowledgment of this meeting any sense of impending climax. He had been away and I had been away, and we were both back again. About his own mysterious affairs he was equally silent. There was nothing, unless it was in the deeper lines of his face and the weariness in which his shoulders slumped, that indicated the other world where decisions were weighed in lives.

Polly drove us to the Farm to celebrate the voyagers' return, and even Philip came, marking this as a great occasion. It was the last weekend in May again and Hazel said, "This is the weekend we always get the awning up." By the intonation at the end of that sentence Adam knew that Hazel considered his return principally important in relation to the traditional getting up the awning on the 30th of May.

Kit had no time for awnings. He had worked out the fate of being left alone, the sole man on the Farm, by proving the value of his beloved equipment. Mechanized, he now did for the village what

Adam's photo of a barren Farm, with the empty Castle at lower right, about 1942.

once these families each had their own men to do. Every day he swore that he wouldn't turn over another field, but every night he was plowing with his headlights on. When he had a moment to himself he would go up to the One-Step-Down Room, which had again become the nursery, take young Kip out of bed—the baby crowing with delight—and carry him off to explain to him the wonders of machinery.

We sat, the diminished family, around the table. Hazel had before her plate a pile of letters—from Donny in training camp, Walt flying over Italy, Brian in hospital getting strong again after a wound, from Timmy and Pierce.

I was haunted that weekend by the dispirited look of the house. The illusion had finally failed; it was now a stage set left standing with the lights off. It looked as if Hazel had grown tired of making the effort of magic and the house of responding. Forty years of enchantments can wear out the most industrious magician. Saturday morning, walking through the dining room, I stopped short. Something was wrong, something more than the failure of spells. Some actual, physical thing had changed. Not the room. The room seemed

229

bigger and emptier. The table! The table was changed. For the first time in all the years I'd known the Farm, the Table, that huge expanse of board which, even empty, had so eloquently spoken of all those it was ready to serve, had become an ordinary family table. The boards it had needed for forty years had been taken out: it was now collapsed to seat a sensibly sized family of eight.

This was no temporary expedient to close up the ranks of the family while the men were away at war. This was to be final. Some of the boys would return, but not to the Farm. They would perch there for a few hours or days or weeks while they readjusted their lives, but as with the tenants of that earlier idyll, war had only precipitated the inevitable. The slow trickle outward would deplete the family, as each man and woman found his or her own need of life beyond the Farm gates grow stronger than the enchantment within. This would have occurred anyhow, another era having ended. Hazel's moral world had at last collapsed. Her larger family was now swept away.

Donny would come back, but only long enough to give Kit, out of his army savings, an automatic milker for the cows in place of Donny's own two hands. Donny, with the example of his father in mind, would not be caught. He was a little tougher of heart than Kit had ever been, but he too would return to the Farm in his own way.

One weekend, on the way up from the Florida Training School, Jude dropped out of the skies in a small monoplane, landing on the meadow where Roney ran. She was off to join the Women's Ferry Service at a secret rendezvous. Her skin was as brown with winter sun as mine was pale. She was slim and sinewy and capable in her natty uniform. She spoke a language of conquest of skies, seas and continents which so diminished my old adventuring that I thought her a new species of woman. The world now was Jude's, and she was as flatly prosaic about it as an old gourmet who has lost his appetite.

She was everywhere on the Farm those few days; drove the tractor, the truck, or flew her airplane in easy interchange. She took Adam and Kit off in the air, or off on the truck for beer, with no awareness of Laurie and me, groundlings. When she bumped into me, she was gentle and kind, and the next moment had hijacked Adam to come up with her as she flew off on an errand a hundred miles distant.

By Sunday dinner I would not exchange a word with Adam.

When I passed him I took care that neither hand nor arm brushed his. It seemed to me the whole Farm was usurped by Jude's vitality. It was Jude's war, her world, and I had no place in it.

The heavy day, the unaccustomed heat, brewed a storm. Rushing downriver, the thunder, lightning, and the rain broke upon us. I retreated to the quietest corner of the living room. Down the stairs rushed the Goddess, in a bathing suit that showed off her long brown legs, her hair flying. She captured Adam at the living room door, whirled him about and cried, "Come along! Let's go out in it! It's magnificent."

I did not know whether Adam had seen me in the gloom, though the lightning lit up even my corner. I saw him take his pipe from his mouth and smile. I would not, were the world never to move again, have let one word of appeal escape me.

"I always like storms myself, I like to photograph the lightning," Adam's judicial voice pronounced. "But just now I have something to do."

"Do it later." Jude pulled him toward the door. "Come on. Get your trunks." Adam had taken his arm out of her strong grasp and in the next flash I could see that he was still smiling and shaking his head, and I knew that positiveness if Jude did not. He wouldn't change the tone of his voice or the warmth of his smile, but neither would Jude budge him.

"You old mossback!" Jude shouted and the house trembled as doors slammed behind her.

In the next lightning flash there he was standing beside me. "That's right," he said, "that's probably what I am. An old mossback. But so are you. So are we both together," he considered. Then his tone changed to a businesslike approach. "Now tell me what's been wrong with you ever since you got off that damned train. You haven't looked at me once."

Who is to account for the storms that brew in women? Twenty-four hours I had kept a sulky dignity. When I got my tongue moving, I burst out: "I will *not* stay here! I can't stay any longer at the Farm. I can't come back here any more. It's too full of you. I don't know where I'll go—I'll go away from this damned Farm"—I meant, though it remained unsaid, "where everything reminds me of you"—"I'm going to go to Gloucester!"

Adam took his pipe from his mouth as though he'd been jolted by the thunderclap. "You're going to go to Gloucester? Gloucester? What are you going to go to Gloucester for? If you have to go, I suppose it's all right. It will be even harder for me to get to Gloucester than it is for me to get here. I thought we would get married next weekend. If you want your husband traveling back and forth to Gloucester, that's all right with me."

Jude, for whom the intoxication of the elements, if she had to exult in them alone, had somewhat worn off, dashed in through the front door followed by both dogs. She did not see us in the dark and pelted upstairs to change.

"I'm not going to marry you," I said, "I'm going to go to Gloucester." Gloucester, chosen at random, had assumed the proportions of an island of new exile. He should have been able to see that what I meant was that I was going to Gloucester because I had to escape from him, never see him any more. I loved him; therefore I must leave him.

Bing, as wet as Jude but not so beautiful, discovered us and leaned against me, batting me with his sodden plume of a tail. "Look," said Adam, addressing Bing, "beat it, will you?" and he gave the dog a firm push skidding him along the floor to speed his exit. "What's this about not marrying me? Of course you're going to marry me. There never was any question but that you and I would be married. Only I don't understand what you have to go to Gloucester for."

Hazel came into the front room looking for Adam. "Darling," she said, "if you'll help Laurie she could get the awning out of the attic and when the storm is over spread it out. Then we could see if there are any bad rips in it."

"Not now, Hazel dear," Adam said gently. "I have something to do which comes first." This was, I think, the first time he had ever denied Hazel anything.

"Why, Adam," and Hazel left us.

"Now you've done it," I charged. "Now you've gone and hurt Hazel's feelings."

"Damn Hazel's feelings." Adam was beginning to lose his patience. "I'm having enough trouble with one woman and her feelings at a time. What do you want me to do—get down on my knees? I suppose this isn't a good enough proposal for you? Isn't it romantic enough for you? I wish I understood women."

"I wish you did!—I'm not marrying you. I *can't* marry you. I can't darn socks and I'm not strong enough and who knows whether I could ever have all the children you ought to have and you ought to go and marry Jude. And that's why I'm going to Gloucester. Because I never want to see you again."

"*There* you are," said Philip, first putting his head into the room and then coming in. "I've been hoping all weekend, Adam, to get you alone long enough to talk about the situation in Europe."

"For God's sake," cried Adam, "not now, Philip" with such exasperation that Philip withdrew as if he'd been stung. Laurie collided with Philip in the doorway, and unscrambling herself came in. "Have you got a stamp, Adam? I want to write to Donny and I thought you'd mail the letter."

Adam had reached the end of his rope. The world was no longer going to manage him. It was now essential to take the world in hand. With a deliberate gesture he took out his wallet, took from it a strip of stamps, handed them to Laurie and demanded, "Will you get the hell out of here and keep everyone else out and shut that blasted door and keep it shut?"

Laurie looked at me, looked at Adam, seized the stamps, and shut the door firmly behind her. I knew that she posted herself in front of it. No one would get by her.

"This damned place!" Then Adam repeated, almost word for word, what Rory had said decades earlier: "There's just too damned much life around here."

After a moment he went on. "Now, what *is* this? I've waited years. Of course you're not strong—but that's only a mechanical problem. You don't decide to marry or not to marry for mechanical reasons—but for love. First I had to wait because you were determined to go off to cover wars, though there wasn't enough left of you to cover a bed! Then I waited while you got yourself patched up and got strong enough to be able to go back into life and make your own decision. I didn't want you marrying me as a refugee because you thought the world was closed to you. I wanted you to go and see for yourself and come back only if it was your first choice. That's why I said nothing to influence you. That's why I said nothing on the picture of the Castle. You were at a crossroad. You could travel whichever way you chose. Well, you came back. After that it was settled, wasn't it?"

I looked at him sheepishly. "But why didn't you *say* something?"

"What was there to say? You've known all along. I said it all years ago. Do you think anything has changed since?"

And so I was, in my turn, carried across the Castle threshold; and learned that all the world may be contained within four walls and that it is said truly, The World is a Wedding.

epilogue

Another Era

A household cannot function without a pack rat's nest. Here I have my desk, made from a discarded door; who could run a life at one of those pigeon-holed contraptions styled "lady's desk"? On this over-large surface, I can push aside bills, account books, pamphlets on pruning, letters that will never be answered as long as I use my pen for scribbling; dictionaries, thesauri, an alabaster heart my husband gave me long ago; various containers of staples, clips, elastic bands, buttons and stamps; a lumpy clay bowl with splotchy blue flowers, fashioned to hold my pens and pencils and an equally lumpy white bunny-bank to match, which is of no use whatsoever and takes up space, except that I love his ears—made laboriously and anxiously and tinted in pink by the small and clumsy fingers of my daughter when she was in third grade. Mothers are the most obsessive of archaeologists, clinging to artifacts of inhabitants now gone on to active lives elsewhere.

I can hear the squeak of the warped casters of my husband's chair as he propels himself backwards to reach for a reference book from the shelves behind him. Lazy man: he has built himself and his desk into a cave of books so that he may reach out in any direction without laying down his pen.

Between our studies, in the hall, lie the two dogs, formerly so lavishly indulged by their young mistress, now jettisoned in the wake of their departed owner. They wait upon us, now, the only arbiters of their comings and goings, each with one eye open and one eye closed. Neither of us can long withstand that patient, passionate longing and they know it. My husband squeaks back his chair and in an instant they are galvanized into cavorting, prancing ecstasy. The big one, a blonde, propels herself against me in gratitude and stands erect to put her paws around my neck. We hit the doorframe together. The smaller one, although seventy-seven in human years, deliriously waggles her rear like a Ziegfield soubrette. I say to them, struggling to recover my balance, "What makes it more fun if we come too? Can't you take yourselves for a walk? If we're along we only whistle to call you back from sniffing and straying." But this is a rhetorical question. I know and they know that it's the companionship that counts. Each of us, my husband and I, stuffs a leash in a coat pocket.

We amble, the four of us, into the College Yard, where there is room for a free run. The dogs attract the citizens of this self-absorbed world. But we, like the ivied bricks of the buildings, the ancient elms still marking the path junctures, are too familiar to be noticed. We stand off the path as each clot of youth jostles past; one does not argue right-of-way with a juggernaut. Sometimes a student wheels at belated recognition of his professor; or another turns about and comes back politely to greet us because he, or she, has sat at our table.

In their wake we catch scraps of excited talk. A wildly bearded one has announced that he's a "heavenist," a condition we are all to share with him when the wicked state will have vanished. His companion, a pretty, gentle girl, proclaims herself an anarchist. I think of the turn-of-the-century "propaganda of the deed" and those wretched madmen obsessed with the belief that it would take only one great last bomb to explode the selfish, the rich, the blind-to-misery, into a celestial enlightenment. Here in the Yard the less ferocious are chattering about "communal living," about the communities they plan to found, or join.

Oh, that persistent hope of cadres of brothers: as if Fourier had never written; as if Robert Owen had never addressed the joint Congress of the United States to display, to much acclaim, his great plans for the New Harmony (it was to last just two short years); as if Nathaniel Hawthorne had not been seduced from his writing table to tend pigs at Brook Farm.

Subject to a foolish indignation, I want to catch at a scarf-end flying by, seize a busily waggling beard, stop in his tracks one of these newly inflamed idealists, and poking him with a didactic forefinger, the green and sprouting youth, announce "But I was a child of those communities of yours!" They would only extricate themselves with less politeness than did the Wedding Guest pinned by the Ancient Mariner.

Still, we who were born to celebrate the efficacy of absolute good

235

grew up to face ultimate evil. We fought, not for a better world, but to survive at all . . . that there might remain to humanity the possibility—now indulged by our children—to dream anew of the millennium.

The Farm Family: The Third Generation

The Farm always had a hold on everyone who was ever part of the "family." It was not to any of us a community of the theory and practice of faith, nor an organized "phalanx" with each having a civic duty à la Fourier, Owen, or Rory Albertson. Rather, it was an extended diversified family.

We lost Hazel and Kit, but Laurie took Hazel's place, not in the same fashion of irresistable charm but with a charm of her own, which is her constant awareness of all things young and growing. Donny, with his wife and children, came back to the Farm and gave it a new frame of existence. A builder in the manner of his grandfather, he built houses on the Farm for all the families. The first was a home for himself and his own family on the top of the hill overlooking the old white farmhouse and the river. The last of Kit's Pittsburgh family were housed in a bungalow on the side of the hill. The second son of Kit and Laurie, born in the war years, built a house for himself and his wife and family on the riverbank, blending in with the trees. When Donny's daughter grew up, married, and had a child of her own, a private apartment was made for her and her family, converted out of Kit's and Laurie's old back bedroom over the kitchen, the One-Step-Down Room, and a hall bedroom. Laurie would never be alone in the big house.

Donny took over where Kit had left off years earlier, guardian of the village as well as of the Farm. We had all admired Kit in his uniform and leggings, riding a fierce motorcycle as chief of the village police; but Donny drives a huge car equipped with siren and flashing light and marked "Police Chief" and "Fire Chief," filling two town offices to Kit's one.

Dutchie had given over machines for the wild and challenging adventure of lobstering in Maine, and Jude ran a university publication in Florida. Walt, too, had gone off. But Norah and Alice, a school-teaching comrade, made the loveliest of gardens around a house in the village just beyond the Farm gates.

In this now-grown third generation, Debby and her husband are deeply concerned in social work in New York City's poorest district—but their children can hardly wait to spend each summer at the Farm. The daughters of my sister Phyllis (herself a psychiatric social worker), one on the West coast, the other on the East, are professionals in the new personal and family problems of a far more complex society than we ever had imagined. Our daughter, Adam's and mine, is both psychiatrist and psychoanalyst in training and in practice in New York. Even the members of this third generation seem to have taken it for granted that their lives must have something to do with serving people. It is as though this had always been a first commandment.

Sources and Guide to Further Reading

This book is based on manuscript and published writings of the chief characters and their correspondence, supplemented by interviews and recollections concerning them. The following list contains the titles of the main published writings and manuscripts of Ralph Albertson, which are not only the main source of information concerning the Christian Commonwealth and the early days of the Farm, but are valuable records of the hopes, ideals, attitudes, and social programs of the decades before the First World War. They may be supplemented by the books written or edited by my father, Philip Davis, which deal with urban problems, notably those of the immigrants and the working schoolboys. On this topic I found much information in some books from my father's shelves: by Jane Addams, Mary Antin, Edward W. Bok, Samuel M. Jones (the "golden rule" mayor of Toledo), P. Kropotkin, Jacob A. Riis, and Lincoln Steffens. I have not attempted to prepare a comprehensive scholar's bibliography of works dealing with this era. But there are some books that I have found particularly useful, such as Oscar Handlin's book on the immigrants and the studies of American Utopian communities by Arthur Bestor and by W. A. Hinds (still valuable, though written a long time ago). Extremely valuable is Ralph Albertson's own survey of American Utopian ("mutualistic") communities (1936), said by Bestor to be "the most carefully documented of all the general tabulations." Of early primary documents, I have listed the works of Bronson and Louisa May Alcott and Edward Bellamy.

The craft of the foreign correspondent in the 1930s is portrayed in Vincent Sheean's book and in Edgar Ansel Mowrer's autobiography (plus the behind-the-scenes account by his wife Lillian), which may be supplemented by Marion K. Sanders's biography of Dorothy Thompson. I have not listed here Walter Lippmann's many books, but only the collection of his early journalistic pieces, published in 1970. Ronald Steel has written a full-length biography of Lippmann, which does not include the documentary material I have presented concerning Lippmann's experiences as secretary to Mayor Lunn of Schenectady.

Finally, on the Spanish Civil War, the most comprehensive account is given in Hugh Thomas's history. I have included in the following list some books written by reporters of that war: Harold Cardozo, Edmond Taylor, and myself. My earlier book, of course, has a much fuller account of my experiences as a reporter during the war.

Much of the Spanish material in this book derives from *My Shadow In the Sun*, published by Carrick and Evans, 1940. It was a book I wrote on a hospital-allowed typewriter as soon as I could sit up in bed. "Wrote" is not the right word; it was practically regurgitated. Although Red Knickerbocker in *Vogue* called it a classic of what the job of reporting entailed, it always left me feeling incomplete. To understand why I so passionately considered it my war, it was necessary to show what in my background insisted that I work myself nearly to death, and why I was furious with frustration because I couldn't communicate, even to those nearest to me. Thomas Mann, in his preface to *Joseph and His Brothers*, called the Nazi war of which Spain was the *entre'acte*, "the outcome of the fate of the World, of Western civilization, in fact of all that I held dear. . . ."

This book on *Innocence* parallels the agony of his experience as an exile from a Germany to which he would never return. It is a large and powerful examination of "beginnings." "No one remains quite what he was when he recognizes himself." What *Joseph* did for Mann, my struggle with *A Fearful Innocence* did for me. The comparison is sound however the dissimilarity in degree.

Addams, Jane. *A New Conscience and an Ancient Evil*. New York: The Macmillan Co., 1913.
_____. *The Spirit of Youth and the City Streets*. New York: The Macmillan Co., 1910.
_____. *Twenty Years at Hull-House, with Autobiographical Notes*. New York: The Macmillan Co., 1912.
Albertson, Ralph. "A Survey of Mutualistic Communities in America." *The Iowa Journal of History and Politics*, 34, no. 4 (October 1936), pp. 375–444.
_____. "Is Civilization at Stake?" Boston: Universalist Publishing House, 1942. (A pamphlet, reprinted from *The Christian Leader*.)

_____. *Little Jeremiads*. Lewiston (Maine): The Cooperative Press, 1903. ("By Ralph Albertson, 'Philosophicus' in the *American Cooperator*.")

_____. "The Christian Commonwealth." (Unpublished history in typescript. A covering, undated, letter of enclosure to Hazel Albertson bears the address: 1415 Singer Building, New York City. Probably written in the early 1930s.)

_____. "The Romance of Jamesport, Written by Ralph Albertson." *The Riverhead News* (Riverhead, N.Y.), July 14, 1944. (Clipping on file.)

_____. *The Social Incarnation*. Second edition. Commonwealth (Georgia): The Christian Commonwealth, Publishers, 1899.

_____. "Three Aspects of Christianity." (Unpublished essay, typescript: dated June, 1942.)

_____. Untitled, unpublished autobiography. (Rough draft in typescript: New York, 1936. The TS is not dated, but on p. 101 he refers to himself as a "man of 69 1/2.")

Ralph Albertson was the editor and/or the publisher of the following journals: *The Social Gospel* (Ralph Albertson, editor: published in Commonwealth, Georgia, by The Christian Commonwealth, Publishers, nos. 1–41, Feb. 1898-July 1901); the *American Cooperator* (Ralph Albertson, editor: published in Lewiston, Maine, by The Cooperative Association of America, Lewiston, Maine, 1902–04); *The Boston Common* (Ralph Albertson, publisher; Livy S. Richard, editor: published in Boston by the Co-Operative Publishing Company, vols. 1–3, nos. 1–52, 1910–13); *The Twentieth Century Magazine* (B. O. Flower and Charles Zueblin, editors: published in Boston by the Twentieth Century Company. [Ralph Albertson, President; Bruno Beckhard, Treasurer], vols. 1–7, Oct. 1904–Dec. 1912). Complete sets of *The Social Gospel* are to be found in the John Crerar Library (Chicago), the New York Public Library, and the Union Theological Seminary (New York City).

Alcott, Bronson. *Fruitlands*. Compiled by Clara Endicott Sears. With Louisa M. Alcott's *Transcendental Wild Oats*. Boston and New York: Houghton Mifflin Co., 1915.

The quotation, attributed to Bronson Alcott, about his responsibility not for one family but for many, does not appear in the obvious sources. A very similar statement appears in a letter from Emerson to Alcott in July 1842, in which he is obviously paraphrasing Alcott's letter to him, written from London: "Why do you say that the way to the East is by the West? The Family is *good*; the neighborhood is *better*; the Communitorium is *best*."

Alcott, Louisa May. *Transcendental Wild Oats: and excerpts from the Fruitlands Diary*. Selections, with an introduction by William Henry Harrison. Harvard (Massachusetts): The Harvard Common Press, 1975.

Antin, Mary. *The Promised Land*. Boston and New York: Houghton Mifflin Co., 1912. (A children's version was later published by Houghton Mifflin [in 1917?] under the title, *At School in the Promised Land, or The Story of a Little Immigrant*.)

_____. *They Who Knock at Our Gates: A Complete Gospel of Immigration*. Boston and New York: Houghton Mifflin Co., 1914.

Bellamy, Edward. *Equality*. New York: D. Appleton and Co., 1897.

————. *Looking Backward, 2000–1887*. Boston, New York: Houghton Mifflin Co., 1890. (Copyright 1888; my copy bears the bookplate "Library of the Christian Commonwealth, No. 911.)

Bestor, Arthur. *Backwoods Utopias: The Sectarian Origins and the Owenite Phase of Communitarian Socialism in America: 1663–1829*. Second enlarged edition. Philadelphia: University of Pennsylvania Press, 1970.

Bok, Edward W. *The Americanization of Edward Bok: The Autobiography of a Dutch Boy Fifty Years After*. 29th ed. New York: Charles Scribner's Sons, 1924.

Cardozo, Harold G. *The March of a Nation: My Year of Spain's Civil War*. London: Eyre and Spottiswoode; New York: Robert M. McBride & Co., 1937.

Channing, William Henry. *The Life of William Ellery Channing*. Boston: American Unitarian Association, 1882.

Davis, Frances. *My Shadow in the Sun*. New York: Carrick & Evans, 1940.

Davis, Philip. *And Crown Thy Good*. New York: Philosophical Library, 1952.

————, and Mabel Hill. *Civics for New Americans*. Boston, New York, Chicago: Houghton Mifflin Co., 1915.

————, and Maida Herman, eds. *The Field of Social Service*. Boston: Small, Maynard & Co., 1915.

————, and Bertha Schwartz (eds.). *Immigration and Americanization: Selected Readings*. Boston: Ginn and Company, 1920.

————, and Grace Kroll. *Street-Land: Its Little People and Big Problems*. Boston: Small, Maynard & Co., 1915.

Handlin, Oscar. *The Uprooted: The Epic Story of the Great Migrations that Made the American People*. Boston: Little, Brown and Co. (An Atlantic Monthly Press Book), 1951.

Herron, George. *Between Caesar and Jesus*. New York: Thomas Y. Crowell & Co., 1899. ("A course of . . . lectures . . . for the Christian Citizenship League, upon the subject of the relation of the Christian conscience to the existing social system.")

————. *The New Redemption: A Call to the Church to Reconstruct Society According to the Gospel of Christ*. New York: Thomas Y. Crowell & Co., 1893.

Hinds, William Alfred. *American Communities and Co-operative Colonies*. 2nd revision. Chicago: Charles H. Kerr & Co., 1908.

Jones, Samuel M. *Letters of Love and Labor*. Toledo (Ohio): The Franklin Printing and Engraving Co., 1900.

Kropotkin, P. *Memoirs of a Revolutionist*. Boston and New York: Houghton, Mifflin and Co., 1899.

Lippmann, Walter. *Early Writings*. Introduction and annotations by Arthur Schlesinger, Jr. New York: Liveright, 1970.

Mowrer, Edgar Ansel. *Germany Puts the Clock Back*. Rev. ed. New York: William Morrow & Co., 1939.

————. *Triumph and Turmoil: A Personal History of Our Times*. New York: Weybright and Talley, 1968. (Autobiographical.)

Mowrer, Lillian T. *Journalist's Wife*. New York: William Morrow & Co., 1937.

Parsons, Frank. *The City for the People.* Philadelphia: C. F. Taylor, 1900.

————, with the assistance of Ralph Albertson. *The Railways, the Trusts, and the People.* Philadelphia: C. F. Taylor, 1905. (For other works by Frank Parsons, see the "Biographical Index.")

Passmore, John. *The Perfectability of Man.* New York: Charles Scribner's Sons, 1970.

Peck, Bradford. *The World a Department Store: A Story of Life Under a Coöperative System.* Lewiston (Maine): Bradford Peck, 1900.

Reed, John. *Ten Days That Shook the World.* Harmondsworth (Middlesex: England): Penguin Books Ltd., 1966. (1st ed. 1926.)

Riis, Jacob. *The Battle with the Slum.* New York: The Macmillan Co., 1902.

————. *The Making of an American.* New York: The Macmillan Co., 1918.

Sanders, Marion K. *Dorothy Thompson: A Legend in Her Time.* Boston: Houghton Mifflin Co., 1973. (Reprint, Avon Books, 1974.)

Sheean, Vincent. *Personal History.* Boston: Houghton Mifflin Co., 1934. (Sentry Edition, 1969.)

Shepard, Odell. *Pedlar's Progress: The Life of Bronson Alcott.* Boston: Little, Brown and Co., 1937.

Steel, Ronald. *Walter Lippmann and the American Century.* Boston, Toronto: Little, Brown and Co. (An Atlantic Monthly Press Book), 1980.

Steffens, Lincoln. *The Autobiography of Lincoln Steffens.* New York: Harcourt, Brace and Co., 1931.

Taylor, Edmond. *Awakening from History.* Boston: Gambit, 1969.

Thomas, Hugh. *The Spanish Civil War.* New York: Harper & Row, 1961. (Harper Colophon Books, 1963.)

Wells, H. G. *The Outline of History.* New York: The Macmillan Co., 1924.

Whitaker, John. *And Fear Came.* New York: The Macmillan Co., 1936.

Biographical Index

The following alphabetical roster gives brief biographical information concerning the chief public or historical persons mentioned in the book. The publications of many of them are listed in the section of *Sources and Guide to Further Reading*. Page numbers following entries indicate major references in the text. For help in preparing these brief biographies, I am greatly indebted to Mina Carson.

JANE ADDAMS (1860–1935). American social settlement worker and peace advocate. Founder (with Ellen Gates Starr) of Hull-House in Chicago in 1889 and its resident director from the foundation until 1935. Jane Addams was president of the International Congress of Women (1919) and was awarded the Nobel Peace Prize in 1931 (sharing the prize with Pres. Nicholas Murray Butler of Columbia University). She and Gerard Swope (q.v.) arranged for Philip Davis to go the University of Chicago and to Harvard. She sponsored and encouraged Ralph Albertson in the days of the Christian Commonwealth. (*pp. ix, 16, 17, 24, 35, 45–46, 75, 83*)

RALPH ALBERTSON (1866–1951). A Congregational minister and social reformer who, in later life, was active in the "cooperative" movement. Studied at Oberlin College and Theological Seminary 1888–91. He founded and managed a Utopian colony, the Christian Commonwealth (in Andrews, N.C., and Commonwealth, Ga.), 1895–1900, where he edited *The Social Gospel*, 1897–1900. Albertson was General Manager of Wm. S. Butler's Department Store in Boston, 1910–12, and was personnel manager of Filene's. He was general secretary of the American Cooperative Association and edited *The American Cooperator* 1902–04. He was publisher of *The Boston Common* and of *The Twentieth Century Magazine*, edited by B. O. Flower and by Charles Zueblin, devoted to social progress and social justice. (*pp. ix–x, xiii, xv, 6, and passim*)

HAZEL HAMMOND ALBERTSON. Wife of Ralph Albertson and daughter of Ernest Hammond. It was Hazel who gave the Farm its abiding character and who kept it going after Ralph Albertson's departure. She was a regular contributor to *The Twentieth Century Magazine*. She was active in the cooperative movement. In later life she was a major force in the Women's Club movement and organized the industrial committee of the Federated Women's Clubs of Massachusetts. (*pp. x, xi, xiii–xv, 6, and passim*)

BRONSON ALCOTT (1799–1888). American educator, author, mystic. Spent early life as a teacher. In 1843 he founded Fruitlands, a Utopian community in Harvard, Mass., which lasted two years. Then, as superintendent of schools in Concord, he was responsible for many innovations, among them calisthenics, singing, the study of physiology, and a parent-teacher association. He was associated with Hawthorne, Emerson, and Thoreau, and was noted for his extreme transcendental idealism. His daughter, Louisa May Alcott (1832–1885) is even better known; her most famous novel is *Little Women* (1868, 1869). (*pp. 9–10, 14, 24*)

BRUNO BECKHARD (1885–1959). Born and brought up in New York City, a member of the Harvard class of 1907. He spent most of his life as a marine automotive engineer, selling and servicing small boats and outboard motors. After being graduated from Harvard, Beckhard was closely associated with Ralph Albertson in many of his schemes and publishing ventures. For instance, from 1910 to 1912 he was treasurer of The Twentieth Century Company of Boston (Albertson was president), which published *The Twentieth Century Magazine*. Later he and Albertson formed a company in New York City called Albertson, Beckhard & Allen. (*pp. 28, 37, 68, 78*)

CARL BINGER (1889–1976). Psychiatrist and lecturer on psychiatry at the Harvard Medical School. A member of the Harvard class of 1910, Binger was graduated from the Harvard Medical School in 1914 and, after service in World War I, became a psychiatrist and a member of the teaching staff in psychiatry at Cornell University Medical College. Later a psychoanalyst, he achieved considerable fame as a result of his appearance as witness for Alger Hiss during the latter's trial, in which he introduced a character analysis of Whittaker Chambers, the chief witness against Hiss. A man of strong opinions, vigorously expressed, he played the role of "God" in the first (private) performance of Archibald MacLeish's *J.B.* (*pp. x, 28, 90–91, 221*)

WALTER BINGER (1888–1979). Engineer, educated at MIT, brother of Carl Binger. Deputy City Commissioner of Sanitation in New York in the administration of Mayor Fiorello H. La Guardia, Binger supervised the construction of the city's sewage treatment facilities and the construction of the Harlem River Drive (now the FDR East River Drive).

During World War II, he was chairman of the U.S. National Engineering Advisory Committee. (*pp. 28, 91, 221*)

CHARLES BONI. Publisher. Together with his brother Albert (Harvard class of 1913), set up the Washington Square Book Shop, where the Washington Square Players was organized, "from which grew the Theatre Guild." The publishing firm of Albert and Charles Boni, launched in 1923, "published Marcel Proust's *Remembrance of Things Past*, and books by Thornton Wilder, Will Rogers, Romain Rolland, Colette, D. H. Lawrence, Ford Maddox Ford, Jim Tully, Upton Sinclair, and the first low-price wide-selling paperback series of the twentieth century." (*p. 26*)

RICHARD WASHBURN CHILD (1881–1935). Author and diplomat. After receiving his A.B. from Harvard in 1903 and his LL.B. in 1906, Child entered the practice of law and from 1915 onward practiced law in New York City. His reputation was made by his short stories, published chiefly in *Collier's* and the *Saturday Evening Post*, and many novels. Child was an organizer of the Progressive party in Massachusetts in 1911 and from 1919 to 1921 he was editor of *Collier's*. Appointed "ambassador extraordinary and plenipotentiary" to Italy, he became an intimate friend of Mussolini, whom he greatly admired. He helped Mussolini to write his autobiography. He found the Italian Fascist movement to embody "gladness, hope, loyal service." On his return to America he helped organize the National Crime Commission and later became active in labor arbitration. He was an ardent supporter of FDR and even organized a Republicans-for-Roosevelt League. (*p. 115*)

PHILIP DAVIS (1876–1951). Social worker, producer of motion pictures, businessman. In his class report, Davis was described as "the Benjamin Franklin of the Class, so versatile is his genius." Born in Motol, Russia, he emigrated to America in 1890, and was educated at Hull-House in Chicago, where he became the protégé of Jane Addams and Gerard Swope. He attended the University of Chicago from 1899 to 1901 and then transferred to Harvard College, becoming a member of the class of 1903. On graduation, he became Associate Director (and secretary) and later Director of the Civic Service House, a "settlement house" in the North End of Boston, of which the founding director was M. Bloomfield. He worked for the Boston School Committee as supervisor of newsboys, bootblacks and school-aged peddlers. He wrote a number of books, notably on "the boy problem" and immigration and Americanization, and was the editor of a pioneering manual, *The Field of Social Service* (1915). After the First World War, he became active in the field of documentary motion pictures, producing films on such subjects as the use of timberlands, the making of cloth, the U.S. Coast Guard, and urban problems. He was long active in the International Ladies Garment Workers Union, first as organizer and then as arbitrator. His autobiography, *And Crown Thy Good*, a paean to his America, was completed and published just before he died. (*pp. ix, xiv, 35–40, 45–50, and passim*)

SAMUEL ATKINS ELIOT, JR. (1893–). Professor of Theatre, Smith College. Grandson of Harvard President Charles W. Eliot, "Sam" Eliot received his A.B. from Harvard in 1913. Studied theatre under Harvard's George Pierce Baker. In his third class report Eliot said that his "play 'The Revolutionist' has been neither produced nor published and probably never will unless a revolution in this country should make it timely." He directed and produced plays at Smith and published a number of books about the theatre. He was also co-author of a book on *Birds of the Connecticut Valley* (1937) and was a regular contributor to *Bird News of Western Mass.* He ended his fiftieth class report with the sentiment, "Love is the leaven in the bitter loaf of this world's public evils." (*pp. x, 25–26, 30, 65, 83*)

JOHN ELLIOTT. Foreign correspondent. Wounded in France in 1940, he was the first casualty among American newspapermen in World War II. (*pp. 134–36, 140, 143–46, 150–51, 153–54*)

GEORGE HERRON (1862–1925). Congregational minister and socialist. Born in Indiana and educated in Wisconsin, he died in Munich. He was one of the founders of the Rand School of Social Sciences in New York City in 1906. (*p. 16*)

EDWIN LELAND JAMES (1890–1951). The *New York Times*'s chief correspondent in Europe in the 1920s. He came to New York in 1930 as the assistant managing editor of the *Times* and was promoted to managing editor in 1932. It was under James that the *New York Times* grew to be the world-covering and influential newspaper that it is today. He held that "the newspaper is the daily story of the progress of mankind"—"the textbook of democracy." (*p. 118*)

ROBERT ["Bobby"] EDMOND JONES (1887–1954). One of America's foremost stage designers. Born in New Hampshire, he was graduated from Harvard in the class of 1910, *cum laude*, and for two years was a graduate assistant and instructor in Fine Arts. He went to Europe in 1913 with financial help from such friends as John Reed and Kenneth MacGowan, and studied the "new stagecraft" with Max Reinhardt. Returning to New York in 1914 after the outbreak of World War I, he began his career of stage designs, developed for the Provincetown Players and later the Theatre Guild. Among his most reknowned sets were those for *The Wild Duck, Hedda Gabler,* O'Neill's *The Hairy Ape,* and *Anna Christie.* He was said (by Mordecai Gorelik) to have been "the founder of the whole present-day tradition of scene design in the United States. He had the gift of combining the lyrical with the dramatic, catching both at their peaks. . . . He had an eternally boyish, zestful presence, an amused scorn of everything stuffy, a romanticism that was real to himself and that he made real to others." At Harvard, "Bobby" Jones took George Pierce Baker's course in drama, the famous "57 Workshop," which during the years attracted many famous men including novelist

Thomas Wolfe; he practiced his costume and set designing in the big front room at the Farm, for impromptu plays and charades. In 1934 he produced "color designs" for two color films in Hollywood: *Becky Sharp* and *The Dancing Bride.* (*pp. x, 27*)

BERTRAND de JOUVENEL (Baron de Jouvenel) (1903–). Diplomatic and foreign correspondent (until 1939), author, President and Director-General of the French Society for Economic Studies and Economic Documentation, 1954–74. He was Professor of the Faculty of Law in Paris (1966–72) and a Visiting Professor at Oxford, Cambridge, Manchester, Yale, and Berkeley. Author of many books on French and American politics, politics and economics, and international affairs, and editor of several journals devoted to the analysis of current problems, he was awarded many honors and prizes. (*pp. 135–36, 139–40, 142, 145, 147*)

HUBERT RENFRO KNICKERBOCKER (1898–1949). Born in Texas, and studied at Southwestern University (Texas) where he got his B.A. in 1917. He went to New York in 1919 with the intention of studying psychiatry, but at Columbia he found that the only program he could afford was journalism, and so he took that and became a newspaperman. After teaching journalism for a year, he went to Germany in 1923, once again with the aim of studying psychiatry, enrolling in the University of Munich. He paid his way by sending occasional articles to the United Press. In 1924 he went to Berlin and eventually succeeded Dorothy Thompson as the Berlin chief of bureau for the *New York Evening Post* and the *Philadelphia Public Ledger*. Eventually chief foreign correspondent of the International News Service of the Hearst newspaper chain. When he was "edged" out of Germany by the Nazis, he became a roving reporter, covering the Abyssinian War, the Spanish Civil War, the Sino-Japanese War (1937), and finally saw the parade of German troops into Austria and then Czechoslovakia. Chief of foreign service for the *Chicago Sun*, 1941–45, he died when his plane crashed in 1949. (*pp. 126, 151, 153–55*)

JULIUS KUTTNER (1892–1951). Engineer, attended Harvard 1909–11, spent a year at Cornell, graduated with an S.B. from MIT in 1915. Designed diesel engines, wrote books on diesel power and motorships, and lectured at the Polytechnic Institute of Brooklyn. As diesel engineer for the Century Steel Company, he designed power systems for steamships and motorships. In his class report, he noted that "I translated Dr. Sigmund Freud's 'Die Traumdeutung' from German into English for Dr. A. A. Brill, at compensation [in psychoanalytic hours] by the page." (*pp. 25, 30*)

LAWRENCE LANGNER (1890–1962). Born in Swansea, South Wales, he came to the United States in 1911. A chartered patent agent, he was a specialist in foreign patents and trademarks, but is best known for his work in the theatre. He was a founder of The Theatre Guild, which produced many of the plays of Eugene O'Neill (including *Strange Interlude* and *Mourning Becomes Electra*), of George Bernard Shaw (*Saint Joan, Back to Methuselah*), and others. He was founder and first president of the American Shakespeare Festival Theater and Academy in Stratford, Connecticut. He was the author of many books on the theatre and on trademarks. (*pp. x, 27–28, 91*)

WALTER LIPPMANN (1889–1974). Author, editor, columnist. In the 1960s, Lippmann had the "unquestioned . . . title of dean of American newspapermen." When he died, James Reston observed that his twice-weekly columns (entitled "Today and Tomorrow") "reached millions of people every day he wrote." He produced "more than 4,000 columns, totaling more than four million words, 20 books." It was agreed that he had "given [generations of] newspapermen . . . a wider vision of our duty," showing "us how to put the event of the day in its proper relationship to the history of yesterday and the dream of tomorrow." He provided an analysis of the crises and ordinary affairs of America and the world that had "a depth and breadth of knowledge that is possibly unmatched in journalism." Through his column (which appeared in 250 newspapers) he molded the opinions of readers throughout the world, including business leaders and statesmen, such presidents as Roosevelt and Kennedy, and—it is said—even influenced Premier Khrushchev of the USSR.

Born and brought up in New York City, Lippmann became an outstanding member of the Harvard class of 1910 (which included such other notables as John Reed [q.v.] and T. S. Eliot). He was greatly influenced by William James, George Santayana, and Graham Wallas (q.v.), becoming president of the Harvard Socialist Club. He worked as a reporter for *The Boston Common*, a reformist journal edited by Ralph Albertson (q.v.). Lippmann married Albertson's daughter Faye in 1917. In 1912 he became executive secretary to the Reverend George R. Lunn, newly-elected Socialist mayor of Schenectady, but resigned after four months. This experience, a turning point in his life and thought, is presented through his letters for the first time in *A Fearful Innocence*. Lippmann was a founding editor, with Herbert Croly, of the journal *The New Republic* in 1914. After service during the First World War on the American Commission to Negotiate Peace, he joined the editorial staff of the *New York World*, eventually becoming editor. When the *World* ceased publishing in 1931, he began to write his column "Today and Tomorrow" for the *Herald Tribune*. (*pp. x, xi, xiii, xv, 25, 31, 47, 64, 70–71, 72, 74, 75–76, 78, 90, 115, 118, 130*)

KENNETH MACGOWAN (1888–1963). Author and educator, member of the Harvard class of 1911. Beginning as a drama critic on the old *Boston Transcript*, he gained fame as a director and producer of plays and then of films—for RKO-Radio Pictures, 20th Century-Fox, and Paramount. He became professor of Theater Arts at the University of California at Los Angeles and was famous for his courses in playwriting. (*pp. x, 27*)

EDGAR ANSELL MOWRER (1892–1977). Foreign correspondent and brother of the head of the Paris Bureau of the *Chicago Daily News*. From 1923 to 1933, he was chief of the Berlin Bureau of the *Chicago Daily News* and elected president of the Foreign Press Association in Berlin. The Nazis pressed for his resignation because of his independent critical position with respect to the new Germany; the Nazis arrested a Jewish Austrian journalist, Dr. Paul Goldman, and released him only on Mowrer's resignation. He was expelled from Italy (1936) because of his frankness about the Mussolini regime, and also from the Soviet Union (1937), again because of his uncompromising honesty. When expelled from Nazi Germany, he was escorted to the train by a platoon of S.S. Hitler's Minister of Information, Joseph Goebbels, once said that he would expend a whole army division on Mowrer's capture, since his articles against the Germans in general, and the Nazis in particular, were considered so dangerous. In his last years Mowrer became Washington correspondent and author of a syndicated column for the *Chicago Daily News*. He wrote many books on problems of national and international politics. (*pp. 122, 125–26, 128–29, 138–39, 160–61, 167, 171, 173, 191, 208*)

FRANK PARSONS (1854–1908). Lawyer, teacher, political scientist, social reformer. Born in Mt. Holly, N.J., Parsons spent most of his life in New England, where he became professor at Boston University Law School. One of the founders, and dean, of the Ruskin College of Social Science at Trenton, Mo. His chief concerns were reforms in currency (the "money question"), and in municipal affairs. He advocated public ownership of local public utilities (gas, electric light, water, streetcar transportation, etc.), direct legislation by the people, municipal home rule, and municipal civil service. His main books include *The City for the People* (1900), *The Story of New Zealand* (1904), *The Railways, the Trusts, and the People* (1905) with the assistance of Ralph Albertson, and *The Telegraph Monopoly* (1899). He was a pioneer in the area of vocational guidance. (*pp. 27, 36*)

LUCIEN PRICE (1883–1964). Editorial writer for the *Boston Transcript*, 1907–14, and for the *Boston Globe*. A member of the Harvard class of 1910. Author of many books, of which the most celebrated is *Dialogues of Alfred North Whitehead* (1954). (*pp. 26, 30, 47*)

JOHN REED (1887–1920). Journalist, born in Portland, Oregon, and a member of the Harvard class of 1910. He became interested in social problems as a result of his association with Lincoln Steffens and Ida Tarbell, famous muckrakers. Was the author of several volumes of poetry and became an editor of the *American Magazine* (1911–13) and the *Metropolitan Magazine* (1913–15). The latter sent him to Mexico as correspondent during the Mexican Revolution in 1914, which he also reported for the *New York World*. He served as war correspondent in Europe for the *Metropolitan Magazine* during the First World War. He was a member of the board of directors and an editor of the radical publication, *The Masses*. In Russia during the October Revolution in 1917, Reed came to know Lenin and became an enthusiastic supporter of the Bolsheviks. His *Ten Days That Shook the World* has long been the classic account of the early days of the Russian Revolution. Returning to America at the end of the War, he became active in the formation of the Communist-Labor Party, and was indicted for sedition. He left America to return to Russia, where he died of typhus. His ashes are buried in the wall of the Kremlin. He is still something of a folk hero in Russia, where a street was named after him in October, 1980. (*p. 72*)

VIDA SCUDDER (1861–1954). Outstanding American educator, teacher of English (beginning in 1892) and professor of English (1910–27) at Wellesley College. Author of many scholarly books on aspects of English literature, she was also active in liberal politics (as a suffragette) and in social movements. Among her books are *Social Ideals in English Letters* (1898) and *Socialism and Character* (1912). She was a friend of Ralph Albertson. (*p. 67*)

HERBERT JACOB SELIGMANN (1891–). A writer, member of the Harvard class of 1912. Became active in philanthropy and wrote articles for magazines on art, literature, and social problems. (*p. 26*)

VINCENT SHEEAN (1899–1975). Journalist with a progressive or socialist political point of view. According to the *New York Times*, he conceived of journalism as not just the process "of getting the story, but understanding it, and through that understanding making it part of the experience of his readers." Working as a reporter on the *Chicago Daily News*, he became a foreign correspondent in 1922 for the *Chicago Tribune*, where he was a friend of Ernest Hemingway. He gained fame in 1925 during the war in Morocco, crossing the desert to interview Abd-el-Krim, the rebel chief. His exciting and adventure-laden autobiographical account of his profession, *Personal History* (1935) was a major force attracting others to the field of journalism. With first name actually James, he was known as "Jimmy." (*pp. 118, 126, 129*)

LEE SIMONSON (1888–1976). Stage designer and art critic. A member of the Harvard class of 1909, Simonson was a student in George Pierce Baker's drama course, "57 Workshop" and a founder of the Harvard Dramatic Club. After serving in the U.S. Army's corps of interpreters in the First World War, Simonson joined Lawrence Langner and others to form the Theatre Guild, for which he designed sets for the next twenty-one years. Later he turned to the opera, designing sets for the Metropolitan, beginning with the four operas of *The Ring of the Nibelung* in 1948. (*pp. x, 27*)

GERARD SWOPE (1872–1957). American electrical engineer, business executive, and philanthropist. After graduation from MIT in 1895, he went to work for Western Electric in Chicago, where he lived at Hull-House. He later joined General Electric and became president in 1922. He served on various boards during the New Deal, was chairman of the New York City Housing Authority, and in 1951 became chairman of the Institute of Pacific Relations.

J. WILLIAM TERRY (1887–1962). Newspaperman, editor, novelist, and lecturer. "J.W.T." was ordained a Methodist minister, but after six years turned to writing and lecturing on world affairs and literary subjects. A feature writer for *The Overland Monthly* of San Francisco, he was a specialist on the Far East and Russia. Managing editor of *The League of Nations Chronicle* during the 1930s, J.W.T. was long an ardent advocate of arms reduction and used his influence to attempt to stabilize world peace. He worked in the editorial department of the *New York Times*, the *New York Sun*, and the *New York World-Telegram*, and was a staff editor for ten years on the *Paterson* (N.J.) *Morning Call*. After his retirement he wrote several novels on life in America. (*pp. 119, 121*)

DOROTHY THOMPSON (1894–1961). Newspaper columnist, lecturer, and radio commentator, described in 1940 as having, next to Eleanor Roosevelt, the "most power and prestige of any woman in America." Her political column for the *New York Herald Tribune*, "On the Record," contained forceful and convincing opinions on the world situation, expressed with vigor, brilliance, enthusiasm, and "uncompromising sincerity." Born in Lancaster, New York, the daughter of a Methodist minister, she worked her way through college, graduating from Syracuse University in 1914, after which she became active in the campaign for women's suffrage (1915–17) and did social work (1917–20). She went to Europe after the First World War, where she began a career of journalism, becoming Vienna correspondent for the *Philadelphia Public Ledger*. In 1925 she was appointed head of the *New York Evening Post's* Berlin office, and in 1928 became the wife of novelist Sinclair Lewis. Forced eventually to leave Germany because of the growing displeasure of the Nazis at her frank revelations, she devoted herself to warning the world about Hitler's plans and ambitions with a fervor that caused her to be dubbed a "modern Cassandra." "On the Record" was widely syndicated and in 1938 and 1939 she had a radio program as well. She reached the highest point of her influence during the years of World War II and the following years, remaining an uncompromising opponent of tyranny in any form, whether from the right as in the case of Nazi Germany, or from the left as in the case of Soviet Russia. (*pp. 117–18, 126, 129, 130–31, 171*)

GRAHAM WALLAS (1858–1932). British political psychologist, active in the Fabian Society and lecturer in political science at the famed London School of Economics, of which he had been one of the planners (along with Beatrice and Sidney Webb). Appointed Professor of Political Science at the London School, he paid four visits to the United States. He lectured at Harvard during 1909–10, and profoundly influenced members of the class of 1910, including Walter Lippmann, John Reed, Carl Binger, et al. Wallas used to describe himself as a "working thinker," and much of his intellectual effort has been said to have been "directed to the attempt to improve the mental processes of those who occupy their minds with public affairs." He pleaded for "a closer association between psychological and political studies"—a goal achieved by Walter Lippmann (q.v.) in his *A Preface to Politics* (1913). He was a Fabian in this thinking, but unlike many of his fellow socialists, who were chiefly "concerned with institutions and systems, " the center of Wallas's concern was for human beings as individuals rather than with human beings in the mass. (*pp. 25, 30, 75*)

HENRY WILLCOX (1890–). Civil engineer. Harvard class of 1912. Founder of Willcox Construction Company, which during the post-World War II years "put up some ten thousand low-rent apartments, mostly for the New York City Housing Authority." (*p. 28*)

CHARLES ZUEBLIN (1866–1924). Writer and lecturer on public questions. Zueblin, a friend of Ralph Albertson and of Frank Parsons, was appointed instructor in sociology at the University of Chicago in 1892 and became professor in 1902. He left Chicago and settled in Winchester, Massachusetts, where he devoted himself to writing and lecturing. He was editor of *The Twentieth Century Magazine*, published by Ralph Albertson. (*pp. 27, 65*)